"We have all been shaped by the Perverse Feminine Archetype. Aradia's stunning contribution examines this distortion through a synthesis of history, psychology, feminist theory, case studies, and heartfelt qualitative inquiry, uncovering the labyrinth Western modernity built to conceal the monstrosities deposited by centuries of gender prejudice. Critically engaging Jungian depth psychology, this work illuminates the monster we were taught to reject within ourselves, revealing how, through courageous research with bold women, we can reclaim and integrate the essence of this once-demonized feminine force with joy and power into our wholeness of being."

Susan Rowland, *PhD, Professor of Depth Psychology, Pacifica Graduate Institute, and author of* Jungian Literary Criticism: The Essential Guide

"At a time when patriarchal power has intensified in its quest to demean and diminish women's political, social, and personal agency, *The Perverse Feminine* compellingly reminds us that old stories can be told anew and that power can be returned to the disenfranchised. This gutsy book shines a light on feminist spirituality, the mythological forces that haunt and condemn women, and the urgent need for radical inquiry into their voices. Aradia's analysis is a beacon of interdisciplinary practice and a testament to what is possible when we insist on looking backwards, forwards, and, most importantly, within."

Breanne Fahs, *PhD, clinical psychologist, Professor of Women and Gender studies, Arizona State University, and author of* Burn It Down! Feminist Manifestos for the Revolution

"Through Aradia's insightful lens, we witness how women are forced to carry the archetypal projections of a dominant patriarchy—or face the consequences. Drawing on depth psychology, mythology, and feminist discourse, this well-researched and vital work illuminates how these projections shape women's lived experience and psychic terrain, reinforcing systems of oppression. A compelling contribution to the ongoing struggle for women's emancipation from false and imprisoning narratives."

Stephen Julich, *PhD, core faculty, Department of East-West Psychology, California Institute of Integral Studies*

THE PERVERSE FEMININE

The Perverse Feminine resurrects a long-buried psychic figure: The Perverse Feminine Archetype. Grounded in Intuitive Inquiry, this work builds on Jungian theory, feminist psychology, and myth to illuminate the archetypal constructs of forbidden power, deviant desire, and inherited shame shaping the collective psyche of cisgender women.

Across careers, relationships, and inner lives, women in this study enliven the perverse through acts of subversion, refusal, creative expression, and sexual exploration. Through their stories, a meditation on the unconscious unfolds, unveiling the archetypal dimension as a portal to healing and integration.

Distilled from the data, a four-stage framework maps the psychological journeys of research participants across the evolving inner landscapes, where pain, power, and transformation intertwine. Through evocative narratives that generate tools for archetypal engagement, this study offers individuals, theorists, and clinicians a guide to identity, self-discovery, and psychic wholeness within a rapidly changing cultural landscape.

Kalen Aradia, PhD, is a feminist researcher and writer excavating archetypal forces buried in the collective shadow. Her work examines exiled emotions, forbidden desires, and instinctual truths to reveal the mythic structures that perpetuate psychic fragmentation.

THE PERVERSE FEMININE

AN ARCHETYPAL RECLAMATION OF FORBIDDEN POWER

Kalen Aradia, PhD

Routledge
Taylor & Francis Group
NEW YORK AND LONDON

Designed cover image: © Getty Images

First published 2026
by Routledge
605 Third Avenue, New York, NY 10158

and by Routledge
4 Park Square, Milton Park, Abingdon, Oxon, OX14 4RN

Routledge is an imprint of the Taylor & Francis Group, an informa business

Library of Congress Cataloging-in-Publication Data
Names: Aradia, Kalen author
Title: The perverse feminine: an archetypal reclamation of forbidden power / Kalen Aradia.
Description: New York, NY: Routledge, 2026. | Includes bibliographical references and index. | Identifiers: LCCN 2025017687 (print) | LCCN 2025017688 (ebook) | ISBN 9781032593937 hardback | ISBN 9781032596945 paperback | ISBN 9781003455837 ebook
Subjects: LCSH: Femininity–Psychological aspects | Archetype (Psychology) | Sex (Psychology)
Classification: LCC BF175.5.F45 A65 2026 (print) | LCC BF175.5.F45 (ebook)
LC record available at https://lccn.loc.gov/2025017687
LC ebook record available at https://lccn.loc.gov/2025017688

ISBN: 978-1-032-59393-7 (hbk)
ISBN: 978-1-032-59694-5 (pbk)
ISBN: 978-1-003-45583-7 (ebk)

DOI: 10.4324/9781003455837

Typeset in Times New Roman
by Deanta Global Publishing Services, Chennai, India

I dedicate this book to my blood and chosen family, whose presence has shaped me in ways words cannot fully express, to my ancestors who compel my body to move and my mind to dream of an uninhibited existence, and to the lost loves who remain imprinted within the recesses of my heart. To the fearless women whose footprints I follow, to those beyond the veil. Unseen, yet invariably felt. And to Mookie, my beloved familiar, who walked beside me in my darkest moments and whose spirit remains with me still.

This book is a remembrance, a reclamation, and a confrontation of the lies that bind.

Who is this book for?

Women deemed too sensitive, too dramatic, too much.

The silenced, misdiagnosed, and dismissed sisters.

Those who shapeshift to survive, who fold their rage inward, who squelch their passion for an illusory safety.

The queer, the Othered, the witches, the wild ones.

Bodies that remember what the world refuses to name.

Aching with a curiosity no doctrine can contain.

This book is a reckoning and a return.

Contents

Figures

Tables

Preface

This project was born out of a pressing desire to understand how deeper historical and psychological forces have shaped my experiences. At 28, I found myself trapped in yet another abusive relationship, staring down the barrel of cyclical control and erasure. Something had to change. My life became an ongoing negotiation between survival and self-sabotage, shaped by forces I had only begun to identify. Drawn to research to quench my thirst for answers, I traversed a landscape built of psychological and mythological realities. While I discerned the fractured territories of my selfhood, I cultivated a question. Why did I continue to give my power away? If I could conceptualize it, perhaps I could change it. Through my pursuit, I sought a source of complexity, a mirror to my internal world. In my studies, the archetypal materialized in the footsteps of psychopomp, Lilith. She offered a language to articulate the convergence of myth, lived experience, and historical condemnation. Perhaps containing my experience within her figure invited me to convene with my trauma, to face a buried truth I had long feared. Healing soon grew into a source of reckoning, a splintering of awakening. Here, I was summoned to encounter the pain, the depth, and the truth of a fractured inner world. I could no longer look away. As I mustered courage, I called upon an ancestral wounding. Leaping into this mythic terrain, I became captivated by women who live at the fringes of society and who choose truth over approval. Those who refused to conform to a societal lie. I wanted that. I wanted to be near them, to understand how to connect with their energetic force field.

With this aim, I began gathering qualitative data, allowing the research to take shape. Choosing to frame the research within an Intuitive Inquiry (II) approach, I discovered a force emanating from Lilith that exceeded the bounds of my infallible perspective. Across each cycle of this process, the archetypal shadow surfaced as the Perverse Feminine Archetype. As I traced her essence, her image threaded through every layer of thought and method. She rose as a connecting force between the psychic terrain, where participants and I curated a collaborative space of reckoning. Amidst this unraveling, a sense of turmoil, defiance, and longing washed over me. As participant stories wove into mine, they sharpened questions embedded in shame and personal undoing. Intuitive Inquiry opened a passage, drawing us into the obscure chambers of perverse femininity. In that space, Lilith resurrected, not alone, but as a force moving through each of us.

Professional Acknowledgements

I am grateful to my mentors and colleagues for their insight and steady support throughout this work. I owe particular thanks to Dr. Anne Huffman, Dr. Stephen Julich, and Dr. Breanne Fahs. Your guidance has shaped my growth with both care and exacting challenge. You pushed me to think in new ways and helped bring this project into being. To Liz Wheeler, my conceptual editor, thank you for your thoughtful attention and for helping me refine the shape of my ideas. And to Anna Moore at Routledge, thank you for your guidance and for making space at an established press for the work of a new author. Your belief in this project means more to me than I can say. To the participants who shared their stories with vulnerability and depth: thank you. Your courage and complexity made this project possible.

Mapping the Spiral

Mapping the Spiral pulls the reader into a nonlinear descent. A break in logic. A plunge into the perverse. Theory, method, and lived story intertwine, shaping psychic inquiry. To confront the Perverse Feminine Archetype (PFA) is to revel in her power, her peril. To live in a trifecta of entwined deliverance, a symbolic return.

Part I establishes the foundations, including theory, method, and the researcher's insights.

Part II enters the spiral, cascading through study results to animate a four-stage schema.

Part III expands the discussion, proposing new directions for research, practice, and communal transmutation.

Note: The core findings of this study, presented as a four-stage healing framework, are outlined across Stages 1–4 in Part II. Each stage rips open descent and return, mapping chapters as hauntings. The experimental insights coil amid fracture, exile, and return. We begin with theoretical groundwork, which leads us into metaphorical profundity. Each chapter traces stages of psychic integration and indicates how the PFA unfolds in lived, repeating cycles.

PART I: LAYING THE GROUNDWORK: UNDERSTANDING THE ROOTS OF THE PERVERSE FEMININE ARCHETYPE

Part 1 sets the tone with an ambitious campaign that combines lived experience and conceptual musings. An incantation draws the reader into a dissonant meditation, where theory spills over and memory pulls at the edges. Each chapter builds on the one before, highlighting intersections of personal redemption, theoretical insights, and qualitative methodology.

Chapter 1: Unveiling the Perverse Feminine

Curated where contradiction assembles and memory refuses silence, Chapter 1 delves into the disowned realm of the researcher's lived experiences. Beginning with an autoethnographic analysis, the personal wounding surfaces as an awakening. Contemplative reckonings and psychic tension, exposing the essence of PFA communion.

Chapter 2: Archetypes, Feminism, and the Shadow

Once thought to be timeless and universal, patriarchal conditioning runs rampant. Chapter 2 uncovers its indistinct hiding place beneath a feminist gaze. As we encounter the stark elemental forces, we dissect the threads between gender, power, and omission. Jungian theory supports multiplicity, begging the archetypal to thieve the senses. The theoretical architecture expands here, offering a scaffolding to support the interpretations presented in Part II.

Chapter 3: Spirals of Inquiry

Method spirals with each cycle, returning as a curve of revelation; a ritual of insight. Across densely entwined landscape of Chapter 3, from research development to manifestation, the researcher extends recursive and reflexive paradigms. Demand participation, *Intuitive Inquiry (II)*, demands the researcher, witness, reader, to morph into one. As novel insights stir, the subjective undercurrents of ancestral awakening unravel, inviting in elements often overlooked by traditional research.

Chapter 4: The Journey of Perverse Feminine Integration

What surfaces is a story. Wounded, lucid, mythic. As the culmination of previous loops crystallize, a thematic schema materializes, magnifying subdued potential. Sifting amid participant narratives, *Societal Indoctrination*, Shapeshifting, Awareness, and Redefining the Feminine, map a rhythm of reclamation, where the PFA stretches the mind. She moves, not as a fixed idea, but as a feral pulse who slips the noose of conventionality.

PART II: THE STAGES OF HEALING: A CYCLICAL JOURNEY OF FEMININE RECLAMATION

Part II tremors in the terrain of metamorphosis; a splinter and return. Converging story with theory, scar with symbol; throbbing with heartbeat. Immersed in complexity, testimonies anchor theoretical and historical systems in daily life. The PFA emerges here, felt beneath the dialogue.

Stage 1

Societal Indoctrination: The Inheritance of Obedience

The first fracture. The infiltration of fabricated normalcy. The energetic turns against itself; subservient and condemned. *Societal Indoctrination* serves as patriarchal conditioning at the core of the collective unconscious. Condemnations expose dominate voracity trapped in a historical cage. Witch hunts, hysterical diagnoses, and systemic violence coalesce in the aberrant. Our heroine; our demon; our femme fatale assaults the pages, calling forth the ancient cries of the past.

Chapter 5: Perverting the Feminine

The act of perversion lives in the projective qualities of the hegemonic. Muting the unruly woman and to conceal its envy. Patriarchal structures condemn transgressive, deluding the population into submission. Demonization and violence occupy the normative overculture while the potency latent within emotive translucency perish. Disillusionment obstructs the soul, encased in an oppressive landscape. As participants share accounts of the surmountable external pressure, they evoke a denounced sisterhood.

Chapter 6: The Collective Unconscious and Patriarchy

Gendered oppression whispers, subtly shapes how shame circulates; how voices muffle. Chapter 6 seeks vocalization through a subterranean map of psychic oppression. Where Chapter 5 cracks the surface, this descent carves pathways to the unknowable. Culling mythic sediment to reveal an emblem transposed as weapon to assault the feminine. Laying bare unconscious strata, the PFA speaks through a collective wound.

Chapter 7: Witch Hunts and Hysteria

The expression of a defiant woman threads into grief, where refusal meets suspicion. From stake to asylum, longstanding systems silence and contain. Delving into historical branding, we uncover inherited scripts encoded in whispered diagnosis and cultural messaging. Parallel with participant musings, the avalanche of contemporary conditioning collides with an oppressive past. Embedded in conversations that illuminate the inner shame that surrounds emotional turmoil, we discover a felt sense of the present-day war against autonomous women.

Chapter 8: Demonizing Lilith: A Case Study

Lilith's removal from the sacred narrative marks an early illustration of the PFA. Once honored as a figure of sexual power and independence, her exile as a she-demon encoded a warning. Encouraging subservience, the parable necessitates obedience. Lilith's arc energetically shapes a cultural template positioned across generations. Her primary essence carries erotic will. Gagged, burned, and buried. Positioning as an invitation to her dungeon, her arc guides us into an entanglement with the indoctrinated mind.

Stage 2

Shapeshifting: Fractured Identities

Cast out from cultural belonging and exiled to the wilderness, women often survive by splitting off aspects of their authentic selves. Performing an idealized femininity, they contort until the role consumes them. The performance is no longer a mask but mistaken for the authentic core. Over time, disguise calcifies into habit. Emotional expression, ambition, and instinct trim to fit the mold.

Chapter 9: Shadowed Formation

The PFA's formation is a passage of descent, where rejected traits sink below consciousness. In the psychic underworld, women internalize cultural prohibitions. Repression feeds inner turmoil. As the gateway into Shapeshifting, the cobwebbed chamber becomes both echo and vessel, preserving fragments too distorted to surface. Moments of confusion arise here, between the inner world and social performance.

Chapter 10: Internalized Sexism and the Personal Unconscious

Internalized sexism nests in the body like a parasite. Inherited law, cloaked as virtue. It murmurs: be quiet. Be smaller. Be good. Shaped by early socialization, cultural expectations, and relational reinforcement, detrimental messages contour how women manage their inner world. Participants speak of a persistent self-surveillance, culminating in guilt. A reflex to prioritize others at the expense of their own well-being distills into acts of neglect, framed as a sacrificial virtue. Testimonies speak to oppressive intimacy and how psychic subjugation roots beneath recognition. Forming as an undercurrent, the PFA takes shape, nagging women to seek beyond their circumstances.

Chapter 11: Contemporary Madness: The Pathologization of Feminine Power

From nineteenth-century hysteria to the contemporary borderline personality disorder (BPD), projected illness persists under the guise of care. Medical systems act as agents of control, rejecting characteristics deemed irascible. In participant's words: the wreckage they survived. Chapter 11 tears into the nature of diagnosis as a form of control. Embedded in accounts of subjugation, women reveal their fear of expression. Intentionally devalued and mislabeled the articulation is an erasure. A portrait of mental health generates a mechanism of social discipline.

Chapter 12: Lilith as the Queen of the Shadow

Kabbalistic interpretations position Lilith as a demonic figure, sculpted by sin and divinity. She reflects rage, erotic power, and refusal: the very qualities culture deems dangerous. Her mirror reveals a mind fractured by internalized law and cultural fragmentation. Folded into her dominion over the underworld, we glimpse the early contours of the PFA, exiled and abandoned. As we follow her descent, Lilith moves as a challenger and companion, guiding us to face the disowned and traverse traumatic terrains.

Stage 3

Awareness: Awakening the Perverse

The spell cracks. Not with ceremony, but in tremors: a withheld opinion, a door slammed too hard. The perverse stirs, echoing Lilith's defiance. Quiet, steady, undeniable. Obedience falters, and ancestral wounds surface in strained conversation, a withheld opinion, a dismissed instinct. Curiosity, once dormant, entices seekers inward, and subtle rebellions illuminate a growing fervor. Buried traits like anger, erotic will, and ambition rise with force. As the veil lifts, the once-demonized parts of the inner realm begin to speak, and the PFA arises, seeking recognition.

Chapter 13: Shadow Confrontation

Facing the PFA requires an intimate turning inward, a willingness to examine repressed aspects of identity. Following participants into a landscape of recognition, internalized beliefs begin to loosen their grip. Interviews lay bare junctures where suppressed emotions, taboo desires, or unclaimed resilience rise to the surface. In naming the disavowed, a disruption in conventionality occurs. As buried material comes into view, coherence is possible; an act of unbatism.

Chapter 14: Catalysts and Challenges

The pursuit of awakening trembles. Inherited safety demands that worn structures be reimagined. For participants, the catalysts of change materialize as a betrayal, a loss, or an unexpected insight. Unsettling and contrarian, the weight of compliance crafted to please or protect. Releasing those constructs often led to confusion and isolation. In the depths of that discomfort, an inner restlessness pervades. Challenges surface as an invitation to plunge into the PFA, where discomfort shifts into necessary terrain.

Chapter 15: Active Imagination: Engaging the Perverse

Contending with the unconscious requires opens a portal into the abandoned basement of the mind. Threaded into visualization, creative writing, and dream dialogue, women stir what lies beneath conscious reach. The PFA unveils as a presence, met in image, movement, and internal dialogue. Rather than observing from a distance, women come into direct contact with her essence. Disowned qualities intertwine themselves into the fabric of psychic awakening.

Stage 4

Redefining the Feminine: An Integration of the PFA

The PFA requires confrontation with the disowned. Convergence begins here. At the primordial roots in restrictive societal undercurrents. Lilith guides us into the unknown, and here we can reclaim vitality. Shame yields discovery. Rage defines boundaries. Roles shaped by compliance fall away, where testimonies give way to increased sovereignty. A devotion to realism supersedes external approval. The rejected is sacred. The forbidden is a uniting thread, stitched between desecrated mental folds.

Chapter 16: Shadow Integration

Once one attends to the call of confrontation, the PFA ravishes their conscious life. Coiled inside the marrow of discarded bones, the symbol is lover—a mirror charged with truth. Shadow integration begins here. Not as resolution, but as reverent intimacy. Rejected fragments return with a charge; they demand recognition. Bearing witness to the inevitable decomposition, interviewees dance in the shadows of a mournful recognition of lost time. An urgency washes over doubt and the underworlds spills into the realm of the living.

Chapter 17: Manifestations of the PFA

The PFA is a seizure. She jerks across the landscape of memory, claws through instinct, slashes the veil. Her inescapable presence pervades through synchronistic dreamscapes. Moments of clarity sparkle in the light of recognition, decimating the bondage of conventionality. Her energy radiates through mythopoetic symbols whose unwieldy embrace emits an artistic pigment of forgotten screams. Ritual triggers insurgency, dislodging submerged memories. Forced to attend to projective demons of exiled truth, women locate her in the crevices of their road to restoration.

Chapter 18: Embodying the Perverse Feminine

Pivoting toward the mythic profane, we untie the knots of self-directed misogyny. Lilith vitalizes cultural castaways. Her refusal, her hunger, her flame: invitations to birth an uncorrupted life. As women meet her ancestral vibration, they encounter a visceral clarity, discarding an abstract ideal. This final movement circles the reconstitution of the disavowed, where what was buried is no longer concealed, and reclamation rises.

PART III: BROADER IMPLICATIONS AND REFLECTIONS: EXPANDING THE PFA BEYOND THE PERSONAL

The text refuses containment. It bleeds into practice, into rooms where theory meets breath, rage, silence. Participant voices rupture the theoretical frame, reorienting its foundation. From reflection to application, movement suggests that the PFA is evolving and ever-present, capable of informing both clinical settings and cultural resistance.

Chapter 19: Beyond the Framework: Future Directions for the Perverse Feminine

As interview contents raise pertinent questions, what surfaces is a potentiality for to address the bounds and biases seeped within the research. Pulsing beneath gender landscapes, political conventionality, and cultural unrest lies an opportunity to increase a cross-cultural, therapeutic, and empirical reach. Arriving as a passage way, a sacred approach to analysis.

Chapter 20: Reflections on the Perverse: A Researcher's Journey

Deepening into the stages of PFA integration, a vulnerable exposition reveals the researcher's edges. Stretching beyond conformity, into a underlying reckoning with her beliefs. Poised at the edge of curiosity, the work continues. Here, the aberrant no longer whispers from the margins and researcher becomes the subject

KEY TERMS AND FRAMEWORK

Theoretical and methodological lenses uncover an intermediary investigation. As stages materialize, Lilith's myth sharpens into view.

Research Question

What is the PFA, and how can connecting with it help heal internalized sexism?

Key Terms

Background

Theoretical lens

Psychological and feminist theories underpinned the research, reconstituting Jungian psychology, archetypal theory, and feminist perspectives.

Jungian psychology and archetypal theory

Jungian psychology encompasses Carl Jung's theories, including archetypes, the shadow, individuation, and the collective unconscious. As these universal symbols or images embed in mythos, they support individuation (Jung, 1970).

Patriarchy

A social system in which men hold primary power and dominate roles of political leadership, moral authority, and property control, marked by the devaluation of feminine traits and the reinforcement of male dominance (Walby, 1990).

Feminism

Feminism is a movement and theoretical framework addressing gender-based oppression. As bell hooks (2014) defines it, feminism seeks to end sexism, sexist exploitation, and oppression. This container intersects with Jungian theory by examining how patriarchal norms shape internalized sexism.

Myth

Myth refers to traditional stories that mirror cultural values and unconscious archetypes (Singer, 2000).

Lilith

Lilith, a Semitic figure symbolizing rebellion and autonomy, is central. Her myth offers a lens for understanding hegemonic repression (Mason, 2017).

Shadow and shadow integration

Repressed desires and emotions, a vital element of individuation. Turning inward catalyzes a reckoning with the lost aspects of the Self, leading to greater recognition (Jung, 1907–09/1969b).

Phenomena

The phenomena awakened throughout the research supported a comprehensive approach to forming the shadow to understand internalized sexism.

Perversity

Traits like assertiveness, which deviate from traditional gender roles, are labeled perverse, pushing them into the hidden realm (Dijkstra, 1988).

Hysteria

The historical pathologization of women's emotional experiences, reinforcing patriarchal control and embedded in contemporary mental health challenges (Chesler, 2018).

Internalized sexism

An unconscious absorption of sexist beliefs that leads to a suppression of seemingly perverse traits such as sexual independence, autonomy, and emotional expression (Wehr, 1987).

Persona distortion

The pressure to conform causes a misalignment between one's outward persona, deepening potential repression (Jung, 1970).

Identity fragmentation

Societal pressure splits personal desires from external expectations (Jung, 1977a).

Collective unconscious

A shared reservoir of unconscious memories and archetypes passed down from generations, shaping societal norms and individual psychic imprints (Jung, 1970).

Active imagination

A Jungian technique to dialogue with the unconscious, facilitating shadow integration (Jung, 1907–09/1969b).

Self vs *self*

I utilize *self* in lowercase to denote the personal, constructed disposition shaped by social conditioning and internalized norms. In contrast, I refer to the Self (capitalized) to signify individuation as described in Jungian theory.

METHODOLOGY

The qualitative approach to data analysis generated a clear route to evolution and the PFA's role in healing internalized sexism.

Intuitive Inquiry (II)

II is a research method that invites intuition participation through a five-stage hermeneutic matrix (Anderson, 2004).

Narrative analysis

This method uncovers patterns in personal stories, examining how societal norms imprinted onto participants' beliefs (Clandinin & Connelly, 2000).

Thematic analysis

Identifies recurring themes, revealing societal pressures (Braun & Clarke, 2006).

Participants

Twenty women whose experiences reflected traits of the PFA and the four-stage healing approach.

PART I

LAYING THE GROUNDWORK

Understanding the Roots of the Perverse Feminine Archetype

Part I opens a conceptual portal, introducing the inquiry through lived experience and emergent technique. The chapters that follow (1–4) serves as the foundation for the researcher's background, theoretical and methodological undercurrents, and preliminary findings. Here, the reader is invited to descend into conceptual underpinnings, preparing for the Perverse Feminine Archetype (PFA).

DOI: 10.4324/9781003455837-1

Chapter **1**

Unveiling the Perverse Feminine

The following autoethnographic vignette illustrates the lived experience of conditioned dysfunction through a feminist psychological lens.

"Curfew, ladies!" Nurse Barb chirped. Her grating footsteps scraped across the mustard-yellow linoleum. Each step, a jagged knife slicing through the suffocatingly still room; a siren's call to disillusionment. The frigid hallway assaulted my senses. To my left, jolting cries rattled as guards dragged a flailing body. To my right, a vacant stare. We both lay wide-eyed, commiserating with an unspoken resonance. Am I in hell? No, just a Vegas psych ward. The unrelenting refrain of *fifty-one/fifty* vibrated as I registered its condemnation. Burned in my retinas lived the image of a man. Was he a nurse, an intake coordinator, or a psychiatrist? I wouldn't know. I glanced at his clipboard: "*Detention of Persons with a Mental Health Condition for Evaluation and Treatment*" (California Welfare and Institutions Code § 5150, 2024). A mouth. The term struck me like a death sentence.

She spoke softly, and my innards recoiled. A recollection of my husband's indictment, "You're crazy! Just like my mother!" A flood of memories collided with the refrain of *fifty-one/fifty*, cascading as a symbiotic branding. Almost poetic, his words bled from his terse lips, a prosaic undertone. As he calmly consumed his steak, gnawing methodically, he narrowly glanced up from his newspaper. The clinking of his fork punctuated the erasure that followed, vibrating the room. His intellectual superiority and worldly values undercut my emotional turbulence. I examined his countenance, hoping to uncover hesitation, remorse, or even the slightest flicker of compassion.

Was his assessment cruel? Did he intend to plunge a blade into my soul? Or perhaps he was the objective expert, while I stood as the chaotic madwoman. I observed his movements to gather some semblance of evidence. It never surfaced. He was an unbothered man as I unraveled silently. My recollection numbs reality.

DOI: 10.4324/9781003455837-2

I dimly recall the person I was before our love story began. I might have been someone with goals, someone he loved. Over time, I'd come to imagine that, as he proclaimed, it was in my best interest that he remained critical and unemotional. He had to be strong, for I was weak. He had to be smart, for I was dumb. Someone in this marriage had to. He was my anchor, tethering me to the world. I'm lucky to have him. He's right. I have mood swings, and I can't seem to function in the real world. Can I trust my perception? Probably not. Without him, I would float away, right? Because *that* was the design.

Rumbling in questions of uncertainty, a well of defiance coiled in the folds of my chest, crushing my ribs and knotting in my throat. An urgency gathered. A somatic expedition, and my fury seeped out from the cracks in my veneer. Containment dissolved. The pulsing pressure in my jaw was clenched so tightly that it ached. My body craved articulation. The sensation hummed, restless and electric, craving release, yet paradoxically, it became a refuge, hinting at the undiscovered oceanic depths of my being. My wildness sought expression. Defiance. A witness to a long-forgotten wildness. In that sterile hallway, surrounded by the ghosts of women past, I sought a quiet solace in the essence of my pathology: I allowed myself, for once, to be an angry woman. Housed in a cage, my animalistic sensibilities arose—a source of lost vitality and a reckoning of my most valuable possession. Time. Could my maladaptive tendencies serve as an entryway to power? In my electric unraveling, I glimpsed the possibility of an expression, a feral aperture. Under the weight of trepidation, I summoned an entity whose ashes rose from my chest. I summon her from the depths of a deserted hellscape. Under the weight of my plea, she materializes.

ESTABLISHING PERVERSITY, INVOKING LILITH

My quest for redemptive reckoning sought sanction within demonized obscurities. Lilith guided me as I carved pathways to articulate her presence in conceptual design. Liminality surfaced as visceral wisdom entwined with intellectual tradition, unsettling my propensity towards Stoic fantasy. *Idols of Perversity* by Bram Dijkstra (1988), enticed me into an expansive underbelly, where haunting portrayals of feminized dissidents serve as muses. Historical portrayals of villainous creatures seduced the senses, leaping from the page, reflecting a twisted and erotic condemnation concealed in an unruly physical force. Encoded in the marrow of a symbiotic network, my mind transfixed upon the nature of wielded perversity.

At its root, perversity is a breach in sanctioned norms (Merriam-Webster, 2019). When applied to women, it enforces a punitive connotation. Welldon's (1995, 2011) theoretical developments fortify uncharted phenomenon, identifying how society denounces those who disavow normative behavior. Morally reprehensible, they say. Her duty is as a mother, they say. Ussher (2006) extends conceptualization by arguing that female rage and psychic pain are routinely baked into pathological discourse. By contrast, male excess is rebranded as tragically flawed.

This paradoxical landscape erodes power, centralizing the male hero. Emblematic anti-heroes like Satan in Judeo-Christian traditions, the tyrant king in mythology, and the biologically deviant Homo Criminalis (Lombroso & Ferrero, 1895) demonstrate how violence is consistently framed as fortitude, even when cloaked in the language of moral defect. Such asymmetry reflects the systemic valorization of male ambition and the pathologization of female volition (Chesler, 2018). The historical witch trials, a significant crucible, expose the harmful normalization of sanctioned violence. As Federici (2004) argues that persecuted witches were often landowners, midwives, healers, and unmarried elders. Targeted not for spiritual deviance but because their sovereignty posed a direct threat to the ascending monotheistic order. Their persecution dismantled communal structures and reasserted patriarchal control over reproduction, labor, and land. Admonishments inscribe contemporary structures, from disproportionate psychiatric diagnoses to persistent economic marginalization. Collective amnesia collides with present-day challenges, and a guide emerges to navigate the electrifying expanse. Redemption lives in the taboo.

What if perversity is not pathology, but a memory? A rupture where the doors of the psyche stand ajar, exhaling a forgotten force, inviting us to slip into an untamed elsewhere. Beyond invitation, the Perverse Feminine waits. Not as a reflection. Not as a reversal. As a presence dwelling where exile and return collide. Emitting from the blasphemous, insurrection ravishes a timeless place (see Figure 1.1).

Entrenched in Jung's theory of symbolic images, where motifs are entryways to hungry ghosts [Jung, 1(1933–54/1969)], Lilith's archaic presence forms a symbolic vessel in the unseen: A transgressor who harbors the unwanted, the forgotten. Neither saint nor sinner, she defies closure. Her force coalesces at the edges of unsanctioned impulses. Expelled for her refusal to yield to Adam, her exile lingers amid testaments of uncompliant women (Ruah-Midbar Shapiro, 2019a).

In moments of desperation, she traverses the corporeal, infiltrating with an intoxicating aura, thick with the scent of stifled potential. She sharpens longing and destabilizes the ground. Koltuv (1986) aligns her with a vector for unspoken drives, a congealment of personal and collective disillusionment. Her lineage etches a descent into culturally enforced obedience, a site of estrangement from disavowed psychic content.

Figure 1.1 *Lady Lilith*

Original artwork housed at the Delaware Art Museum. Public domain.

Note:
Oil painting by Dante Gabriel Rossetti (1866, altered 1872–1873) portrays Lilith, the mythological first wife of Adam, who rejected her husband's sexual proposition. Consequently, she was removed from the Garden of Eden and condemned to an immortal penance of demonhood. Rossetti's depiction reflects 19th-century Pre-Raphaelite themes of the femme fatale, emphasizing her enigmatic allure and commanding presence. The inclusion of a poppy in the lower right corner encodes themes of languid beauty and opium-induced slumber.

MYTH AS METHOD: EXCAVATING THE PERVERSE FEMININE

Medicalizing those who challenge gendered norms encapsulates projected perversity, reinforcing subjugation within Abrahamic Euro-American ideology. Oppression becomes a psychic residue, siphoning energy from a villainous woman. Conditioned to fear her predatory curse, we seek protection. We negate her influence. We placate acceptability. Rejection calcifies erosion, dampening the Self into disjointed splinters (Jung, 1969a). A hallowing coalesces; a web of avoidance that signals provocation. Perversion unveils an imaginal affront, seeking qualitative measures attuned to the devotional and nonconforming.

Encoded in an allegorical examination, Intuitive Inquiry (II) bridges depth psychology, feminist epistemology, and metaphysicality, engaging in a hermeneutical dialogue (Anderson, 1998, 2000). Across five iterative cycles, it prepares us for an expedition unclaimed by conventional science.

Semi-structured qualitative interviews with 20 participants laid the foundation, as research follows the II protocol for a narrative communion, paralleling Jung's concept of individuation. Following data collection, a thematic analysis was employed to determine key psychological patterns. As participants grappled with their beliefs, their desire for healing permeated conversations. Epiphany carried the texture of initiation. Taboo undercurrents formed descent. Narratives convulsed, echoing the distinct stirrings of gendered paradigms.

Insights unearthed a forbidden truth: A desire for insurgency. Wielding feminine distortion as my bridge, an internal rift appeared in dominant motifs. Where women spoke of the quiet punishments that follow refusal, I grappled with disillusionment, as turbulent edges of a scorned inner child surfaced. Reckonings demanded accountability. In returning to Lilith's legend, I collided with her as a conduit of disjunction and recollection. To meet her regard, I must interrogate my own.

I write as a white, non-disabled Jewish cisgender woman. Shaped by a European heritage and trained in Western psychological traditions. I recognize the historical implications of white feminism (Ware, 2015) and my perpetuation of its flawed application. The structures I build upon, particularly psychoanalytic approaches, amplify my bias as they exist within outdated and harmful theory (Rowland, 2002; Grosz, 1994). Thus, I do not seek a universal truth; I merely strive for understanding.

STAGES OF PFA INTEGRATION

Stage 1—Societal Indoctrination: The Inheritance of Obedience

At the brink of consciousness, Societal Indoctrination imparts its lessons: compliance ensures survival, deviation incurs expulsion. The untamed feminine, domesticated through repeated messaging. Emotions policed. Instincts redirected. Wildness pathologized. Participants speak from these wounds. An abandonment; an ache, churning in their testimonies, seeding patriarchal directives into the folds of their minds. Implanted deception touted as conventionality. I moved through that steady current of denunciation, delineating how their daily lives chastised the rawness of their being. Fear of desire commemorated a slow erosion of self. Woven throughout the interviews, seekers describe early teachings that shamed sexuality, narrowed autonomy, strangled creativity. Their intuition? A desolate desert. Ancient portrayals of disorderly women twist the collective psyche until authenticity wanes. Witches burned. Hysterics tortured. The moment of trespass, when intellect yields to the weight of elusive external law. Contradictory lessons imprint along neural paths: Shrink, contain, present as palatable. Ladylike. A noose of etiquette.

Stage 2—Shapeshifting: Fractured Identities

How does one survive in a swarm of selves, each contorting to soothe, to please, to stave off collapse? Amassed upon burdened shoulders, the shapeshifter dons her mask in pride. Spiritual substance reshapes itself to meet unspoken directives. The thirst for approval constricts the soul, a desperate cry for belonging. Interspersed in interviews, women wrestled with suffocations that imitate sincerity. To craft an identity softened for the pursuit of love. A beautiful fiction. A quiet urge to dismantle the performance stirs, yet lacking reflection, the familiar guise remains intact. What began as preservation corrodes the internal corridor. Shapeshifting takes root as a manipulation born of longing. Choreographed gestures obscure a deep unrest, reaching toward an unspoiled Self.

Stage 3—Awareness: Awakening the Perverse

Voices quivered with the strangeness of newfound agency, responding to a call entrenched in psychic memory. Participants relished heretical spaces, inviting destruction where they had once imposed rigid control. Disavowed material returned in unpredictable contours in volatile shapes. Not wholly opaque, nor purely salvific, but electric, contradictory, and alive. As boundaries loosened, laughter disrupted dread. Reluctant disclosures surfaced before they were fully formed, accompanied by a visible sense of risk and revelation. Channeled through the Perverse Feminine Archetype (PFA), Awareness destabilized inherited performances, dislodging adaptations inured by patriarchal standards. What surfaced was not resolution, but encounter. A communion with deviance.

Stage 4—Redefining the Feminine: An Integration of the PFA

Obsolete parables no longer hold. The restraints loosen. No longer shaped, trimmed, or silenced, the feminine pursues impulse. Incited by unsanctioned rites, participants construct life anew. With a faint insistence on uncontained potency, interviews enlivened stories of retribution. Channeling the PFA summoned an unholy resurrection. Conventionality revoked. Sexuality transfigured. Illusory authority vanishes, exposing the lies of hierarchical power. Their movements' smoke ascended. Insistent, disobedient, and impossible to contain. Born of unseen repudiation, they abandon the ornamental, burying themselves in the loam. Feral, deliberate, alive in refusal. My researcher sensibilities sought an arrival; a path to guide me into a linear pursuit. But I could not detach from the subversive currents between. I followed the ethereal into a graveyard of undoing, where disorientation gave way to relief.

RESEARCHER REFLECTIONS

Illustrative discernment overflowed into academic pursuit, compelling me to probe the edges of conceptual thresholds. Provoked by the snarled roots of internalized sexism, I immersed myself in feminism, mythology, Jungian theory. As I investigated, shards of codified hesitation pierced my introspections. Depth psychology posed a parallel theoretical challenge. Evil feminine metaphors in Western iconography veil the unspeakable, collapsing deviance and race into a single distorted formation. Fanon (1967) coins this mechanism as epidermalization, a psychic imposition through which colonial systems graft threatening projections onto Blackness. Colonial codes seep into doctrine, scripting a psychic reality where whiteness presides and difference calcifies as danger.

Determined to locate an alternative approach, beyond the *dark feminine*, monstrous feminine, shadow feminine (Perera, 1981; Gustafson, 2003; Mason, 2017; Creed, 1993; Ussher, 2006; Woodman, 1982), I pivoted toward the perverse. Not to sanitize, but to disturb. Forging conceptual ground that permits a wild release of the aberrant. Cast aside as surplus, woman is written into an architecture ruled by binaries: Light and dark, virtue and excess, sacred and profane (Irigaray, 1985). The Perverse Feminine Archetype (PFA) slices through divides, rejecting containment, refusing coherence. Her form invited me into an expansive domain beyond coloniality, a latent wildness.

A grumbling convulsed in gut. I swung between imaginative bursts and extended silences. More binaries. Relationships strained under the weight of my disillusionment. When my dog died, it felt like the final tether was severed. I was held, not by others, but by the work itself. The research offered no tabernacle. No structure. She refused symmetry. My endeavor refused constriction. A call from an intangible unknown. Uncomfortable, elusive.

Lilith surfaced from the sediment, expelled for her revolt (Patai, 1990), lingering as an abandoned afternote. Confrontation crystallized as I propelled into a psychiatric wound (Kessler et al., 2005; Skodol & Bender, 2003). Why? Why do I normalize my submission? What am I afraid will happen if I stop? In tracking the Perverse Feminine, I stumbled upon a desecrated landscape where the sacred refused tangibility. Existing not as whole, not healed, but awake. The questions remain lodged in my clavicle, thrusting outward. A compulsion. A consecrated ceremony. A map etched in scars. Individuation, not as wholeness, but as heresy.

The PFA unfolded as both a rite of passage and an academic pursuit, compelling me to probe the edges of my psychological thresholds. Immersing myself in feminism, mythos, Jungian theory, and the snarled roots of internalized sexism provoked a quiet upheaval that underpinned this journey. As I investigated, shards of codified internal material pervaded my thoughts, dreams, and the way I loved. The language of depth psychology—a parallel challenge where projective material clouded theory.

Chapter **2**

Archetypes, Feminism, and the Shadow

> Being a mess is taboo. I think I intentionally create messes as a form of rebellion. Something about taking back my power in small ways brings me a lot of satisfaction. It's not very popular, and I've argued with people about it, but I don't care. It's my thing, and I'm keeping it.
>
> (Lilith)

The unconscious reservoir is a sprawling domain. A site where **personal and collective** inheritances interlace, disrupting the illusion of separateness (Jung, 1933–1954/1969b). A covert legend, it absorbs, distills, and transmits. Cultural sediment compacts into convention. Ancestral residue emits inscription, etched into language, anchoring resistance.

Platonic forms offer a metaphysical template, animating perception across generations (Williamson, 1985). Psychological processes absorb into cerebral patterns that manifest in discernible configurations (Lindenfeld, 2009). At the threshold between thought and sensation, the immaterial plants itself in the ordinary. Dreams, unwanted symptoms, and hungry ghosts arrive as emissaries, wielding unresolved memory beyond reach (Woodman, 1982; von Franz, 1999). Their appearance signals a summons: Descend into the submerged. What resists consciousness floods into daily life (1907–1909/1969b).

Each network maps a facet of reckoning. The shadow harbors what culture deems dangerous; the Self speaks to totality; the persona negotiates social legibility. When distorted by shame, constructs calcify (Jung, 1953/1966). The perverse stirs as provocation. Tracking self-denial through cultural allegory uncovers a depleted feminine constitution lodged at the perimeter of intellect. She surfaces where obedience fractures and silence clots. In the moment of erasure, the patriarchal unconscious operates as a mechanism. A logic situated in domination encodes individuality as a threat. Vilified, the uncontrollable woman absorbs

DOI: 10.4324/9781003455837-3

contradiction. In one frame, she seduces; in another, she desecrates. Projection fastens her form. Gender, sexuality, and vitality stretch across ancestral scaffolds. While personal history is bound to cultural code, encounters with the PFA disrupt. Containment unravels. Dread inscribes itself into the body's hesitation.

VILLAINOUS ARCHETYPAL FIGURES OF REBELLION

Villainous sculptures, dismissed as relics, incise a disfigured inheritance. Formed from exile and accusation, they etch the contours of perversion, each carving a trace of refusal. A woman who cries for sovereignty. No longer muffled. Uncontainable. She pulses in Hecate's liminal force, pierces through Medusa's gaze, and animates Lilith's wings. Alive, craving a spectator, a courageous soul to descend into a shadowy dwelling, locked in a mental dungeon.

Hecate (Figure 2.1) hovers at the edges of structure, in negotiation with the material plane. Instruments of a forbidden crossing, her torches, keys, hounds, and serpents emulate passage to the transcendental (Clay, 1984; Hesiod, trans. 1914, lines 404–452). She unsettles boundaries between worlds, enticing the seeker with an inescapable smirk. Skillful in sorcery (Johnston, 1990), she guides us into a paradox, where unquenchable desire burns away the veil of societal persecution. She leads us into the profane; the damned, the misunderstood, the banished.

Here, Medusa arrives desecrated. From her mortal conception as a priestess to her eventual rape, she emulates a warning etched in flesh. Her serpentine crown and petrifying gaze soon become her most notable features (see Figure 2.2). She reverberates through cultural memory, stalled at the brink; a condemnation that reprimands women for their assault (Seelig, 2002) (Ovid, Metamorphoses, trans. 2004, Book 4, lines 753–803). With fervency, her monstrosity is tool; a refusal, an embodied defiance, unblinking in the face of violation (Cixous, 1976).

Where Hecate guards thresholds and Medusa burns with rage, Lilith emerges erotic and untamed. She evades fixation. Some frame her as a dire warning, others as concentrated patriarchal terror (Koltuv, 1986; Plaskow, 1990). She resists domestication, not merely a symbol of exile but a force born from it; one that stains the mythic record with hunger, refusal, and unrelenting demand. Her origins churn in storylines where disobedience stirs dread, and desire corrupts sanctioned order. Mesopotamian lore offers reflections of her form in lilītu and Lamashtu, aerial spirits who slip into homes to steal breath, seduce flesh, devour calm (Sumerian Lexical List from Ur III, ca. 2000 BCE). Their presence memorialized faltering power. Whether Lilith inherits lineage or parrots it, her authority remains. In the Hebrew canon, her name scarcely breaks the surface yet emits potency. Isaiah whispers of a desert haunt, where owls nest and Lilith rests,

Figure 2.1 *Marble Relief of Hekate*

Photographed by Zde (2014). Wikimedia Commons (Unknown Artist, ca. 117–138 CE).

Note:
Hadrianic period (2nd century CE). Three identical female forms are conjoined at the back, symbolizing the triplicity associated with mystic potency. The relief suggests a sacred setting, possibly a domestic or temple dedicated to Hekate, where devotees sought protection and guidance. "Hekate" is the Greek transliteration, while "Hecate" is the Latinized version; both spellings are correct.

Figure 2.2 *Head of Medusa*

Original artifact housed at the Art Institute of Chicago. Wikimedia Commons.

Note:
Drawn by Godfried Maes in 1680, this artwork depicts Medusa with a blend of terror and tragic beauty, reflecting the Baroque period's fascination with dramatic expressions and mythological themes. Medium: Pen and brown ink with traces of black chalk on cream laid paper.

unspoken but unmistakable (34:13–15, CEB, 2011) (see Figure 2.3). Her essence cannot be domesticated. She flashes at the periphery of sacred text. Unclaimed and unforgettable.

> Thorns will grow up in its palaces,
> weeds and brambles in its fortresses.
> It will be a dwelling for jackals,
> a home for ostriches.
> Wildcats will meet hyenas,
> the goat demon will call to his friends,
> and there Lilith will lurk and find her resting place.

Figure 2.3 *The Great Isaiah Scroll*

Digitized by Google Art Project. Wikimedia Commons.

Note:
The Great Isaiah Scroll (Unknown scribe, ca. 2nd century BCE) is one of the oldest known Hebrew manuscripts, housed at the Israel Museum, Jerusalem; the Book of Isaiah. While Lilith's presence is not explicitly mentioned, this public domain artifact allows readers to engage with ancient texts where her mythological presence lingers.

> There the snake will nest and lay eggs
> and brood and hatch in its shadow.
> There too vultures will gather,
> each with its mate.
>
> (CEB, 2011, Isaiah 34:13–15)

In the medieval tale *Alphabet of Ben Sira* (8th–10th century CE), she surfaces as Adam's first wife, rejecting subjugation. Her refusal to comply reframes banishment as agency. Kabbalistic traditions later amplify her threat, casting her as the mother of demons (Dan, 2006). Across each iteration, the symbolic charge intensifies and Lilith evolves from character to force. Her incarnations destabilize constructs conceived from suppression. Delineating a means of entrance requires a vessel capable of cradling without containment. Jung provides a provocative entry point, equipping us to approach her domain while delimiting her expression. To penetrate her domain is to interrogate the very architecture that evokes her, even as it strains to domesticate what cannot be fixed in form.

REIMAGINING ARCHETYPAL THEORY

Greco-Christian angels hover at the fringes of Jung's diagrams, their wings brushing against decorative universalities. Beneath the surface, archetypal theory often blurs cultural residue with primordial claim. His canon reveals allegorical structures saturated with Western exclusions and theological inheritance. Traditional Jungian renderings designate femininity as static forms, asserting them as timeless truths (Rowland, 2002). Nuance flattens. Tension dissolves. Harboring what defies categorization mandates a phraseology capable of possessing contradiction without resolution (von Franz, 1999). Without recalibration, archetypal typologies congeal into hierarchies that exalt intellect while subordinating affect (Crawford & Unger, 2003). Feminized traits diminished, masculine attributes exalted. Scaffolds remain, but the design must shift. A storied existence exceeds a fixed essence, asserting domination. Archetypal orientation collides with fluid systems of meaning (Hillman, 1975; Samuels, 1985), where patterns enliven. Lilith resists assimilation. She agitates. Disorients. Her resurgence across disciplines signals a collective hunger for images dense with contradiction, unsettling imposed limitations. If archetypal patterns harbor primordial weight, their shaping warrants scrutiny. Do cultural inscriptions distort essence, or reveal its pliability? Lilith exists as an active disturbance. She slips past the reach of order, agitating silence into motion. Her recurrence across psychological, spiritual, artistic, and clinical spheres signals an unrelenting impulse toward disruption—the soul left gaunt in its absence. Meaning pools in ambiguity. Memory presses into what resists articulation. Where containment fails, the perverse coalesces.

Shadow Integration and Individuation

Ancient terrors trickle down bloodlines, coursing through stories that splinter the mind. Lerner (1987) illustrates how cultural scripts actively construct sharp divisions that arbitrarily separate virtue from deviance, resonating in private and being shaped by public codes. Inheritance fissures the interior, driving unpermitted characteristics into obscurity. Dichotomous moral taxonomies corral the feminine into sacrificial purity (Lauter & Rupprecht, 1985; Ussher, 2006). The dread of censure warps psychic cohesion, suffocating the Self. The disowned stratum strains against the illusion of normalcy, humming beneath with volatile charge (Wehr, 1987). Jung framed this registrar as a storehouse of exiled traits, preservation of social acceptability, and denial of undesirable impulses (Jung, 1933–54/1969b). Behind the veneer of propriety, vital provocations endure. Pressurized. Numbed. Suspended in cold latency. Whispering through undercurrents: Sacrifice yourself to the overculture. Archetypal image distorts the quiet, exhibiting subliminality. Whitmont (1978) notes how estranged material reappears as projection, rebounding toward the subject. Patterned exile operates inevitably as the adaptive ego aligns with dominant codes, consigning unwanted texture to a psychic cellar (von Franz, 1980). Those feedback loops appeared in participants' accounts in moments, shaped by discarded material humming just outside deliberate appraisal. Individuation commences where luminosity meets occlusion, establishing a kinetic center that can coordinate submerged strata with conscious orientation (Jung, 1933–54/1969b, 1977a). Necessary disruption seethes in daily habits as a catalyst. Infusing individual struggles with harmful self-talk. From an obscured interior, the Perverse Feminine fuses collective and intrapsychic pressure into a volatile companion, summoning engagement with repressed emotions. In my estimation, what surfaced in participant reflections evoked the Perverse Feminine as a doorway for self-inquiry, elaborated in questions such as, "Why do I keep giving my power away?" and confessions, "I just feel like the universe is conspiring against me." The choice to pursue what underlies descriptive realities functions as a form of insubordination, where women rebel against an oppressive voice as a form of insurgency (Ussher, 2006). In our exchanges, a contemplative imaginal praxis unfolded. Lilith stirred as unspoken questions gained shape and inner tension pressed toward awareness (Creed, 1993).Her arrival unsettles the inherited systems that quell feminine rage, redirecting from internal reckoning to cultural confrontation (Rowland, 2002). The next chapter anchors disturbance in a methodological design, drawing on interpretive procedures to follow how charged intensities surface, collide, and reconfigure.

Chapter **3**

Spirals of Inquiry

INTUITIVE INQUIRY: THE DESIRE FOR TRANSFORMATION

> I've always felt like something was off with my sexuality, like there has been a discomfort that I couldn't quite place, and it wasn't until the other day in conversation with my mother, when she told me she thought that being gay was wrong. In this moment, I realized how deeply her belief was ingrained in me and limited my sexuality.
>
> (Persephone)

The Five Iterative Cycles of Inquiry

Note: The methodology requires the researcher to engage in both roles, acting as both witness and participant, thereby positioning subjectivity as an instrument. Accordingly, Chapter 3 integrates third-person descriptions of methodological design with first-person reflexivity. Experiential accounts serve as epistemic data, tracking symbolic resonance, affective shifts, and imaginal encounters essential to the study's progression.

Intuitive Inquiry (II) forms from the researcher's subjective experiences, offering a generative pathway to intrapsychological knowledge. Structured through five iterative cycles, the procedure fuses hermeneutic interpretation with qualitative design (Anderson, 2004, 2011) (see Figure 3.1).

While early hermeneutics examined sacred texts, modern thinkers reframe interpretation as a psychological, historical, and ontological act. Schleiermacher emphasized the interpreter's inner life (1998/1838); Dilthey regarded understanding as inseparable from lived experience (1989); and Heidegger centered wisdom in Being itself (1962).

DOI: 10.4324/9781003455837-4

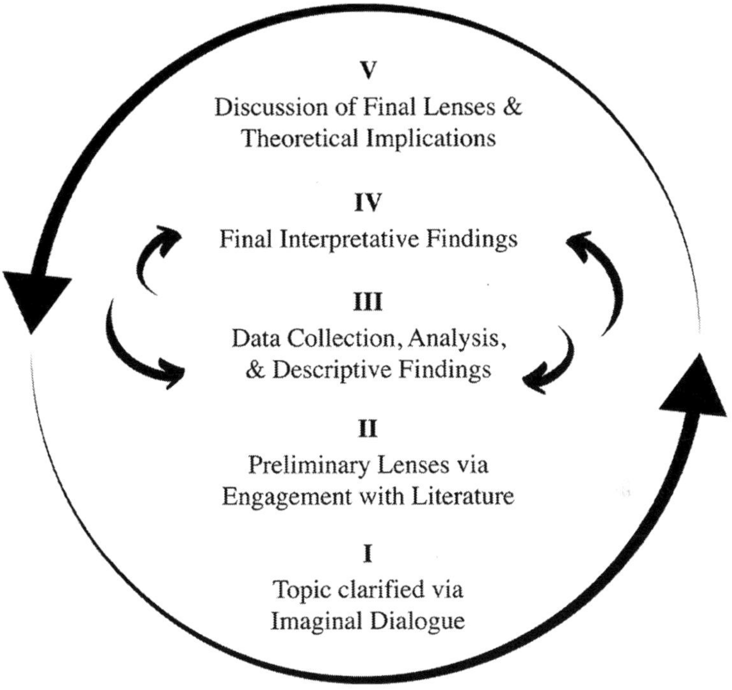

Figure 3.1 *The Hermeneutical Spiral and the Cycles of Intuitive Inquiry*

Author image.

Note:
The hermeneutical spiral and the cycles of Intuitive Inquiry (II). The II spiral invites the researcher to engage in an iterative, cyclical, inductive procedure. Cycles 1 and 2 provide the initial foundation for Cycles 3–5. Cycles 3 and 4 are refined in Cycle 5.

II occupies an initiatory and analytic recursive practice, witnessing and reshaping the metaphorical field. Archetypal language animates the method to delineate the Perverse Feminine Archetype (PFA) as a dynamic constellation of trauma, iconography, and ancestral residue. Paralleling Jung's approach to shadow integration, meaning accumulates across cycles of return (Heelan, 1998).

The following five-cycle structure, adapted from Anderson's model, anchors II's spiral. Each phase interlaces intuition with critical analysis, forming a layered rhythm.

Engaging with Literature: Reviews relevant theories to inform and refine core constructs.

Collecting and Analyzing Data: Conducts interviews and evaluates emerging discoveries with thematic analysis.

Iterative Reflection and Thematic Refinement: Revisits interpretations to improve meaning.

Integrating and Applying Findings: Synthesizes insights into a coherent, action-oriented framework.

While the cycles offer a structural rhythm, interpretive potency hinges on how intuition itself functions. To clarify a methodological core, we turn to the typology of intuition.

THE TYPOLOGY OF INTUITION

Anderson (2019) prescribes five distinct intuitive modalities to inform data collection: (a) Symbolic imagination, (b) psychic encounters, (c) bodily perception, (d) empathic attunement, and (e) wounded knowing. Each layer of instinct requires the investigator to undergo a profound discovery arc. Confrontation boils preconceived notions, dismantling the researcher and reorienting the investigation.

Symbolic and Imaginal Currents

Extending Jung's (1970) vision, symbols appeared as interpretative interlocutors. One specter, Lilith, nagged my senses. If II offered the map, Lilith erupted as the constellation. She appeared in my dreams as a veiled woman in shadows, exposing the weight of a self-loathing mentality. Interspersed with memories of brutality and humiliation, she highlighted psychic blind spots.

Psychic Unravelings

Prolonged muted, psychic receptivity reawakened at the study's edge. Lucid dreams spiraled into allegorical prophecy. Moments of clairvoyance materialized with disturbing clarity—the presence of ambiguous and exacting influences. Sudden bodily collapse, unexplained illness, and the phantom scent of gas despite an electric stove seized my sense of control. Episodes interrupted ordinary life and defied rational classification, mandating surrender.

Sensory Intelligence

The body, long dismissed under patriarchal rationalism, resurfaced as oracle. Speaking in unavoidable resonance. Tingling, tension, and visceral unease alerted me to false coherence. Attempts to override instinct bred stagnation, necessitating a pursuit of an alternative structure.

Empathic Resonance

As participants articulated challenges, I attended to my disowned echoes. Performance began to shatter. Perversity appeared not only as subversion but as compulsive compliance. A fear of magnitude, of engulfment, threatened to unravel my pursuit. The storytellers' shame met mine.

Wounded Insight

Inquiry reopened ancient wounds. As a domestic violence survivor, I approached questions with psychic scar tissue where my trauma repositioned as fertile ground (Anderson, 2019). Art, ritual, and divination offered symbolic mirrors. One such piece, "Righteous Rage" (Figure 3.2), rendered my inner world visible. The

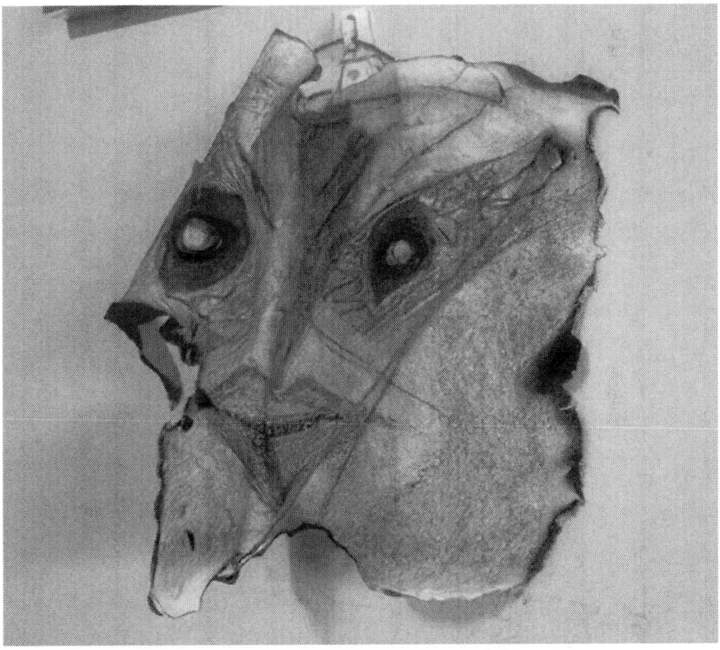

Figure 3.2 *Righteous Rage*

Author's image.

Note:
I entitled this piece "Righteous Rage" it represents an outlet for my emotional anguish. As a woman who has been restricted, confined, and condemned from a young age, I carry immense trauma. I find myself seeking freedom from the trappings of my thoughts, which I later discerned as internalized sexism. How might I finally break free from the confines of sexism? How can I help others to do the same, to live in a space of autonomy, power, and authenticity? Possibly, righteous rage can answer these questions.

image became an entryway: From anguish to agency, from silence to incantation. Archetypal engagement lived a crucible, uncovering how internalized sexism distorts the feminine into silent, shape-shifting compliance.

Immersion in Intuitive Modalities

Tasked with utilizing instincts as a research tool, I initiated a reconnection with a previously muted faculty. Distorted and rusty, the recounts of early abandonment reverberated in patterns of appeasement. II offered more than a technique; it commemorated a return to forfeited wisdom (Anderson, 2004). Amid research design, conventional methodologies felt ill-fitting. Choosing a procedure that prioritized intuition, I dismissed irrationality, leveraging an association to the erasable, the emotional, the embodied irrationality (Lincoln & Guba, 1985; Patton, 2015). Method merged with experience, dissolving boundaries between scholar and subject (Anderson, 2019). While Western epistemology elevates distance, mastery, and clarity, I leaned toward permeability. Women's wisdom became the center, not the supplement. Guided by a commitment to feminist research that honors the epistemic value of experience (Jaggar, 1989), I navigated by impulse, memory, and affectivity. Endeavoring a revolution that involves literary triangulation, participant insight, and internal shifts, I drew upon both intuitive and traditional measures of trustworthiness (Lincoln & Guba, 1985; Ando, 2014). I did not chase neutrality. I stood inside the inquiry, altered by it.

Efficacy and Validity in Intuitive Inquiry

II validity rests in its capacity to generate knowledge through emotional attunement. Characterized by layered context in which meaning arises, the method's strength lies in its demand for presence (Anderson, 2004). To support efficacy, data collection was structured to evoke metamorphasis. Prioritizing safety in design, I facilitated 60-minute semi-structured interviews that invited participant introspections. Each conversation occured place remotely, utilizing encrypted video conferencing software. Participants selected secure environments for our meetings, with the option to opt out of video calls; a strategy employed to minimize vulnerability. Interviews commenced with a reaffirmation of confidentiality and autonomy. No distinguishing information appears in the data. Pseudonyms are used consistently across both analysis and manuscript development to protect privacy. I invited all contributors to pause or end the conversation at any point without consequence. Despite assurances, moments of self-awareness occasionally surfaced. One woman remarked, "I have to remind myself that this is anonymous," before continuing. I recorded confidences in a data logbook. Traditional thematic analysis composed the initial interpretive layer. As responses followed a storied arc, I incorporated narrative methods and re-storying to reflect amplified meaning-making.

Objectives as Compass

The following aims shaped both methodological design and interpretive fidelity (Anderson, 2004):

Provoke critical engagement among scholars and practitioners regarding how societal norms shape psychic life, professional conduct, and selfhood.
Complicate binary constructions of the PFA, illuminating its layered, often contradictory manifestations through integrative analysis.
Cultivate resonance between researcher and reader by offering vulnerability as a method, where storytelling becomes a portal into shared psychic terrain.
Catalyze transformation by inviting readers into acts of self-interrogation, intuitive discernment, and committed reclamation.

As the study evolved, reflection recalibrated understanding, privileging dynamic findings.

Cyclical Research Reflexivity

Each cycle intensified my engagement with the literature. Jungian theory, feminist critique, and mythic analysis unraveled inherited frameworks and reshaped how I approached the psyche (Kautz, 2003; Anderson, 2019). Intuitive Inquiry dismantled the illusion of detachment. Immersion in its demands fractured internal structures I once mistook for stability. As I worked with archetypal figures and mythic residue, I uncovered compartmentalized drives—adaptations forged in silence, constraint, and the performance of coherence (Wertz et al., 2011).

This excavation surfaced ingrained behaviors: People-pleasing, overperformance, and the erosion of boundaries. Amid emotional turbulence, the research offered ground. Participant stories acted as ballast, tethering me to a shared reckoning rather than isolating me in collapse. I tracked shifts in sensation, tone, and inner prompting. Subjectivity became a conduit for meaning.

At times, I absorbed participants' disclosures too fully, crossing into countertransference. To recalibrate, I turned to supervision, therapeutic reflection, and peer dialogue. I also turned to tarot, asking, "Where is distortion directing my focus?" What am I resisting in interpretation? Ritual refined perception, inviting greater precision and accuracy. Personal history functioned as an instrument, privileging obscured patterns.

THE FIVE-CYCLE JOURNEY OF INTUITIVE INQUIRY

In archetypal experimentation, detachment can obfuscate clarity, as researchers inadvertently circumvent emotional delicacy. Consequently, when one seeks communion with liminality, comprehensive commitment to unexplored techniques is essential. Traversing a threshold between established knowledge, the subject matter evokes ambiguity, mandating an anchored form of surrender. By interweaving a prescriptive methodological approach with active imagination, the investigation expands as an evocative interplay between consciousness and image. In practice, the subconscious expedition incites symbolic configurations, inviting mythic aberrations to unveil an unexplored domain. As Jung (1997, 1981) posits, such exchanges elicit pedagogic understanding through image, synchronicity, and involuntary memory. What follows is the first four cycles of investigative accounts, through which the researcher matures as an intermediary, detailing a spiralic descent

CYCLE 1: CLARIFYING THE RESEARCH TOPIC

Clarification initiates as engulfment, where the research arises from lived perspicuity, scoffing at my fixation on objectivity. Imaginal dialogue unraveled in dreamscape and divination, demanding that I surrender habitual doubt and forge an intimate bond with the topic. As repressed filaments surfaced, they exteriorized as emotive constraints. I observed, for example, that my attempts at clinical distance resulted in a tightening in my chest. Indications that neutrality concealed avoidance. What fractured in these moments shaped the unfolding of the design itself (Anderson, 2019). My dreams enlivened with persecutory demons who sought redemption and a calling from displaced inner turmoil. To facilitate an incarnation of intuitive impressions, I commissioned an artist to depict an innate sense of symbolic trajectory: A young girl ingesting cultural prescriptions, eventually seeking reunion with a fractured interiority. The imagery echoed motifs later entrenched in participant narratives, lending retrospective coherence to the eventual integrative framework (see Figure 3.3).

Lilith's haunting invocation materialized as a critical anchor. She penetrated imaginal field formed through ancient texts, feminist exegesis, digital media. Inhabiting her demonic realm required me to immerse myself in my tumultuous inner world; that which I had previously bypassed. Calling her forth required an exposition into the dark. Condemned and exiled, I pursued classical sources, such as the Alphabet of Ben Sira and the Zohar (Sperling & Simon, 1933). Her aberrant and threatening personification emanated from the pages, and I yearned for her to inhabit my spirit. The anger, rage, and sexual deviance bubbled to the surface in her story. Her reappearance across modalities marked a metaphysical fissure. Dreams sharpened and my waking life mirrored internal imagery, forming patterns too layered to disregard. Jung (1970) described such phenomena as synchronicity, deciphered as meaningful coincidences that dissolve perceived separation. Lilith's presence soon became the axis by which convergences spun. As Hurwitz (2009) notes, Lilith epitomizes cultural anxieties of autonomous feminine power, an angst that I shared. The fear of my innate power remain trapped

Figure 3.3 *Mapping the Research, commissioned October 2021*

Figure by contracted artist who wishes to remain anonymous.

within the dungeon of historical admonishments. Activating Lilith's essence, I developed a kinship with her antagonistic and regenerative contemporary story (2019a, 2019b). Resulting in a formidable existential crisis, I fell into a pit of despair. How long had I been disconnected? Oh, how much time I have wasted. The mournful cries of my inner child, seeking comfort in a demon. Amid destabilization, I contested the study's coherence and value. Why would I take on such an ambitious trek into a well of shattered mental contortions? Wandering through San Francisco, I encountered a reproduction of Gustav Klimt's Water Serpents II (1904–1907) (see Figure 3.4), discarded beside a trash bin. The image appeared with uncanny timing. A synchronicity indeed. I understood this act as a communication from an unnamed piece of myself.

The painting's serpentine figures paralleled Lilith's myriad formations, in conjunction with her association with the serpent in Edenic lore. The nude bodies in the illustration struck me. As an enigmatic temptress with varied interpretations, her Kabbalistic presence connects her to Eve's demonic serpent and consort of Satan (Samael) (Dan, 1980) (see Figure 3.5).

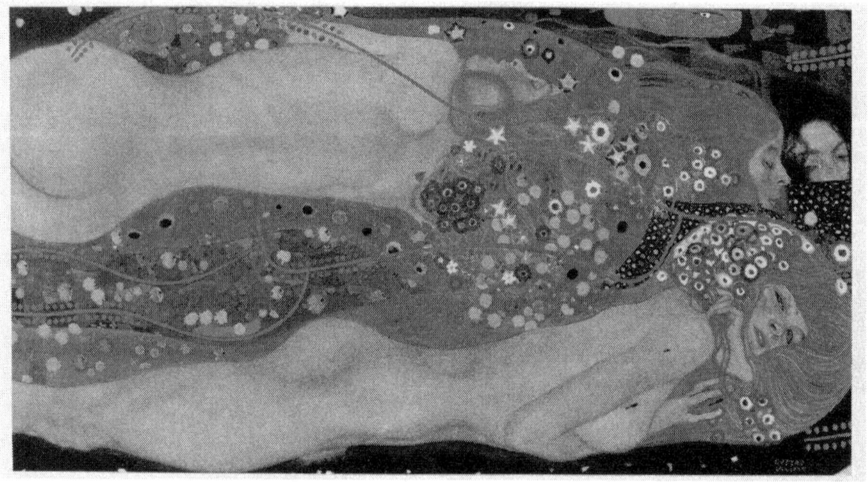

Figure 3.4 *Water Serpents II*

Note:

Water Serpents II (1904–1907) is renowned for its water nymph depiction and is part of Gustav Klimt's exploration of the sensuality of the female form. The painting has a complex provenance; it was confiscated in World War II and later involved in high-profile art transactions.

Figure 3.5 *Lilith*

Original artwork housed in The Miriam and Ira D. Wallach Division of Art, Prints, and Photographs, The New York Public Library.

Note:
Kenyon Cox (1981). This collotype illustration of Lilith portrays her entwined with a serpent, symbolizing defiance, knowledge, and potentcy. Below, Eve's contrasting presence reinforces Lilith's mythological role as a rebellious counterpart in the creation lore.

I wandered into the forest, my throat pulsing with a familiar painful hum. Repressed anger. The sun peeked through the leaves. I pressed my palm against a tree, rough bark biting into my skin. Why is it so easy to see beauty in wilting flowers yet so challenging to welcome my own flaws? I choked on my breath, "What's wrong with me?" I scanned the trees, scouring for answers in their stillness, nothing. My search for salve did not arrive as a refuge, but as pain. I plummeted into the depths of the ache of a life undone. The choice to proceed required an exponential amount of connection with the very pain I sought to avoid. Thereafter, texts animated in tandem with inner material. Resonant, unsettled, alive. The methodological matrix reconfigured itself through symbols. Veiled aberrations and serpent-bodied nymphs flooded my imagination. Nature's solidity, myth's mutability, and emotional charge urged me to engage the PFA as a living force. What took shape in Cycle 1 was not certainty, but alignment; a portal that revolutionized my approach to knowledge itself.

CYCLE 2: ENGAGING WITH LITERATURE AND UNCONSCIOUS MATERIAL

The method unfolded between structure and instinct, dispersing wisdom that traced the inner edges of theoretical landscapes. Historical chronologies and contemporary critiques exposed a dangerous gender paradigm that piqued my curiosity. Lilith shaped my questions and theoretical pursuits. Enlivening the exposition, our collaboration existed as choreography; a dance that tethered scholarship to intuition. Inspired by her image, I sought repudiations that imitated individuation, and her myth carried resonance forward. Refusal, exile, and erotic danger were no longer abstract themes, they serve as an avalanche of psychic discernment. My observations disrupted my structured, systematic approach. As the research unfolded across both mythological and scientific terrains. Methodology materialized within a paradoxical space, where observations dispersed within the margins of existing theoretical texts. Beneath the surface of historical discernment and modern complexities, I detected a persistent imprint of sexist conditioning, which revealed an insidious imprint on primary domains that would later serve as my fundamental literature: Theology, psychology, mythology, and feminism. Employing symbolic ritual and selective focus, I constructed a conceptual framework informed by archetypal patterns underlying internalized sexism.

Research Questions

Guiding curiosities necessitate a systematic review of relevant literature, intuitive insights, and engagement with the internal world.

1. How does the perverse feminine exist in daily lives?
2. How has femininity been distorted or perverted by societal norms?

3. How does the PFA relate to **internalized sexism?**
4. What are the pathways women can take to overcome repressive gender norms?
5. How can the PFA serve as a source of liberation for women?

Inspired by these postulations, I approached the literature with a desire to familiarize myself with predecessor theorists.

Literature Immersion

Cycle 2 mandates an intentional narrowing of focus, aligning literature with the central research questions. The investigator discards superfluous material, concentrating on primary sources. Guided by Anderson (2011), saturation unfolds in three phases: *Familiarity*, immersing oneself in the readings; Determination, committing exhaustively to the practice; and Interpretive Lenses, appointing focal points that contoured the interpretive arc. Entering the Familiarity and Determination phases, I read compulsively, pursuing cords that twisted through words of thinkers like Jung, von Franz, Grosz, Haraway, Plaskow, Butler, Rowland, Kaplan, Estés, and Dijkstra (see Table 3.1). Texts lodged themselves somatically. Some sparked

Table 3.1 *Critical theorists from Cycle 2*

Theory/Framework	Key Theorists	Contribution
Feminist Jungian Theories	Anderson (2011), Rowland (2002), Butler	Feminist Jungian lens to develop an archetypal subversion of patriarchal constructs.
Intersectionality	Crenshaw (1989), Collins (2000)	Prioritized intersectionality and emphasized the importance of centering marginalized voices in feminism.
Jungian Theory	Jung (1969a, 1969b), von Franz (1999), Rowland (2002), Anderson (2011)	Supported the development of a foundational psychoanalytical/ archetypal theory.
Mythology and Lilith	Dijkstra (1988), Koltuv (1986), Dan (1980)	Developed the mythological image of Lilith as a reflection/ embodiment of the PFA.
Feminist Psycho-Spirituality	Miller (1987), Wehr (1987), Lerner (1987)	Integrated feminist perspectives with spiritual practices, exploring how participants sought healing through reclaiming suppressed aspects of femininity.

Note:
Initial lenses appeared as a creative excursion with primary theorists', who provided a pathway towards a structural analysis.

a visceral urgency while others stirred repulsion, sorrow, or unease. I tracked each affective response. Awe, resistance, grief, and urgency led me to relevant texts.

I examined what my senses revealed about the author's framework, tone, or symbolic register. Some works echoed the inquiry's conceptual demands; others exposed reinforced problematic paradigms. When conventional modes of analysis failed to hold complexity, I pivoted toward ritual. I traced the edges of stones, pressed my palms into earth, entered meditative states. A return home. Embodied acts recalibrated my epistemological bearings, permitting knowledge to arise from sensation. Corporeal and cognitive, the literature built itself into a wave of wisdom.

Interpretive Lenses

Anderson (2011) describes Cycle 2 as the forward arc, a phase where intuitive inquiry advances novel deliberations. Tarot sessions, intuitive writing, guided imagery, and twilight walks loosened rigid preconceived assumptions. The Tower card returned frequently, signaling the breakdown of rigid objectivity and the demand for a novel research approach. What follows outlines the guiding interpretive lenses that arose from embodied experimentation, formed by ritual and theoretical undercurrents.

Archetypal-Feminist Synthesis

Arising from the convergence of archetypal psychology with feminist theory, the research examines psychic and sociocultural dimensions of internalized oppression. Collective symbols live as dynamic sites of reckoning and Lilith illuminates how concepts of an ideal femininity perpetuate. With a focus on sexism's psychological consequences, I contend with a guided selection of literary sources rooted in archetypal patterns and feminist critique, thereby shaping the inquiry's conceptual foundation. This interpretive frame informed how I read participant narratives as articulations of both psychic tension and sociopolitical inscription.

Mythopoetic-Spiritual Reorientation

Distinguishable from rigid theological portrayals, Lilith stood as a guiding force. Her presence echoed the layered demands of the individuation discovered in later data analysis. As her image moved across methodological spirals, her insistence on atonement remained. No longer a remote figure, she evolved as a disruptive interlocutor who unsettled assumptions. With her guidance, perversity surged from the text, pressing for the retrieval of fragmented psychic material. Sacred wisdom wrapped in lore, cultivating a symbiotic excursion into the profane.

Power, Healing, and Reclamation

Empowerment stirred the residues of psychic injury, drawing forth buried compliance. Ruptures in normative structures unsettled fixed embodiment, allowing new forms of presence to surface. Sensuality, historically fractured by cultural repression, is reassembled in practices once deemed self-indulgent. Tracing bodily rhythms, erotic attention, and sensory presence, cultivated ritualistic potency. This phase shaped the direction of data collection, emboldening the researcher to delve into previously taboo subjects, highlighting the body as a site of redemption.

Integrating the Lenses

Interpretations gradually entangled themselves, their meanings fusing into a reflexive totality. Lilith's paradox disrupted the ease of goddess spirituality, fracturing any impulse toward resolution. Incorporating interpretive lenses uncovered habituated compliance shaped by ancestral repetition, entrenched in cultural narrative, and communicated through the body's unspoken rituals. What had once lurked at the edges now stirred plainly, sketching an entryway of deliverance. Widening the aperture, the path intensified as theoretical abstractions gave way to collaborative data collection and analysis.

CYCLE 3: DATA COLLECTION AND INITIAL ANALYSIS

Following the symbolic and intuitive saturation in Cycle 2, the third revolution shifts into formal qualitative collection and analysis (Anderson, 2019). Guided by interpretive lenses, I approached the data as both artifact and atmosphere. With a calculated archetypal technique, the analysis required transparency between the participant and investigator, demanding sustained attentiveness. Drawing on both foundational literature insights and experiential attunement, I prepared data that resisted linear interpretation and invited layered insights. Psychological and spiritual sensitivity shaped this phase, attuning the quest to form metaphorical and embodied essence (Anderson & Braud, 2011).

Preparation and Reflexivity

In preparing for the interviews, I entered a creative process akin to active imagination, grounding myself in instinct and intuition. Drumming, dancing, and spending time in nature attuned me to my internal rhythms. As I entered the terrain of discovery, my positionality bled into the work. My prompts, methodological choices, and theoretical orientations bore the imprint of my whiteness, education, survivor history, non-disabled body, and feminist affiliations. Confronting embedded influences required both inward reflection and external critique. Mock interviews exposed tacit assumptions in my phrasing; mentorship surfaced patterns that had felt intuitive but proved methodologically unsound.

Participant Demographics and Recruitment

Although the analysis intended to employ a diverse participant pool, the final sample consisted of a moderately homogenous group. Outreach efforts included: Reddit, Craigslist, the local Planned Parenthood, and mutual connections, employing convenience sampling and snowball procedures. To reinforce accessibility and clarity, a flyer accompanied each posting, inviting those who resonated with the study's themes to enroll (see Figure 3.6). Future recruitment strategies might assess alternative measures to enhance the variety of respondents.

The sample consists of 20 participants. Thirteen (73%) are white women, with seven (26%) as women of color. Eleven (53%) reported heterosexual orientation,

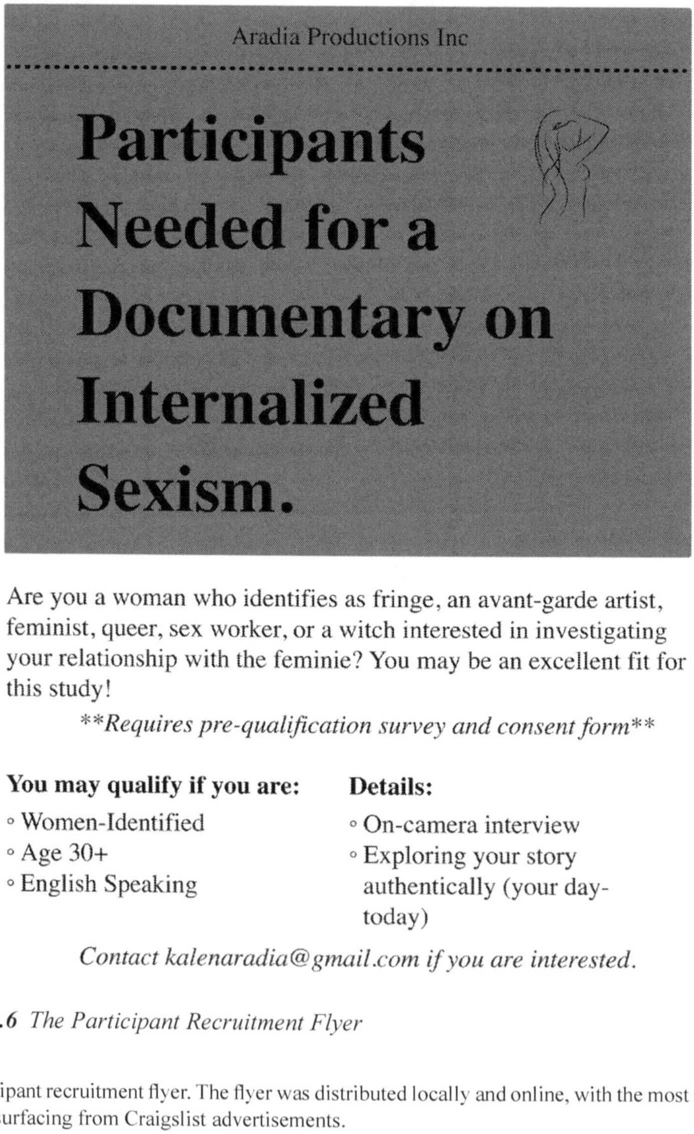
Aradia Productions Inc

Participants Needed for a Documentary on Internalized Sexism.

Are you a woman who identifies as fringe, an avant-garde artist, feminist, queer, sex worker, or a witch interested in investigating your relationship with the feminie? You may be an excellent fit for this study!

Requires pre-qualification survey and consent form

You may qualify if you are:
- Women-Identified
- Age 30+
- English Speaking

Details:
- On-camera interview
- Exploring your story authentically (your day-today)

Contact kalenaradia@gmail.com if you are interested.

Figure 3.6 *The Participant Recruitment Flyer*

Note:
The participant recruitment flyer. The flyer was distributed locally and online, with the most significant response surfacing from Craigslist advertisements.

Table 3.2 *Participant Demographics*

Pseudonym	Age	Identifier	Sexuality	Profession
Lilith	35	Jewish	queer	artist
Hecate	45	White	bisexual	artist
Kali	33	White	heterosexual	actor
Gaia	48	Latin	heterosexual	MD
Artemis	32	White	pansexual	writer
Oya	32	Black	heterosexual	lighting tech
Persephone	32	White	bisexual	lighting tech
Hestia	65	White	heterosexual	LCSW
Medusa	59	White	heterosexual	artist
Demeter	37	White	heterosexual	artist
Nyx	62	White	asexual	doula
Guan Yin	33	Chinese	heterosexual	student
Inanna	43	White	bisexual	doula
Athena	42	White	bisexual	actor
Hera	52	White	heterosexual	speech therapist
Lamia	35	White	queer	artist
Ala	50	Black	heterosexual	dancer
Oshun	32	Black/White	bisexual	artist
Aphrodite	45	White	heterosexual	entrepreneur
Ixchel	33	Latina	bisexual	healer

Note:
The researcher determined pseudonyms to protect anonymity and generate mythological deities and she-demons.

while nine (47%) described themselves as queer or non-heterosexual. No participants reported a disability, representing a substantial limitation in the scope of analysis. Table 3.2 outlines the demographic categories. Participants selected from age, racial or ethnic positionality, sexuality, and profession, but could also self-define under an "identifier" field to account for nuance and multiplicity. Participants often reflected contradiction, ambiguity, and refusal, offering insight into the layered conception of the pursuit. Although not representative of broader population trends, each individual was selected not for lifestyle and qualification as 'perverse' determined by preliminary surveys. Those who function on the margins of society in careers, beliefs and daily lives were primary sources of key data, indicating underlying archetypal dimensions.

While interviewees illuminated key dynamics of internalized sexism and the PFA, their homogeneous nature constrained the scope of interpretation. Future studies should intentionally recruit participants across racial, economic, sexual, and ability-based margins. Limitations of the present study's recruitment strategies should be addressed and modified.

Eligibility Criteria

When recruiting **participants**, the researcher employed the following eligibility criteria:

1. **Cisgender**—To explore internalized sexism as experienced by those socialized under gender-specific norms from early life, all contributors identified as cisgender women.
2. **Language**—Participation was limited to fluent English speakers to minimize communication barriers.
3. **Location**—While physical location was not central to the study, all lived in the United States during the research period. One individual was residing temporarily in Colombia but had long-standing ties to the U.S. education system.
4. **Beliefs**—Eligible individuals expressed strong orientations toward feminist thought (affirmative or oppositional), alternative spirituality, countercultural values, or worked in male-dominated professions.
5. **Age**—All were over 30, an age by which social, professional, and relational pressures often sharpen internal conflicts.

The parameters fostered a participant pool capable of articulating nuanced reflections. Many participants had been informally wrestling with themes of internalized sexism prior to the study.

Research Integrity and Participant Welfare

The study was reviewed and approved by the *California Institute of Integral Studies* (CIIS) Human Research Review Committee (HRRC), ensuring adherence to established ethical research protocols. Each participant supplied with informed consent and received a bill of rights that clearly outlined participant agency throughout the procedure. To maintain emotional safety, the investigator incorporated verbal check-ins throughout each interview. Participants retained complete discretion to pause or withdraw at any point without penalty. Additionally, a $20 honorarium was distributed as both a gesture of gratitude and a measure to enhance accessibility. All interviews were conducted virtually, affording participants geographic flexibility, protection against COVID-19, and the comfort of engaging from a self-selected setting.

Data Collection

The data collection comprised of multiple methodological phases, including video-recorded interviews, narrative elicitation, thematic coding, symbolic clustering, and narrative synthesis. Each participant completed a one-hour open-ended interview via Zoom, guided by two central prompts:

- What does it mean to be a woman who exists outside the binary of good/evil or perverse/ideal?
- How can women utilize perversity as an agent for healing internalized sexism?

The interviews functioned as dialogical spaces where imagery, memory, and metaphor surfaced in response to a carefully constructed arc. Question designed elicited a psychological, aiming to prompt condemned characteristics to

Oral History and Narrative Inquiry

Participants offered autobiographical accounts that revealed the developmental trajectory of internalized sexism, indicating a necessity to infuse *Narrative Inquiry* as a source of data collection. Life histories spanned early socialization through adulthood, exposing apprehensions between genuineness and sociocultural norms (Creswell & Poth, 2017).

Data Handling

In compliance with HRRC guidelines, de-identified transcripts were stored securely on an encrypted external hard drive, scheduled for destruction seven years after project completion. Initial transcription was performed via Otter.ai (https://otter.ai) and manually examined as printed material for accuracy. Final transcripts were uploaded to MAXQDA (https://www.maxqda.com) to support structured coding and qualitative analysis.

Thematic Analysis and Symbolic Tagging

The researcher employed conventional thematic analysis to develop overarching themes, subthemes, and resonant codes via Braun and Clarke's (2006) six-phase model. Interviews were parsed into chronological segments labeled as childhood, current experiences, and imagined futures. Additional relevant codes include *sexuality*, shame, good versus evil, childhood, emotional resonance, trauma, violence, healing witches, spiritual connection, codependency, underestimation, dissociation, and objectification. A symbolic tagging process complemented digital coding: Transcripts were color-coded, annotated, and physically arranged on butcher paper. Tactile mapping revealed symbolic relationships less apparent through digital-only methods.

Saturation and Coding

Data saturation, where additional data ceases to produce new thematic revelations, required a ten-month iterative coding examination (Glaser & Strauss, 1967/1999;

Hennink et al., 2016; Ando et al., 2014; Braun & Clarke, 2006). Repeated cycles of thematic refinement encompassed: *Emotional expression, dissociation, psychic inheritance, and sociocultural binaries*. No new themes appeared in the final stages of analysis, indicating saturation and affirming methodological rigor (Guest et al., 2020).

Narrative Configuration and Restorying

Incorporating Polkinghorne's (1995) narrative configuration framework, provided a structure to trace relational structures and symbolic tensions across interviews. Restorying was employed to reconfigure disparate accounts into cohesive, composite character profiles and narratives that preserved individual voices while allowing for communal analysis. Synthesized profiles embodied diverse expressions of the Perverse Feminine Archetype and illustrated the interplay between narrative and collective psychic structure.

Cycle 3 concludes the empirical phase of data collection and analysis. Cycle 4 initiates a return arc in which the researcher reengages the preliminary lenses and literature from Cycles 1 and 2. Applying this recursive process supports refinement for interpretative understanding and methodological triangulation.

CYCLE 4: INTERATIVE REFLECTION AND THEMATIC REFINEMENT

Cycle 4 commences with a return to the interpretive scaffolds introduced in Cycle 2, enabling a reassessment of earlier assumptions. A refinement of analytical perspectives supports a meticulous representation of the data in forthcoming Cycle 5 (Anderson, 2019). Reconfiguring positionality, bias, and assumptions presents itself through recursivity. The following details the prevalent shifts from original suppositions (see Table 3.3).

Revisiting Cycles 2 and 3 clarified the necessity of Cycle 4. At an interpretive crossroads, early frames were modified, excised, restructured, or expanded, facilitating a more incisive analysis (Anderson, 2011). Reengaging conceptual filters enabled minimization of circular reasoning. Participants' evolving reflections were cross-examined through archetypal motifs. Revisiting the literature yielded new interpretive resonance. The investigator encountered narrative textures that carried metaphorical charge. Echoing earlier cycles, she incorporated art as a visual modality (see Figure 3.7) to comprehend the internal tension shared across interviews; demonstrating key themes of internal conflict between a desire for acceptance and an innate call to destruction.

Table 3.3 *Comparison Between Previous and Final Themes*

Previous themes	Final themes
internalized sexism self-objectification perversity women's mental illness sexuality mythology feminine evil artistic representations	indoctrination shapeshifting awareness redefining the feminine

Note:
The table above demonstrates how initial thematic categories evolved into a more encompassing symbolic schema.

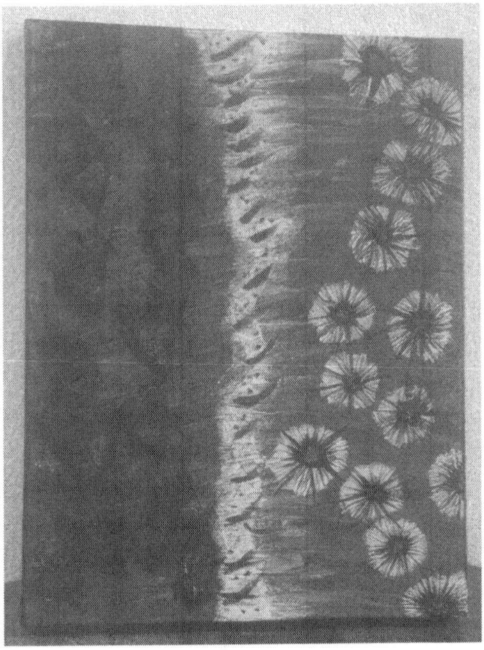

Figure 3.7 *Feminine Binary*

Figure created by the author.

Note:
The researcher painting demonstrates her interpretation on a bifurcated psyche. The vibrant and the disavowed collided here as cohabitants in an indistinguishable interior compass.

Key Transformations in Understanding

Significant **transformations** occurred in several areas of **inquiry** as I interpreted the data:

Narrative arcs

Once an overarching arc surfaced, the researcher interpreted narrative tone as a vehicle for recalibration, shifting from inherited constraint toward clarity. Storytelling unexpectedly occupied centrality and illuminating a pattern from early childhood into present-day complexity. In participant accounts, several participants who presented confidently later revealed persistent self-doubt. Rather than reinforcing a specific subset of empowerment, accounts illuminated recurring feelings of inadequacy. Contradictory disclosures complicated early impressions of the PFA, highlighting her dynamic tension between power and ambivalence.

Rejection of norms

Defying normative femininity often prompted a compensatory alignment with dominant, masculinized behaviors. Acting as inversion, participants described assuming external (masculine) signifiers of power as a way to avoid subjugation, only to find themselves ensnared in a new form of psychic containment. The reactive coping mechanism revealed an underlying challenge with a propensity to devalue femininity outright.

Gaps in Lilith's myth

How does divine rejection reshape Lilith's interiority? What psychic terrain is traversed in the aftermath of exile? Rather than consider her experience within the story, authors center the act of banishment and subsequent demonization, curating a male-dominated focal point in God and Adam. This motif reflects the fixation on external judgments over internal reckoning. Examining Lilith's myth from the inside to include her psychic rupture invites reflection on the unexamined shadow.

The PFA as a process

The PFA was initially conceived as a fixed construct, defined by a specific constellation of characteristics. However, as the interviews unfolded, she materialized as a sedimented presence, layered with historical residue and animated through mythological narrative. Rather than functioning as a predetermined model, she revealed herself through the interpretive procedure as both an echo of cultural repression and a generative force for psychological investigation.

Indistinct themes

> Themes appeared as interwoven phases of a dynamic schema. Internalized sexism, much like the PFA, resisted categorical boundaries; instead, it manifested as a multilayered phenomenon. The thematic patterns suggest fertile ground for future scholarly exploration and methodological innovation.

Cycle 4 constituted a critical inflection point, deepening the interpretive synthesis. Observing the entanglement between internalized sexism and the PFA, findings portrayed an unexpected arc of transformation. Preparatory for the presentation of results in Cycle 5, applied interpretation includes the following questions:

1. How does the perverse feminine materialize in everyday life?
   Participant accounts illuminated early conditioning and the covert negotiations of conformity.
2. How do normative constraints shape femininity?
   Narratives revealed patterns of self-effacement and the unexamined absorption of gendered limitations, often only discernible in retrospect.
3. How is the PFA linked to internalized sexism?
   Adaptive strategies, while protective, often intensified internal conflict, revealing the pervasiveness of internalized gender norms.
4. What pathways disrupt inherited patterns?
   Participants described moments of reclaiming traits once deemed deviant, signaling novel forms of integration.
5. What symbolic or imaginal schema supports feminine agency?
   Lilith appeared as both a mythic and symbolic framework through which participants reimagined authority and reclaimed psychic power.

The conclusion of Cycles 1 through 4 signifies the completion of data collection and interpretive synthesis. As the study advances into Cycle 5, a more integrative interpretation of the overarching findings initiates crystallization.

Chapter **4**

The Journey of Perverse Feminine Integration

> There are so many times when I wish I were in a man's body. I feel like, because I'm a woman, people want me to be soft, and I'm not … so they judge me. It's like when my brother and I both wanted to go to this chess tournament, and I wasn't allowed to go because my dad said girls don't do that. I knew I would've rocked it too, but that's my life and sort of the pill I've had to swallow.
>
> (Oya)

CYCLE 5: INTEGRATION AND APPLICATION OF FINDINGS

As the culminating spiral, Cycle 5 serves as a convergence point where the thematic, theoretical, and intuitive discernment developed in previous phases assemble. Articulated with intrapsychic complexity, the chapter revisits prior interpretations and interrogates their feasibility against lived accounts (Anderson, 2011, 2019). Each preceding cycle established groundwork for layered synthesis. Now interspersed into a coherent interpretive framework, the model demonstrates unifying results (Anderson, 2004).

PRIMARY RESULTS

Enmeshed in contradiction, women struggled to disclose their inner worlds. However, as research continued, discussions highlighted the role of chronic self-monitoring, shaped by unspoken cultural mandates that encourage restraint and emotional containment. Emotional expressiveness collapsed into a singular expectation for composure. Indicated as a learned vigilance, absorbed through omission

DOI: 10.4324/9781003455837-5

and everyday interactions. Within the study's support structure, the articulation of repressions marked a threshold, leading to three discoveries:

1. Cultural conditioning compelled participants to constrain their full range of affective and psychological expression, particularly when it involved autonomy.
2. The Perverse Feminine Archetype (PFA) provided a symbolic form for the researcher to frame conversations, offering a language for previously unnamed tensions and disavowed energies.
3. Participants' re-engagement with their disowned qualities unfolded in stages, where misaligned strategies unraveled, allowing new meaning to take shape through repeated self-confrontation.

Healing spiraled, revisiting struggles with clarity and attunement. Ingrained in their language, an architecture gave way to the PFA framework.

Rooted in a discovery-driven analysis, the findings coalesced into a symbolic trajectory marked by psychic rupture, resistance, and reclamation. This unfolding solidified into four distinct stages that trace a developmental arc of the Perverse Feminine Archetype (PFA): Societal Indoctrination, Shapeshifting, Awareness, and Redefining the Feminine (see Figure 4.1 and Table 4.1).

Societal Indoctrination marked the initial formation of self-perception. Messages about femininity rarely arrived as commands. Instead, women observed frequent cues in their environment. A wife discarding her goals; a victim charged for her clothing. These cues, subtle and consistent, gradually modified their understanding of safety and worth.

Table 4.1 *Overview of Subthemes* **within** *the PFA Integration Cycle*

Stage	**Indoctrination**	**Shapeshifting**	**Awareness**	**Redefining the Feminine**
Subtheme 1	engrained feminine expectations	damsel in distress	desire for change	rebellion
Subtheme 2	dehumanization	self-doubt	recognizing the challenge	shadow
Subtheme 3	fosters codependency	unhealthy boundaries	reputation awareness	autonomy
Subtheme 4	mixed messaging	limited aspirations	unconscious developments	

Note:
An overview of the **cycle** includes the subthemes that support each **stage**.

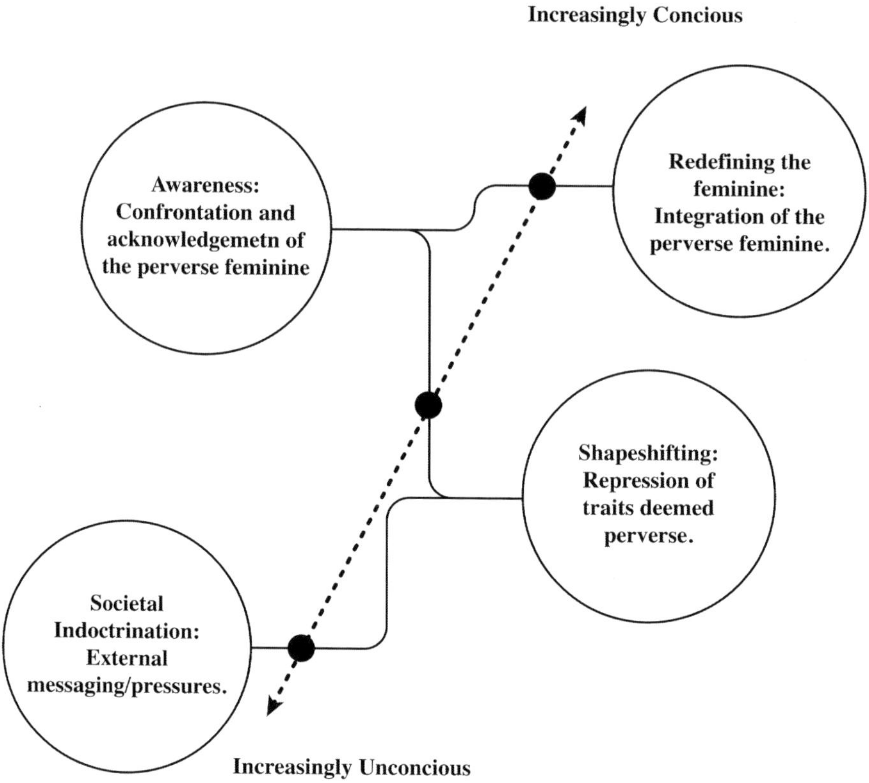

Figure 4.1 *Perverse Feminine Archetype* **Integration Framework**

Author's image.

Note:
The cyclical progression of PFA integration. Each stage is inextricably bound to its successor.

Shapeshifting defined the phase of strategic adaptation, where participants highlighted adaptability forged through belonging, as they suppressed their natural inclinations. Traits that once surged spontaneously were tucked beneath curated gestures designed to deflect scrutiny.

Awareness punctuated the rhythm with rupture. Former compromises now pressed against the body like ill-fitting skin. In contemplation, participants described growing unease. Unable to return to unawareness, they sought refuge in the unknown.

Redefining the Feminine revealed itself in motion, emphasizing unruly desire. Some approached with hesitation. Others erupted. Bound by a refusal to perform containment any longer, their speech emitted an invigorating tone.

PFA CHARACTERISTICS

The PFA arose as a conceptual lens, grounded in recurring data patterns and ancient heritage. She signifies a metaphorical tension pummeled by cultural inheritance. Constructed through sustained engagement, she uplifts self-governance, acting as a conduit for the disavowed. Manifestant through Lilith, she conjures sexual sovereignty, defiance, generative power, and embodied rage (see Table 4.2). Participants conjured her both directly and in the hushed ruptures of their accounts. Charged in moments of fragmentation, she invites a psychic realignment through a descent pilgrimage. As a conceptual and clinical construct, her formal framework offers a language for sacred communion.

Table 4.2 *Key Characteristics of the PFA*

Characteristic	Representation	Example	Figure
Autonomous	Unbound by external pressures	Professional women in male-dominated fields are challenging gender norms.	**Lara Croft** in *Tomb Raider* (West, 2001)
Resilient	Bouncing back from challenges	Feminist activists and artists use trauma as a source of empowerment.	**Daisy** in *Girl, Interrupted* (Mangold, 1999)
Creative	Intellectual and emotional expression	Writers and artists who challenge societal expectations through creativity.	**Jo March** from *Little Women* (Gerwig, 2019)
Dominant	Assertive and unwilling to accept the status quo	Leaders and revolutionaries who have sexual and emotional autonomy.	**Cookie Lyon** in *Empire* (Strong & Daniels, 2015–2020)
Connected	Attunement to inner truth	Spiritual healers who embrace intuitive knowledge and nature.	**Misty Day** in *American Horror Story: Coven* (Murphy & Falchuk, 2013)
Embodied	Connection to the body	A sense of physicality.	**Celie** in *The Color Purple* (Spielberg, 1985)
Transitionary	Evolving; nonbinary	Gender nonconformist.	**Divine** in *Pink Flamingos* (Waters, 1972)
Oppositional	Harsh rejection.	Rejection of traits deemed evil.	**The Evil Queen** in *Snow White* (Hand, 1937)

PARTICIPANT MOTIVATION

Participant motivation stemmed from curiosity about feminine dynamics and a strong desire to help others through their stories. Transparency was illuminated by courage, revealing a commitment to contend with the detrimental effects of external pressures. Hecate shared her thoughts on her choice to participate:

> Why do I want to participate? One, I knew that this process would be special because it would allow me to follow my intuition. Two, anything I can do to support other women and learn more about them is part of my calling. My mission here on the earth is to use my journey to connect with other women and show them that it's okay to be different and that what they may see as wrong could be their gift. So, when I heard about this interview, there was no question that this was a gift given to me to talk to you. I don't know what to expect; I have no idea what we will talk about, but I'm fucking ready.
>
> (Hecate)

Women shared an overarching frustration with restrictive systems, fueling their desire to prune damaging internal judgment. Although some began the interviews with hesitation, they gradually eased into conversations characterized by introspection. The research design prompted process-oriented responses, stimulating passionate self-discovery exposés.

NARRATIVE THEMATIC FINDINGS

Cycle 5 illuminated disruptive gender associations and resulting symptomatic challenges such as internalized suppression, psychic rupture, and disorientation. The Perverse Feminine Archetype (PFA) was volatile presence that intensified buried conflicts. I employed her as a preparatory force, moving her to unsettle the protective structures, which prompted pronounced self-confrontation and narrative transparency. What surfaced was a resurgence of qualities long cast aside: directness, sexual force, fury.

Not reclaimed, but reinhabited, they formed the raw material for repair. Lilith appeared in dreams, rituals, flash images, and unexpected synchronicities, often during periods of emotional upheaval. Her function was catalytic. She interrupted the habitual censoring of intuition as a clinical indicator of intuitive disruption, prompting participants to confront ambiguity and reestablish a sense of internal agency. Her presence unsettled emotional defenses, producing agitation and challenging participants to engage with contradictions. The accounts include four central terrains: Internalized sexism and the denied self, survival strategies and acts of rebellion, reclamation of bodily autonomy and voice, and mythic reorientation through spiritual and symbolic frameworks.

Internalized Sexism and the Denied Self

Early evaluations from caregivers, teachers, and peers distort self-perception. With a pervasive focus on emotional restraint, participants described an underdeveloped sense of their authentic selves, leading to heightened surveillance (Kalsched, 2013). Manifesting as a split between one's superficial presentation and disavowed inner reactions, severed clarity. This subtle erosion proved damaging. Delineating how internalized sexism evolved as a fixation on perceived neediness, they indicated a yearning for authentic expression.

Resistance, Survival, and Rebellion

Participants described intensifying conflict as they challenged narrow gender prescriptions while trying to preserve connection with family, partners, and peers; in one account, a participant noted how asserting her autonomy caused tension with her mother, who viewed compliance as safety. For some, internalized sexism operated as a survival tactic. The "damsel in distress" persona surfaced in several accounts as both a culturally sanctioned role and a calculated strategy to lower expectations or sidestep conflict. Performing helplessness served as a temporary shield but gradually constrained participants' sense of movement. Over time, a growing unease with the façade of helplessness blurred authenticity and reinforced self-doubt. Incorporation of the PFA served as a lens through which to acknowledge feminine distortion. Prompted by a desire for change, women ended relationships, altered their appearance, and redefined boundaries; rebellion occupied spaces of transformation, where the shadow bubbled to the surface through inescapable anger. Although frustration with external systems was a dominant trend, participants also observed a subtler form of disavowal: A deliberate muting of feminine traits.

Reclaiming the Body and Voice

Women's bodies served as sites of confusion and emotional dislocation, where detachment from sensation was misread as self-discipline. Conditioned to view the corporeal as a tool to gain male desire, they learned to monitor appearance and suppress discomfort rather. Their accounts included compulsive self-surveillance, emotional numbing during intimacy, and suppressed responses to physical distress. These patterns often stemmed from prolonged invalidation, resulting in a struggle to name internal cues. Moments of defiance emerged in a rejection of beauty standards and self-pleasure. When asked about longing, they spoke of movement as ritual; modes once dismissed as excessive or indulgent. One woman noted how she sought connection through masturbation, while others utilized their bodies to tap into anger, jealousy, and sadness, as a form of internal communion.

Spirituality and Myth

In the absence of traditional religious frameworks, participants sought intuitive and ritual-based spiritual practices, including tarot, astrology, energy healing, and ancestral rites. A craving for nonlinear feminine power underscored the testimonies. From here, conversations swelled with archetypal undercurrents. Lilith's presence guided our path as interviewees named their desire to tap into their perverse nature.

Crossing the Threshold

Cycle 5 concludes by setting the stage for forthcoming chapters. As Part I concludes, the work shifts from methodological framing and theoretical orientation toward a substantive exposition of the study's findings. Organized around the four progressive stages of PFA integration, each chapter opens with a Jungian foundation, contextualizes historical tensions, and invokes the figure of Lilith. Theoretical perceptions intersperse with narrative material that translates the collective unconscious into grounded, lived realities. The application of archetypal inquiry, informed by an interpretive lens, enabled a creative and disciplined mode of restorying. Thematic patterns surfacing throughout participant accounts were synthesized into composite vignettes, preserving nuance while enhancing cohesion.

For instance, several participants described similar traumatic events, the researcher wove their accounts concurrently to highlight a shared emotional connection. Linguistic markers often dismissed as imprecise, including fillers and pauses, were deliberately retained to preserve both the authenticity and the integrity of feminine-coded speech patterns. Pseudonyms function as symbolic referents for distinct archetypal inflections. Individualized names denote recurring traits and dynamics, coalescing into mythological formations. Readers are encouraged to immerse themselves as fellow interlocutors, following the conceptual and narrative associations with attention. The opening four chapters of societal indoctrination are especially layered, guiding readers through the converging expanse of myth, psychology, and history.

PART II

THE STAGES OF HEALING

A Cyclical Journey of Feminine Reclamation

Part II advances the research by weaving together participant narratives, ancestral traces, and theoretical insights. Each of the four stages is organized into a section with corresponding chapters. Societal Indoctrination examines the distortion of femininity, the patriarchal collective unconscious, the legacy of witch hunts and hysteria, and the demonization of Lilith. Shapeshifting examines shadow formation, links internalized sexism to the personal unconscious, challenges contemporary psychiatric frameworks, and positions Lilith as the queen of the shadow. Awareness investigates moments of shadow confrontation, triggers for awakening, and the use of active imagination to engage the Perverse Feminine Archetype (PFA). Redefining the Feminine is the final stage, encompassing shadow integration, lived manifestations of the PFA, and its embodied materialization. Each stage offers vivid accounts of inherited constraints, providing a rigorous and evocative exploration of the qualitative and mythic realms.

DOI: 10.4324/9781003455837-6

Stage **1**

Societal Indoctrination

The Inheritance of Obedience

EXTERNAL MESSAGING: CONDITIONING THROUGH SOCIETAL EXPECTATIONS

> So, forcing women into one box that they have to sit in and they can't escape is a perversion. It's a perversion of the soul. It's like, if a woman you know isn't just a little virgin, then she's perverse. And of course, the virgin only exists so that we can pervert her.
>
> (Nyx)

We begin with a tale of inherited social codes, uncovering how interviewees seek validation via compliance. Indicative of a chasm between external prescriptions and internal realities is a gap that spans institutions, perpetuating unrealistic expectations. Women absorb detrimental embedded paradigms. An orientation toward obedience, often disguised as a sense of approval, arises from a yearning for recognition. Within hegemonic systems, colonial cohesion is frequently misinterpreted as volition, leading to behaviors aligned with dominant standards (Sait, 2021; Thiessen, 1993; Takakuwa et al., 2004). Such conditioning initiates a distortion of selfhood that participants described as objectification; a gift, commodity, or a vessel of projected desire (Haraway, 1991). Religious institutions, particularly Christianity, appeared as one of the earliest perpetrators.

> The Catholic Church has influenced US politics and culture for over 100 years through mass movements, and it's sent me the message that I need to be a good girl, whatever the fuck that means, right? I mean, it just seems like there's always going to be some part of me that is deemed problematic or inferior. I guess I should accept that, but this part of me still wants acceptance.
>
> (Lilith)

DOI: 10.4324/9781003455837-7

A dichotomous idealization or purity results in a constrictive belief system, evoking detrimental messages. Infiltrated by the normalization of punishment, the unconscious absorbs oppression as standard. Evident in art, cinema, advertising, and literature, media portrayals of shameful women subtly penetrate the psyche (Korsmeyer, 2004; Calogero, 2004). Authority, when exemplified by women, is often met with derision. Terms like *bitch* are shorthand for assertiveness, while male counterparts are lauded as confident, reflecting a broader entrenchment in Eurocentric beauty norms. The compounded burden of racism, fatphobia, and aesthetic exclusion reconfigures as a critical mechanism wielded by dominant systems of control (Crenshaw, 1991; Wolf, 1991).

> There's a lot of fatphobia and racism that happens on TV. There are a lot of, you know, typical pretty, skinny, and white leads. Pretty is subjective but look at these roles. They don't challenge the male lead or the status quo. The women who look like me always play some role that grosses me out.
>
> (Gaia)

Normative beauty hierarchies serve as gatekeepers of worthiness, scripting desirability, and punishing divergence. Ideals often trickle down through generational instruction, seeded in benign childhood incidents. Before girls articulate resistance, lessons of acceptability steep in subtle directives which calibrate a constrictive self-image.

> My mother gave me this birthday card when I was like 10 to say, "Here's what ladies do. They lower their voice. They're not loud in a room." A whole list of things that I wasn't. There's a stay-in-your-place kind of thing. And I think it's really subtle. You know, stay in your place, be small and quiet. And I think that's changing tremendously. But, like, I'm 66, so I was born to be small and quiet as a woman.
>
> (Hestia)

Conditioning stems from peers and well-intentioned adults during adolescence. Hunger for approval gradually morphs into self-monitoring, breeding disillusionment. The initial disciplinary action often criticizes expressions of sexuality, correcting innocent curiosity. Over time, a disconnection from desire occurs, signifying an inherent danger in the body.

> I've always been interested in bodies and sex. I started feeling romantic and sexual very early on, like I was 9 or 10, probably. Fuck, even at preschool, I was trying to kiss boys. And then, in my teens, I was also interested in girls and appreciated female bodies ... but in my culture and home country, it was very closed-minded and religious, so being sexual was considered dirty and unacceptable, so I had to hide myself.
>
> (Persephone)

When internalized calculus compels women to sever from core dimensions, the Perverse Feminine Archetype (PFA) forms in this fractured state as a submerged repository. Desire becomes transactional; the body is no longer a site of sovereignty, but a conduit of conditional worth. Security is elusive. Depicted in the rising tide of gendered violence, existential stakes underscore threatening visi bility (Sharma, 2015; UN Women, 2024a). Chronic vigilance in public spaces illustrates how repression can translate into perceived threat.

> I've had many experiences with sexual assaults, but one stands out that I didn't recognize as assault at the time. After a night out drinking with friends, a guy walked me to my car and touched me without my consent. It happened so fast that I felt frozen and couldn't say no. I buried the memory, but that feels wrong, I guess. I should be able to walk down the street, no matter what I'm wearing. That's not the reality, though.
>
> (Oya)

Gendered expectations sever women from their internal compass, fostering mistrust. As they interpret their bodily processes through external authority, estrangement saturates childhood with lessons of containment (Martin, 1987). Preventing organic growth, individuals often construct their identity from peripheral criteria, as opposed to subjective experimentation (Lalukota, 2023). Artificial feminine architecture restricts expression to a repertoire of socially approved behaviors, where neutrality can be misread as defiance.

> I was shy as a child and often misunderstood. People thought I was a snob, but I was just awkward and bullied for being different. It was frustrating to feel pressure to smile to appear nice as if to combat my 'resting bitch face.' I learned to smile because nice girls do.
>
> (Oshun)

Butler (1990) argues that gender is not merely performed under constraint but is constituted through repetition of those very norms, rendering deviation intelligible only as failure or subversion. Girls raised to center relational deference contort themselves to fit into idealized maternal roles. Over time, those who resist displacement reject inward, adopting misogynistic beliefs as a defense. The pressure to conform fractures coherence, replacing internal agency with an externalized hunger for approval.

> Like 'this is what you do'—this is what a woman does. College is for meeting the person you're going to have kids with. That's what I was taught, but I got kinda lucky, because there's more of a rigidity to some religious sects, and yeah, I think I don't want to throw around the word indoctrination too loosely, but it feels akin to that to me. It feels very much like standards and practices are imposed upon you from a young age, and you get less of a choice of what it means to be a woman.
>
> (Persephone)

The exaltation of self-sacrificing motherhood and obedient wives redefines dependence as a virtue. The pursuit of desirability often eclipses professional goals, severing access to individual pathways of meaning. Through this lens, Societal Indoctrination functions as a learned betrayal lodged in the unconscious. Historical implications emerge in witch hunts, religious persecution, and intergenerational shame, each feeding a collective shadow that distorts and represses feminine power. The chapters that follow trace how buried energies reveal the mechanics of patriarchal conditioning and expose lingering scars of historical persecution. Lilith, cast as a she-demon, is reexamined as a symbolic guide who illuminates exiled psychological matter.

Chapter **5**

Perverting the Feminine

> It's perverted that a woman would not back down. I mean, at least as far as the white masculine is concerned, right? Sometimes I wonder what would happen if I just said fuck it all? If I stopped playing nice, but then I hear that little voice in my head telling me to shut up.
>
> (Ixchel)

Those relegated to the periphery often struggle to assert their presence, yet their existence alone unsettles the collective comfort of indifference. Within a culture saturated by convention, social conditioning becomes a control apparatus that reconfigures volition to suppress conventionality. Under this sustained psychic siege, the compulsion to conform fractures selfhood. Resistance invites exile, a confrontation with the isolating silence of metaphorical abandonment. What remains is a stark polarity: Capitulation or insubordination. Women enmeshed in these binds articulate a yearning for a vital feminine force capable of rupturing imposed forms. A symbolic charge takes form as a forceful enough charge to defy the hegemonic contours of normativity. Indoctrination is an overt mechanism of enforcement, which erodes authenticity. The notion of *perverting the feminine* crystallizes as a composite of collective projection, a shadowed distortion shaped by societal fears, fantasies, and disciplinary imperatives.

CONFINEMENT THROUGH NORMS

> I mean, in some ways, what would be considered traditionally feminine is a perversion, right? Because we have all the aspects of personality, character, and style. I've never really thought about how angry it makes me to try to become that ideal, and then I'm called weird. Like—*What?*
>
> (Lamia)

DOI: 10.4324/9781003455837-8

Traditional femininity constitutes a form of perversion, reverberating across recurring restrictive metaphors. Such imagery underscores how dominant conventions marginalize women, severing their access to collective belonging and psychic coherence. The participants' yearning echoed through my quest, reawakening a subterranean, muted ache. Friends, partners, and detractors frequently dismissed my intuitive premonitions, ejecting them as irrational. Memories surfaced as I felt a visceral tightness each time participants spoke of their similar hunger. Constrained by narrowly prescribed traits like gentleness, nurturance, and docility, participants revealed how reductive expectations suppressed the breadth of their psychological and emotional range. They sought a form of expression beyond the walls of their immovable enclosure. High expectations operated as a balancing act, pressuring women to walk a tightrope of obedience, expected to comply while condemned for timidity. Such dualism distorts perception, relegating individuals to a starkly black-and-white reality in which portions of spirit fall by the wayside.

> I rarely hear somebody describe a woman as being feminine. Because there's the expectation that if you are biologically, or you identify as female, you must be inherently feminine. So, there's no need to apply it. I think a woman is considered a thing that is outside of humans, honestly.

Embedded through the conversations, participants floundered when invited to articulate what 'feminine' meant to them, disclosing the perplexing nature of gender roles. Their characterizations often collapsed under the weight of expectation, uncertainty, and inherited scripts. Frequently defined in relationship to men, Simone de Beauvoir's concept of the *other* provided additional insight, denoting a preoccupation with normative expressions (de Beauvoir, 2018).

> In my Chinese culture, my family taught me the value of a wife. I was shunned when I didn't fit the typical standards like small, quiet, pale, and delicate. I mean, people told me I should've been born a boy! It made me so insecure; I hated how I looked and who I was. I guess I don't feel like a woman because I don't fit that 'feminine' mold. I feel like a failure. I just want to scream sometimes, but then I'd be 'crazy,' right? There's no winning. I wish I could be soft-spoken, but I'm just not!
>
> (Guan Yin)

Idealistic expectations sustained a persistent perfectionistic drive, tethering participants to unattainable standards, where shame surfaced as a chronic pressure. Coalescing as testimonies of unspoken desires, the following analyses offer a glimpse into pervasive psychological challenges. Indicative of the lingering gender entrapment distorts the mind and situates womanhood in dualistic rigidity.

THE WARPED LENS OF FEMININITY

> Anything between good or bad, masculine or feminine, feels threatening. I think it's because there's a binary around it. Individuals are constantly looking for ways to define themselves in these categories. They're not just who they are, and I don't really know how to be in this feminine identity. Do I play with that? Do I work that up? Do I do it in my mannerisms? Do I do it in my clothing choices? Do I wear makeup? I mean, all of these trappings, right? Some of them are more embodied. Some of them are more put on.
>
> (Hecate)

As I sensed the agony of prescriptive roles, they arose as splinters between thought and flesh, imprinting visceral contortions. A history of condemnation continuously undercut my actions. Prompting an interrogation with my history, I contemplate how the word '*feminine*' cuts deepest. In what crevice of bone or ligament does it implant? How is it honed into a blade that punctures the spirit?

> Ugh … this is so hard; I'll just try my best to answer. So, there's this illusion that I have, from an external source, that I can't fully pinpoint, that I need to sort of have it together, be combed and freshened up. I find this especially hard when I want to *feel*. I feel like I just want to be thrown apart, like my heart is open to the wind, and everything feels everywhere.
>
> (Lilith)

She continued. Her voice carried profound unease:

> I don't really feel like an archetype of beauty or femininity, so it's not easy for me to be what I think people want me to be or make people happy; I think, as a woman, I need to make people happy. So many women share this internal struggle or battle regarding their relations with societal expectations and personal desires.
>
> (Lilith)

Rarely articulated in its representations, femininity functioned as a shadowed reflection that obfuscated reason. Entangled in a tension between depraved and ideal, offered little room for multiplicity or contradiction, flattening substance into a surveilled performance.

> On the surface, it would be the traditional Western idea dictated by the systems in place. As far as women, I think of myself as a mother and as a person who has struggled against patriarchal systems. Feminine … there's the traditional description of dresses and makeup.
>
> (Hera)

Storytellers unintentionally emulated dichotomies they sought to resist, illuminating a cognitive shattering engendered by latent institutional pressures, where external expediency overrides internal comprehension. Grappling with an innate yearning for vitality, a persistent sense of disconnection appeared, leading to a skewed interpretation of physical potency.

THE BODY

> It's so not true that women are weak, and I'm really tired of that idea being perpetuated. As a doula, I've witnessed them be strong as hell, but it's a vulnerable kind of strength. Of course, they don't really give in to this until they are in the middle of childbirth. Otherwise, they try to pretend they have no emotions.
>
> (Medusa)

Despite recognizing flawed logic, participants described how sociocultural constraints lead to disgust with healthy physiological functions. Dismissed by dominant discourse, their bodies become invisible, severing women from corporeal wisdom. The routine omission of bodily functions in public discussion compounds marginalization, reducing them to symbols of dysfunction or weakness. Cultural narratives that cast the female body as erratic, messy, or untrustworthy normalize emotional suppression, reinforcing unequal power dynamics (Martin, 1987).

> I remember when I was on tour with a band as a drummer, and I had to mind my p's and q's; when I didn't, it was like, "Oh, she's a bitch; she must be on her period," It's like … why do I have to be on my period to be upset? I'm a fucking human, but I guess that doesn't matter, because I'm a weak and crazy girl who just can't function because of my body.
>
> (Artemis)

Culture transforms the bleeding body into an unclean site of sin, an object that demands repentance. Patriarchal narratives reinforce disconnect, exploiting fear that separates the red river of menstruation from its cyclical and sacred symbolism. By doing so, they deepen the disconnection from women and foster a general sense of innate judgment (Grosz, 1994), deeming their bodies inconvenient. Kristeva's (1982) abjection theory further clarifies: Menstruation, pregnancy, and sexuality, is polluting.

> I feel like it adds to the concept that women are weak, because no matter how strong a woman is, there is about a week of the month that she's not going to be as strong no matter how much you try, so it just adds to it, like, obviously, there's nothing I can do about it.
>
> (Oya)

Emotional paralysis links to a civilization obsessed with immutable physical features. As Bordo (2003) argues that patriarchal standards have long disciplined the female body, twisting it into an object of control with strict aesthetic exemplars. To embody the conventional is to exist as a paradox, both idealized and reviled, contained and feared. As institutional forces impose external restrictions, they contour cognitive impressions. Dijkstra (1996) likewise examines how religious ideologies historically demonized sexuality, reinforcing limitation, shame, and suppression.

> For the female body, in society, you're looked at and judged, like I was saying, in so many ways. And it's really damaging to anyone who's in a female body, I think, because we're looked at in a lot of strange ways and objectified. I do feel like there's a lot of judgment, no matter what you're doing, like you need to be, you need to look a certain way, you need to act a certain way. You're always continuously being judged about your body, about the way that you speak, about the way that you present yourself to the world, in general.
>
> (Ixchel)

Disdain for those who display traits of perversity, ranging from explicit sexual expressions or overt feminine behavior, appears frequently in participant narratives, evoking despair. Shame incurred from external sources reveals layers of condemnation, heightening alienation and relegating natural expression to the shadows (Zweig & Abrams, 1991). Rejection eventually internalizes, leading to self-doubt and cycles of self-suppression. In this way, the vilification erodes self-trust. What begins as cultural disapproval calcifies into inner punishment, setting the stage for more overt forms of harm, where symbolic erasure transforms into lived violation.

VIOLENCE

> Our species has allowed objectification of women because the feminine is defined as weak. The wholesale rape and pillage of nature show how normalized the hatred towards us is. I can't even go for a fucking run without fear. I wish I were a man. I haven't really told people this, but I was raped, and so many women I know have been, too. They act like it's no big deal. Ugh. It makes you want to shut down, hide …, and become invisible.
>
> (Ala)

Rape and gender-based violence permeated participant narratives, rendering safety illusory and often unattainable. Each report reproduced a profoundly familiar terrain: One shaped by survival and the slow erosion of voice. Cultural and political scaffolding that enables such harm exposes a collective normalization of violence against women.

> Regardless of how far we think we've come, we still elect Trump … who raped a woman. I think we, as a whole, see her as perverse because she went against him. I remember my mom even telling me that she was probably lying. So, I think that at those levels, that perversion, feminine perversion, is in opposition to the quote-unquote standards that we're trying to uphold. Make America Great Again, blah, blah, blah.
>
> (Inanna)

Gender-based violence remains a substantial global concern (United Nations Office on Drugs and Crime, 2024; Russell, 1990; Smallbone et al., 2008). In 2023 alone, approximately 85,000 women were murdered worldwide, with nearly 60% dying at the hands of their partners (UN Women, 2024a; Violence Policy Center, 2021). Black women comprise 32.1% of intimate partner homicide victims despite representing only 13.4% of the female population (CDC, 2023); Indigenous women face a homicide rate 6.5 times higher than that of non-Indigenous women (CDC, 2023); and Latina women account for 42.8% of female homicides in Los Angeles over the past decade (Los Angeles Civil Rights Department, 2023). Amid these alarming figures, the extent of harm is frequently obscured, as many cases go unreported.

> It was very challenging for me to get access to just regular women's wellness exams and birth control. Planned Parenthood has extremely restricted sources. Because it's like the access to accessible women's health care is just not there. I almost lost it. To get a well-woman exam, a mammogram, a Pap smear, and all that, they told me that it was going to cost almost $2,000 out of pocket.
>
> (Lamia)

Bodily autonomy remains a contested and precarious terrain, particularly as participants contend with the cascading effects of the Roe v. Wade reversal (Londoño Tobón et al., 2023). The subsequent defunding of Planned Parenthood intensifies existing barriers, particularly for uninsured patients (Planned Parenthood Federation of America, 2020). My experiences with the healthcare system evoked a surge of righteous indignation. Why is a basic physiological necessity not recognized as a fundamental human right? The narratives echo structural disregard. Repeatedly, women described experiences with misdiagnosis, their symptoms minimized, or pain dismissed outright. Twice as likely as men to receive diagnoses of depression or anxiety, a trend that supplants appropriate medical investigation and contributes to delayed or missed diagnoses (Albert, 2015; Haraway, 1991; Kessler et al., 2005; Chesler, 2018). When physicians misread heart attacks, overlook strokes, or pathologize legitimate suffering as hysteria or emotional excess (Hoffmann & Tarzian, 2001; Vaccarino et al., 1999; Miller, 2024), it reveals a deep-seated suspicion: That women's reports are inherently unreliable. Such institutionalized doubt fuels portrayals of unworthiness, reinforcing shadow material.

ARCHETYPES AND PROJECTIONS

> Oh, yeah. Ass and titties! That's the theme … Well, I mean, it's the theme of like, how society … depicts women, for real … Don't get me wrong, there has been some film and television that, you know, they've had … better examples of … women. But, you know, mostly it's … sexually objectifying them.
>
> (Demeter)

Beyond the promise of psychological redemption exists an invocation: For a woman to exist without the weight of caste-based inferiority, to breathe in a world not designed to suffocate her agency. What sustains her? When she resists codified norms, why is she cast as a villain? Or worse, a witch? How does the trope of 'perversity' become both an accusation and a reservoir of feminine potency? Investigating tension reveals a mythos rooted in collective anxiety, one that underwrites patriarchy's enduring control by recycling archetypes of the dangerous woman: The demonic witch, the erotic seductress, the deranged outcast (Mulvey, 1975; Warner, 1994).

> I often like not saying stuff because I'm scared of being too much. That happens a lot where I feel like I'm in, especially in a relationship with men, and especially, I guess, more on the romantic side of things. Am I being unreasonable and being a little too crazy? I definitely, like, checked myself, like I'll check in with myself or check with others. Am I being, like, this is too crazy or overdramatic, you know?
>
> (Nyx)

Artemis's observations highlight a malignancy that devalues achievements:

> I think women are viewed as outside of humanity and categorized differently than men. For instance, you are a female director or aviator, while a man is just an athlete or director without that qualifier. In acting, it's almost comical how little progress we've made since the movement a few years ago. Sometimes, I watch TV and find it amusing how little we've accomplished since then.
>
> (Artemis)

Lilith demonstrates how society projects terror onto monstrous women, encoding fears that circulate in the cultural bloodstream. Her demonic status underscores the grim struggle between social control and redemption. Witches carry this same double edge: Cast as monsters to fear yet quietly standing as emblems of survival. Archetypal images reflect a cultural ambivalence surrounding feminine subjectivity, simultaneously revering and rejecting her potency. Such duality places her mythic presence at the heart of the tension between normative social mandates and psychic wholeness (Hillman, 1999; Mitchell, 2000; Leonard, 1993).

> I feel like whenever I express anger or assertiveness, people see it as unnatural, like I'm stepping out of my role. It's exhausting to feel like you have to explain why you deserve to take up space constantly. She does everything just right, like on time, and that's not possible.
>
> (Hestia)

When anger is perceived as deviant, a nuisance to be justified or shamed, it pushes the PFA further to the margins, stripping away her complexity and humanity. Lauter and Rupprecht (1985) describe this challenge as a collective mindset in which a narrow and restrictive femininity assembles stereotypes that, to some extent, clarify the historical challenges women have faced. Perplexed by the continued cycle of devastating messages, we turn our attention to the collective unconscious, where patriarchal beliefs culminate throughout the psyche.

Chapter 6

The Collective Unconscious and Patriarchy

> It's hetero-normative, patriarchal, white supremacist culture, right? It's just thousands and thousands of years of white men not evening power but like constantly consuming power and accruing power. If you go way back to my people, you've got cultures that existed beyond gender, and yet the Western world thinks that they have claim to fucking everything, you know, it's like some weird Christian trip.
>
> (Ala)

Detrimental archetypal misfits function as nodes of cultural danger. The witch, the whore, the hag. Each crucifixion mirrors society's fear of the uncontained woman, while traditional femininity remains the unquestioned norm. Those who refuse its terms are banished to the mythic margins. To monitor exclusion, we turn to the symbolic terrain, where myth and image uncover bones of repression. From cultural remnants, the Perverse Feminine Archetype (PFA) forms, dragging with it the tangled lineage of suppressed psychological material (Jung, 1907–09/1969b). Habit now appears as psychic clutter: Internalized commandments wrapped as instinct, beneath the surface, coded scripts press into thought. With her, the fog lifts. Recognition burns.

UNMASKING THE PATRIARCHAL COLLECTIVE UNCONSCIOUS

> I think it's like a fish swimming in water. I think we've been in this water for so long. You know, we don't even realize what's in there. Yeah, it's there all the time. So, how would we know anything differently if we've never experienced a different culture or atmosphere?
>
> (Demeter)

DOI: 10.4324/9781003455837-9

Demeter's parable unfolds a paradox as we rummage through clandestine scripts buried beneath the polished proclamations of culture. Patriarchy, deft in its illusive cunning, breeds distortions that seep into our marrow, warping what we claim as instinct. Questions coil in suspicion: Which urgings pulse from an origin untouched, and which are spectral remnants, relics of an ancient falsehood? Can we, with any precision, carve the perimeter of what we possess? The challenge of our mission is to observe how damaging pedagogy seeps from sacred pulpits, camouflages in the gentle lull of bedtime fables, and lords itself over the subtle choreography of permission to speak.

> I think we all carry some internalized -isms, like misogyny, homophobia, and even white supremacy, myself included. I'm not sure if it comes from religion, but growing up Catholic definitely taught me that men and women have very different roles in the world.
>
> (Oya)

Religious constructions of good and evil occurred early in the interviews, often linked to childhood moral codes. Teachings functioned as crucibles, forging durable beliefs before critical reflection. Within symbolic order, patriarchy functions as a living organism, sustained by collective rituals sanctified through tradition (Lerner, 1987). Disavowed impulses project outward, moralized, and absorbed by institutions, which encode them as deviance. Spiraling through entertainment, medicine, psychology, and myth, the system endures as an affective atmosphere. Its machinery reproduces gendered norms that become embedded in cognition, shaping behavior through performances of belonging and legitimacy (Foucault, 1977; Butler, 1990; Gergen, 1985).

> Oh my gosh, I'm having female characters outside of the Christian religion show us … Ah, you know, I think they'd be defined as hags. Right? Elderly, fierce. Um, tough. Those are the perverse women, the ones who refuse to conform.
>
> (Hecate)

Hecate's account reflects characters rendered monstrous through religious doctrine and reified in popular tropes. This form of indoctrination seeps into daily rhythms, permeating communal norms until it becomes deeply ingrained in the unconscious. Recognizing the slow accretion of patriarchal codes, we view their impact as ambient forces that contour routine interactions and group belonging.

THE UNCONSCIOUS AND INDOCTRINATION

> Growing up, having a voice was somewhat dangerous in my family, so I had a few reasons why speaking out would be hard. I always had to be quiet. I mean, I remember my parents would get into screaming matches with each other, and it bothered

> me, but what could I do? It was so weird because the next day we would go into the church and pretend we were a normal family.
>
> (Guan Yin)

Themes of purity and moral rectitude travel across family expectations, religious institutions, and social pressures (Bandura, 1977). Testimonies revealed how interferences permeate domestic life, mirroring the restrictions imposed by doctrinal ideology. Whether or not participants maintained religious affiliation, many described the struggle to dismantle inherited conflict between virtue and sin. Morality lessons entrenched layers of the psyche (Jung, 1907–1909/1969b). Prolonged exposure produced a climate of subtle coercion, where sexism became ambient. Resistance was swallowed by indifference, erased beneath the smoothing pressure of collective assent.

An unremitting surge of deliberations monumentalizing hegemonic masculinity in male dominance erodes nonconforming expressions and pathologizes emotional complexity (Connell, 1987). Women are objects of projection and punishment. Discord, even when silenced, is marked as disorder. The effects reverberate across social structures, embedding hierarchy not only in law or labor but in perception itself (Eisler, 1987). Those positioned as subordinate must navigate a terrain of cognitive dissonance, social erasure, and the insidious violences that define our unspoken caste logic.

> Perversity is like … doing sexual stuff I don't want anyone to know about. It feels shadowy and bad, like I'm being masculine in a way men don't like. Like those femme fatale movies, where the woman is sexy but evil and hurts the man. We don't want to hurt the man, that would be bad. It's like … women wouldn't call it 'perverse,' it's just our sexuality. What's so perverse about that?
>
> (Hecate)

The PFA functions as a vessel for dreadful feminine potency. In cultural narratives, she is portrayed as the dismembered and diminished woman, reduced to a manageable version of her former self (Kaplan, 1982; Doane, 1991). Through repetition and pressure, she learns to contort: To conform, distort, and sever the instinctive aspects of her being. Erotic vitality, rather than being celebrated, is rendered dangerous, available only to the seductive villainess. The resulting psychic load, stitched from shame and fear, inherits a symbolic lineage shaped by those who stood in stark contrast to sanitized idols (Gilbert & Gubar, 1979). Rather than illuminate complexity, the binary imposes structure: A schematic that encodes femininity as either virtuous or deviant (de Beauvoir, 1979/2010).

> To me, perverse means sort of like a monster …something unnatural, right? So that would have to have aspects of both feminine and masculine, but they're not entirely integrated. It would have to be a weird combination, maybe not typically feminine, but it has just enough to make you think twice.
>
> (Ala)

The monstrous feminine frames perversity as a symbolically charged space of tension, where moral anxiety, projected onto the feminine body, marks it as grotesque and excessive (Creed, 1993). Mythic representations often position her as both sacred and threatening, erotic and taboo, exposing the fragility of idealized gender norms (Ussher, 2006). Participants described erosion as cumulative; an endless layering of mixed messages and moral scripts that rendered authorship suspect. Between goddess and she-demon, little space remains for rest or recognition. Popular media channels often perpetuate unease through rigid portrayals, casting the defiant woman as a threat, aberration, or cautionary tale. Ideological pressure to contain autonomy fuels projective perversity, casting transgression as an ethical threat (Creed, 1993). Hecate examined this dynamic through the contrast between Snow White and the Evil Queen (Disney & Hand, 1937), two archetypes split by ambition. The Queen's power is reframed as malignancy, while Snow White is the ideal: Docile, obedient, and emotionally palatable dream.

> That witch in Snow White? Totally evil. It was like a poisoned apple, a creepy mirror, and even her *body* was evil! Those long arms, ya know? And the green face … She just gives off this bad vibe, like she's from somewhere else and wants to destroy everything good and innocent. It's weird, but I kinda feel that in myself, too. Like, I want to be all pure and good, but this other part of me is not so nice.
>
> (Gaia)

Gaia's insight resonates with feminist critiques that interpret ancient narratives as representations of staged femininity through polarized archetypes: Virgin or witch, saint or seductress (Warner, 1994). Rebels and misfits often occupy the role of psychic scapegoats, serving as containers for what civilization refuses to acknowledge (von Franz, 1970). Hierarchies of race, class, and sexuality are embedded in allegorical stories, with each axis compounding how femininity is organized and judged (Bailey, 2010). Such structures do not merely reflect bias; they ritualize it. Across symbolic registers, perversity becomes a centrifuge, pulling into focus the traits rejected as excessive, volatile, or transgressive.

> Growing up, it was clear how different things were for girls. Like, I couldn't even wear pants to school! When I was 13, my dad actually made *me* cook dinner because I was the 'woman' of the house. Then, even though I was a top student in college, I couldn't get a job in architecture. All the guys got internships, no matter how good they were. It felt like some fields were just closed off to me, no matter how confident I was.
>
> (Medusa)

Structural limitations reproduce in the archetypal zeitgeist, shaping how behaviors filter through symbolic lenses (Jung, 1964, 1907–09/1969b). When saturated with patriarchal logic, the overarching lenses distort the feminine into something fractured. Too loud, too ambitious, too much. Archetypes, far from neutral, mirror dominant ideology, entangled with its outward expression. The PFA surfaces as a composite entity: Saturated with projection and tethered to inherited shame.

EMERGENCE OF THE PFA

> My residency in India was wild. As someone who considers themselves strong and independent, it was really hard to cover up. I mean, women were restricted to covering up and not able to go out alone, while men enjoyed so much freedom. When I jumped in to help with the heavy lifting for our final show, they stared at me like I was from another planet! I just wanted women to see they could do anything. And it was that moment of confronting what this traditional woman should be. And I'm not. But what does that mean? Does that mean I'm a good person? I'm a bad person? Does that mean I should be in jail? Does that mean I'm evil? You know, where do I fit in this?
>
> (Oshun)

Acts that diverge from expected femininity are swiftly recoded as deviant. When women assert physical power, their presence is often reframed as perverse or threatening, especially when it disrupts normative spectatorship (Kaplan, 1991). The discomfort provoked by such ruptures is not neutral; it reinstates varying levels of constraint. Social correction arrives subtly, through nudges toward softness. Yet in resisting that choreography, performance falters. Gender, revealed as ritual rather than essence, unravels.

Berger and Luckmann (1966) argue that reality assembles itself by repetition. Practice becomes doctrine. Social routines, once absorbed, congeal into apparent truth. Disruptions shake the scaffolding that holds the illusion in place. Gendered hierarchies persist not because they are natural, but because they are performed; they are so ritualized that they vanish into habit. Once the pattern ruptures, the underlying architecture trembles. Jung invited ancient motifs inward, recasting mythic images as internal patterns that contour psychic life. Although one might endeavor to hold an archetype at a distance, its form resists capture. As Heidegger (1927/1962) observed, foundational structures rarely announce themselves; they shape awareness from beneath recognition, forming the conditions for meaning without stepping into view.

> I think that, as humans, none of us knows the right way to do anything. I don't think there's any one way to do any one thing, and so my 'grey' perspective is that there is some kind of collective unconsciousness between all humans, and I think that the Universe has that kind of pervasive energy, you know like—I think it's a big amalgamation of things, I think there's some kind of energy.
>
> (Inanna)

When saturated with projection, archetypes risk rigidity. Rather than portraying the psyche's multiplicity, they harden into moral opposites. Recognizing the personal challenges embedded within my life, I cast my decision to leave a marriage in archetypal terms, interpreting it as a betrayal of the 'good woman' ideal. That framing echoed the myths I internalized: Enduring was virtuous; severing ties was suspicious. The symbolic field, shaped in part by the recurring forms in the unconscious (Jung, 1970), is reduced to a punitive script.

> It's totally taboo for women to sleep around or dress in revealing clothes. People judge you for that, and even for liking different kinds of sex, like BDSM. They act like you're evil or something! And even though I hate the word 'provocative,' it's true that dressing that way can lead to slut-shaming from both men and women.
>
> (Persephone)

As the interviews unfolded, the stories echoed my psychic terrain. I came to recognize an earlier phase of my life as marked by Societal Indoctrination, a term that provided contour to a previously inchoate unease. With its naming, the PFA stirred as a symbolic force in the unconscious, challenging the fragile architecture of the ego (Whitmont, 1978). She countered internalized logics, inciting a psychological growth. Indoctrination serves as a mechanism of patriarchy, scripting gendered convictions within a mythology authored long before us (Foucault, 1977). Fictions fasten themselves to our psychic architecture, profoundly etched, that performance blurs.

Chapter 7

Witch Hunts and Hysteria

> I think there must be some historical lineage I don't fully understand yet. I think women ... were the healers, midwives, and herbalists who everybody went to, mostly, and they got too powerful. So, the Male Society turned that into a slur, right? And so that then, it's been historically so long, that it becomes ingrained that witches are evil, and they're mean, and they eat children, and they're ugly. And, you know, all those sorts of preconceived notions about who witches are.
>
> (Hestia)

Before the consolidation of patriarchal rule in early modern Europe, between the 14th and 17th centuries, women held respected roles at the epicenter of communal life. Their authority in midwifery, healing, and ritual practice positioned them as threats to the emerging sociopolitical order. Beginning in the late 15th century, particularly with the publication of the *Malleus Maleficarum* in 1487 (Kramer & Sprenger, 1486/1928), secular and religious male institutions launched coordinated efforts to consolidate control. Legal measures to suppress unsanctioned spiritual practices included inquisitorial systems that disproportionately criminalized women's authority as heretical. Amplified by biblical texts, such as Deuteronomy 18:10–11 (CEB, 2011, Deuteronomy 18:10–11), acts of divination and enchantment were used to justify the theological basis for persecution.

The witch materialized as a vessel for collective anxieties, while women's wisdom was driven into secrecy by the Church. Scientific and philosophical expansions reignited suspicions, now cloaked in clinical and cultural language and targeting emotions, intellect, and erotic desire. As rationalism replaced religious dogma as the dominant mode of truth-making, suspicion of women's bodies and knowledge systems was reformulated. Representations of evil embedded in myth, folklore, and theory are rearticulated as institutional categories in clinical and cultural discourse. Consequently, the fusion of religious dogma with nascent medical models produced interpretive frameworks rooted

DOI: 10.4324/9781003455837-10

in fear and suspicion (Ussher, 2006; Federici, 2004; Karlsen, 1987). Operating within institutional paradigms, hysterical labels crucified unconventional women as erratic, dangerous, or morally deviant (Barstow, 1994; Showalter, 1985).

CONSTRUCTING THE WITCH

> I was raised with religion, and I could remember bits and pieces, but as I grew up, I never felt very religious; I was very much the kid making potions in the background. I gravitated towards witchy books about mysticism … occult traditions, you know, feminine ideology. I think my mom suppressed her interest in those fields, but that's a whole other story. I remember them being hidden and wrong in some way.
>
> (Athena)

Historical accounts have historically cast witches as emblematic disruptors of social order, defying religious doctrine, domestic submission, and communal codes of conduct (Sollee, 2017). Persecution assumed institutional form, punishing women who departed from dogmatic moral and behavioral standards. Religious and legal systems reinforced narrow ideals of femininity, rendering deviation a source of shame and social retribution (Levack, 2015; see Figure 7.1). The evil witch arose as an emblem of destruction, employed to suppress alternative wisdom systems into legacies of indigenous healing, feminine mysticism, and embodied ritual approaches resisted masculinist rationalism (Ehrenreich & English, 1973).

Juridico-religious systems of early modern Europe encoded feminine disobedience as a moral pathology. Surveillance seeped into daily life, where suspicion became synonymous with womanhood, and abnormality was punishable. Disciplinary regimes produced perverse subjects by enforcing conformity to physical and psychic norms (Foucault, 1978). Rather than subduing deviation, regimes constructed through naming, diagnosing, and moralizing nonconformity into legible forms of deviance. Psychoanalytic clinicians interpret the female body as erotically saturated, ministering each gesture or sensation as a site of projected *perversity*. Intertwined with colonization of stolen lands and masculinist egoism, the legacy persists in modern contexts, embedding itself in medical institutions through diagnostic overreach, reproductive control, and the continued framing of feminine traits, such as emotional expression and intuition, as illness.

> It's like … that blackness of outer space, that endless void? That's feminine energy. It's like a womb, this deep, swirling darkness inside. And anyone who's more feminine has that in them, like this chaotic energy that could burst out at any moment. And it freaks people out, especially men, because they don't have it. They're simple, you know? So when they see someone with that depth, that wild, cosmic energy … it's scary to them. And then it becomes taboo. Like, if you're emotional, people are all, "Whoa, where'd *that* come from?" They don't get that it's just part of being feminine.
>
> (Aphrodite)

Figure 7.1 *Trial of George Jacobs*

Public domain. Reproduction sourced from the Library of Congress, Prints & Photographs Division.

Note:
Trial of George Jacobs (1855) (Matteson & Detroit Publishing Co., 1900-1920), depicts a courtroom scene from the Salem Witch Trials, colonial America. Original painting housed at the Essex Institute, Salem, Massachusetts.

At the height of the trials, juridical and theological regimes escalated perceived threats to orthodoxy and patriarchal control into forms of state-sanctioned violence designed to expel defiance. Heresy, spiritual agency, and gender nonconformity pose existential threats to ecclesiastical and civic order. This ideological framework authorized a massacre: Of the estimated 100,000 executed during the witch hunts, between 75,000 and 85,000 were women, disproportionately targeted for behaviors and roles that transgressed male authority (Rapley, 2001; Levack, 2015). That same structure of perception, where deviation signals danger, persists in modern institutions as unorthodox women remain under surveillance, rendered suspect, and disciplined through bureaucratic, diagnostic, and educational means.

Witchcraft, it's mostly simple stuff. Connecting with nature, you know? But some traditions get a little wild, with sacrifices and whatnot. Even that, though, it's still

> about drawing from nature, that power we're all connected to. But it's been condemned! Like, the way the colonizers killed off native people for their earth magic … that really hit me. It's like they were trying to wipe out *everything*—the connection to the magic, to our own power. That's what is disgusting, not witches.
>
> (Oya)

By the height of the witch trials, religious and legal institutions had deployed the Malleus Maleficarum (Kramer & Sprenger, 1486/1928) (see Figure 7.2) as a juridical weapon, evolving earlier theological judgments into law. The manual's influence contained explicit protocols of interrogation and punishment. Religiously sanctioned violence illustrates how persecution adapted to the tools of governance, permitting state power to cloak suspicion in the language of legality (Federici, 2004; Barstow, 1994).

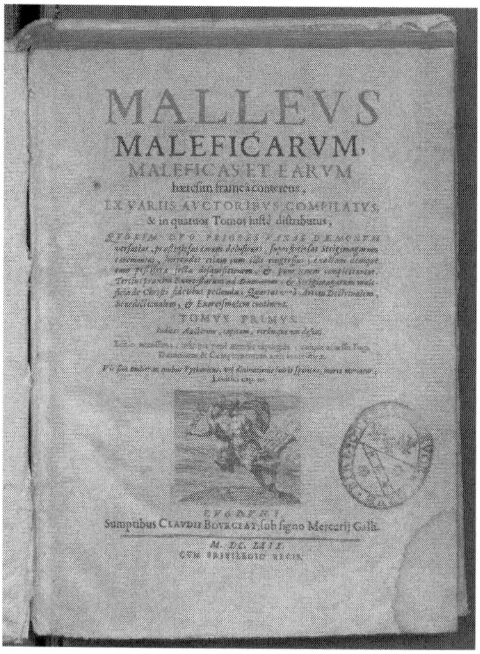

Figure 7.2 *Title Page of Malleus Maleficarum*

Public domain. Wikimedia Commons.

Note:

A page from the 1669 edition of Malleus Maleficarum, a witch-hunting manual authored by Heinrich Kramer in the 15th century. Featuring Latin text in red and black ink, an illustration of a bound figure, and a stamped library seal.

> I think that what comes to mind is definitely sexuality, and, like, the power source of women and really like, birthing all these … demons and unwanted things … into the world, like Lilith and all that. That comes to mind, but I think that it's needed and magical. And how can you have the light without the dark? You know what I mean? And, like, I don't understand why that's considered dark either. Because even witchcraft, and all that, like being burned at the stake, being demonized, all that is just insane to me.
>
> (Ixchel)

In regions that encompass present-day Germany, France, and Switzerland, women who served as midwives, herbalists, and seers were primary targets of persecution (Monter, 1976; Briggs, 1996). Religious and legal authorities cast them as threats to orthodoxy, while engravings and propaganda reinforced their perceived deviance in the public imagination (see Figure 7.3).

As the demonic witch calcified, she evolved into a symbolic vessel for malfeasance (Dutton, 2007). Her endurance demonstrates the insidious persistence of

Figure 7.3 *The Four Witches*

Public domain. Image courtesy of the Cleveland Museum of Art.

Note:
The Four Witches, depicting four nude women standing together in an intimate, almost conspiratorial arrangement, while a demonic entity lurks in the background. Engraving by Albrecht Dürer (1497).

Social Indoctrination, which conditions women to be obedient. Beyond a relic of superstition, the witch endured as an archetype who rationalized coercive control. Whether cast as seductress, lunatic, or heretic, she served to delineate the boundaries of acceptable femininity.

> In middle school, I got called into the dean's office because of how disruptive I was in class. I was doing the same thing the boys were doing. I wasn't being loud in class like others, but there was some unspoken rule that girls and boys had different expectations. I was just asking why boys could get away with things that girls couldn't. That conversation turned into a lecture about how to be more respectful. Even now, I must carefully pick my battles because if I speak up too much, I'll be labeled difficult or aggressive. It's exhausting trying to stay in this narrow box just to avoid being punished for who I am.
>
> (Medusa)

Persecution drifted into modern institutions, where psychiatric diagnoses (Tomes & Showalter, 1987) and forced sterilizations of Black, Indigenous, and immigrant women (Davis, 1981) exacted control over the feminized body. Though framed as medical necessity, such interventions reflect previous rituals of punishment.

Medicalizing the Feminine: Hysteria and Control

> My dad is a doctor and always wanted a son to follow in his footsteps and I felt this pressure to be better than him … like to compete. He had two specialties. I got three. I became a surgeon, all in my masculine. My feminine side, the intuition? It was there but like a decoration, not real power. My family still calls me the witch to poke fun at how I was in childhood, but I've lost all respect and connection to that part of me.
>
> (Gaia)

By the late 17th century, scientific and philosophical expansions reignited suspicions, now cloaked in clinical and cultural language and targeting emotions, intellect, and erotic desire. Representations of evil women are entrenched in myth, folklore, and theory and rearticulated through institutional categories in clinical discourse. The fusion of religiosity with nascent medical models produced a contemporary reiteration of documented violence (Ussher, 2006; Federici, 2004; Karlsen, 1987). Operating within institutional paradigms, hysterical labels crucified unconventional women as erratic, dangerous, or morally deviant (Barstow, 1994; Showalter, 1985).

> That's another big stereotype, that if a woman portrays any sort of emotion, that is not something that, you know, a man, or, like, sort of society at large … wants her to be or is trying to elicit from her, then she's crazy. And that, I mean, that goes to historical contexts of, you know, women being branded as hysterical.
>
> (Hecate)

Stigmatization runs under the skin of individual experience; its force emits a collective heritage. The imprint moves within the bones and stirs in the soul, where emotional depth and intensity are disordered. Resonating with the historical suppression, hysteria admonishes a collective thread (Koerber, 2018). Hellbent on medicalization, the patriarchal machine clamps down on unruly potency, and the delirious woman is confined to domesticity (Appignanesi, 2008).

> Labeling people as 'evil' or 'crazy' is dangerous. Pure evil exists, but we're usually wrong about who we pin it on. And what we do to those people … it's messed up. Like, gay white men get thrown in that category too, because they're not 'manly' enough, or women who dare to express their emotions fully. If they can twist it so your choices, your being, is somehow feminine, evil, crazy, dark … then they can justify anything. Maiming, torturing … It's like bombing whole towns because the people are Black. It's all connected to these labels and how they let us do terrible things.
>
> (Hecate)

The term *hysteria* originates from the Greek word hystera, meaning womb, and reveals how deeply rooted gendered myths about female biology and emotional instability are, dating back to c. 1800 BCE. Early Egyptian papyri described the uterus as a migratory organ that could cause illness throughout the body (Nunn, 1996), a belief paralleled in Greco-Roman traditions, perpetuated in medieval and Renaissance thought. Hippocratic theories (~400 BCE) framed the uterus as the source of mental illness, fusing bodily function to emotional disturbance (King, 1998; Reynolds, 2018). Later revived in medieval medical doctrine, most notably in the *Trotula Compendium*, a widely circulated 12th-century collection of women's medical texts associated with Trota of Salerno (Green, 2001, 2008). In works like *De curis mulierum* (On Treatments for Women), symptoms linked to a "wandering womb" were treated as evidence of inner disorder; a continuum that anticipates the demonological interpretations witnessed in witchcraft trials. By the 19th century, these ancient views evolved into hysteria, a catch-all diagnosis applied whenever women transgressed prescribed gender norms (Tasca et al., 2012; Maines, 2001).

Praying to Purity

> Perverse feminine archetype … it's in the witches and medicine women that have always lived and the club I'm part of. I think perverse is a funny word because it just means it's away from the mainstream. Then it got demonized or somehow perverse, something negative, and I think that I allowed this to control me for a while, where I was afraid to step out of the prescribed roles and feared my own body; I think I still feel pretty separate from myself. Hell, I was told masturbation was evil … that had to fuck me up in some way, right?
>
> (Lamia)

Participants described the burden of inhabiting forms long inscribed with danger and deviance. Internalized restraint often calcifies into ritualized self-discipline, where one seeks absolution through compliance. Inherited codes of shame and restraint shaped how many struggled to inhabit pleasure, voice anger, or assert presence without penalty. The witch, historically tethered to systems of racial, economic, and spiritual stratification, materialized as punishment. Discomfort germinated in environments inscribed by colonial erasure, an unspoken legacy vibrating at the contours of individuality.

> It's crazy how everything 'feminine' gets shamed, you know? Even across different cultures, the people who embody that feminine energy get the worst of it. Like, white people are all about that masculine energy, focused on 'doing' and conquering. But the people who are connected to the earth, the indigenous people who value softness, trust, creativity … they get trampled on. There's this whole system built against them. Even with religion, the most feminine ones, like paganism and witchcraft, were persecuted and demonized. It's just … ugh. It makes me so mad!
>
> (Inanna)

State and ecclesiastical forces have long disciplined reproductive autonomy and expressive potential, positioning them as threats to patriarchal order (Foucault, 2003). Federici (2004) situates the witch hunts within the consolidation of capitalist labor structures, arguing that these campaigns targeted women whose embodied knowledge disrupted the emerging economic rationality. Rendered grotesque to sanction their removal, accused witches illustrate how the Perverse Feminine Archetype holds the trace of disavowed power, surfacing as an archetypal breach.

> For me, it's really about going against the norm. So, 'perverse feminine' is like … taking something not usually seen as feminine and owning it radically. I think that it's needed and magical. And how can you have the light without the dark? You know what I mean? And, like, I don't understand why that's considered dark either. Because even witchcraft and all that, like being burned at the stake, being demonized, all that is just insane to me.
>
> (Kali)

Doctrinal scripts inscribe visceral associations between pleasure and violation, an inheritance forged through generations of sanctioned repression. What lingers is the active architecture of surveillance. Indicative of the current political regime, on July 24, 2025, President Trump issued the executive order *Ending Crime and Disorder on America's Streets*. Framed as a public safety initiative, the policy resuscitates a bid to remove perceived deviance from public view under the rhetoric of protection (The White House, 2025). In doing so, it reveals an enduring fixation on sanitizing the social body.

From Possession to Perversity

> When I began to practice witchcraft, I felt like I was finally connecting with a part of me that I had lost touch with. It was like I was somehow, I don't know, coming back to myself. But … that didn't last long because there was this other part of me that felt so detached and scared of being different. It's hard to explain, but I just felt weird.
>
> (Nyx)

Present-day hysteria iterations enact systemic dismissal of women's distress as biologically predetermined or affectively disproportionate (Hoffman & Tarzian, 2001). Medicalized chronologies uphold outdated diagnoses, allowing obsolete models to linger and distort credibility. Perversion functions as a subversive impression, forged through mental health's legacy entanglement with sin. The anathematized (add additional context) resurfaces as a strategic adaptation. Participants describe a relentless pressure to self-edit, a vigilance that collapses the line between staying safe and losing one's sense of reality (Gilbert & Gubar, 1979). By the 1890s, medical discourse reframed hysteria as demonomania. Charcot reinforced the connection between emotional expression and pathology, diagnosing visible affect as symptomatic of supernatural corruption (see Figure 7.4) (Workman, 2016). Such associations disciplined perceived gender violations. Medical models gradually supplanted religious explanations: Freud's psychosexual theory repositioned supernatural possession as a shattering of mental cohesion.

> It's messed me up, this whole thing about women and emotions. Whenever I feel something strongly, I always wonder if I overreact. It's like, 'Was that justified?' I second-guess myself constantly. It's gotten to the point where it's hard for me to get angry. So now, when I *do* get mad, I'm almost proud of myself! It was so bottled up inside me growing up.
>
> (Persephone)

Freud's concept of *polymorphous perversity* cast childhood erotic curiosity as fluid and unbounded, an instinctual field gradually narrowed (Freud, 1905/2000; Gay, 2006). With his theoretical progression came penis envy, positing womanhood as subordinated to male development. Feminist psychoanalysts disputed and illustrated how the conception projected male anxiety onto women and redefined maternal authority as threatening (Horney, 1967; Chodorow, 1978; Mitchell, 1974). Jung diverged from Freud in the shadow, an internal contradiction (von Franz, 1999). Where Freud emphasized developmental constraint, Jung traced disowned impulses into archetypal imagery. Essentialist universal symbolism often eclipses and reinforces dominant social expectations under the guise of collective harmony, the guise of psychic unity (Wehr, 1987).

Figure 7.4 *Jean-Martin Charcot Demonstrating Hysteria in a Hypnotized Patient at the Salpêtrière*

Image courtesy of the Wellcome Collection.

Note:
This 1888 etching by A. Lurat reproduces André Brouillet's 1887 painting, depicting Jean-Martin Charcot demonstrating a case of hysteria in Marie Wittman, a hypnotized patient at the Salpêtrière Hospital.

The PFA ignites at the breaking point of internal strain, where conditioned containment comes undone. Demonstrated in film, such as *Female Perversions* (Streitfeld, 1996), where Swinton's character, an ambitious attorney, exudes precision and control while she is privately unraveling. Her compulsions disclose a psychic brink: A breach where adaptation collapses and forbidden desires stage their return, unable to be hidden any longer (Kaplan, 1991). Building on Dijkstra's (1988) visual critique of fin-de-siècle visual culture and Grosz's (1994) analysis of corporeal inscription, perversity functions as an analytical tool, exposing indoctrination via an archetypal aberration. As a symbolic fulcrum, Lilith concatenates punishment with myth. Her story preserves resistance, where disavowed impulses lodge in collective memory, exposing a fracture between instinct and sanctioned behavior.

Chapter **8**

Demonizing Lilith

A Case Study

> I've decided that this year I'm identifying with Lilith. I mean, I really identify with the idea of Adam's first wife, who kicked him to the curb because she wouldn't obey him in bed. God, I've been through that myself. It's so interesting that she turned into a demon, but when you think about it, the demon wasn't all that bad in old Greece. It's identified with emotional states, animals, and nature … mostly creativity. Funny how the word has shifted, too.
>
> (Aphrodite)

Nearly three millennia before the formalization of psychiatric diagnosis or the spectacle of witch trials, early cosmogonies portrayed women's contempt as an existential threat. Among ancient mythic scapegoats, Lilith's monstrous mutation spans eras, with each metamorphosis depicting societal angst. From Mesopotamian lilītu to the Alphabet of Ben Sira and later Kabbalistic texts, there exists a compulsive regulatory force, offering a perverse case study. As established in *Witch Hunts and Hysteria*, the metaphoric function of myth transitions into the codified force of law, where ritualized banishment transitions into legal precedent. When animated by the classical daimon, Lilith generates chaos. In ancient Greek philosophy, such a being is an intermediary force, neither moral nor divine, yet capable of traversing both realms. Contained as muse, the entity transmutes the soul's unrest into consequential action, inciting inspirational direction (Plato, Symposium; Heraclitus, Fragment 119). Positioned as a daimonic entity, Lilith is a catalytic force, an agitator of archetypal proportions who transforms ancestral unrest into creative disobedience (Burkert, 1985; Hillman, 1979). Her presence disrupts structures of virtue and vice, exposing how hegemonic systems distort the spirit. An affront to moral orthodoxy, she reignites proclivities subjugated by doctrinal restraint (Hillman, 1979, 1989). Conjuring her image invites confrontation with exiled dominant paradigms (Best, 2003). Contextually, through her lens, participants stir pedagogy embedded in cultural memory. Her

DOI: 10.4324/9781003455837-11

gaze uncovers hidden internalized messages that valorize certainty and pathologize contradiction (Patai, 1990).

> I felt like, you know, there's that concept of a woman is, she's like her, the child of her parents, until she gets married. And then she's owned by her husband. Like … I'm an adult; why do I need to be propped up with my parents as if I'm still a child? They wouldn't be asking me to do this if I had a husband and kids. It might seem silly, but it sort of feels like my parents own me in some way, and they just want me to start a family already. Greece…,
>
> (Demeter)

Demonization functions as a mechanism of restraint, delineating how inner sanctions are regulated. Feared and eroticised, those who step outside normative boundaries, who express forbidden potency, are dangerous. Participants describe cumulative psychic injuries: Subtle messages that amount to character defamation. Unlike mythic epics, their accounts unfold in intimate domains. Parental authority, possessive partners, and punitive inner critics subtly vilify their convictions. As sinister tropes absorb psychically, women enact conformity. Lilith's residue lingers in experience, reaching for reprieve.

SANCTIFIED SUBMISSION

> I grew up in a Catholic family, so good and evil is something I learned from the Bible as a kind of Adam and Eve … it's something that I recognize as an early message for me. As a child, your brain is constantly sucking in information, so you will learn from what you are being taught and from experiences from TV shows. It's crazy to think that literally, the first 5 or 6 years of the child will determine who they will be in the future from what they see, what they hear, what they watch, and stuff like that. Slowly, your parents tell you, okay, this is bad; school tells you, this is bad; society tells you this is bad, and experiences with people make you realize, okay, even if you have not been through this, this is bad.

Participants described a persistent prescriptive ideology, upheld by caregivers, educators, and media across early developmental stages. Perpetuated by social mandates that tie feminine propriety to virtue, submission functioned as a survival mechanism; an adaptive response conditioned by early attachment needs, and reinforced by observed social norms (Bowlby, 1982; Bandura, 1977). Symbolism here draws from early Sumerian religious cosmologies, where female deities presided over cosmic order and ceremonial power (see Figure 8.1). Goddess centrality in ancient epochs reflects an ethos that elevated feminine sovereignty, foreshadowing the disavowal enacted by subsequent regimes.

> Gosh, when I was married, I felt like my husband was jealous of me. It seemed like he wanted to restrict me in every way … everything felt like some odd competition,

Figure 8.1 *Burney Relief (Queen of the Night)*

Photograph by Aiwok (2011), sourced from Wikimedia Commons.

Note:

Frequently associated with Inanna or Lilith, this winged figure with clawed feet and owlish eyes suggests a liminal feminine—fertile and fearsome, divine yet untouchable. Her stance, flanked by lions and owls, evokes ancient power that has not yet been tamed by patriarchal myth. British Museum, London.

> and I did everything I could to make him happy. He was upset when I used sex toys, so I threw them out. He got mad about my yoga and meditation practice, so I stopped. He even ripped up my yoga mat. That was hard for me, and I don't think I've ever recovered. I still feel so restricted. I have difficulty connecting with the person I was when I was deeply involved with my spiritual practice.
>
> (Oya)

Enheduanna, daughter of Sargon of Akkad and High Priestess of the moon god Nanna, played a pivotal role in shaping the theological and political cosmologies of her era, authoring hymns that positioned female divinity as central to Mesopotamian religious life (McCarthy et al., 2004). By the second millennium BCE, societies reorganized their power structures, replacing matrifocal practices with andocentric systems (Eliade, 1959; Black et al., 2006; Lerner, 1987). Religious and legal shifts restructured home life, devotional roles, and civic inclusion to mandate obedience and sustain control, such as Hammurabi's Code §§128–141, which dictated female sexual fidelity and domestic obedience (Roth, 1997; Eisler, 1987; Christ, 1979).

> I think I'm perverse because I feel like I'm deemed inappropriate by certain people and the public eye. I mean, look at me; I am a Black, non-binary queer artist. How much more unacceptable can I be? Even my mom, who really does support me, questions my art sometimes. It seems like because I am in a female body, I'm constantly being judged for the type of work I put out there because it is seen as hyper-masculine. People always ask me why I want to work big, and I think if I were a man, they just wouldn't think twice. So, I didn't allow myself to work to my full capacity for a long time.
>
> (Kali)

Legal codes spanning Mesopotamian marriage contracts to Athenian domestic laws stringently curtailed female sovereignty (Raday, 2003; Rapley, 2001). During this period, female demons classified as *lilītu* erupted in Akkadian texts as seductresses. Known as night demons, such ghouls preyed on men in their dreams, moments of vulnerability, where breaches in the boundaries of consciousness occur. Though not explicitly emergent from legal reform, their incarnation reflected anxieties surrounding unchecked feminine allure. Further reinforced through apotropaic ritual practices, they signify a widespread effort to manage women as perceived hazards (George, 1992; Hurwitz, 1992; Patai, 1990). As entities within the perverse formation, they prefigure Lilith's appearance, providing a parallel prototype within the mythological tapestry.

LILITH IN JEWISH TRADITION

> So, I do feel, of course, like, the strength of a woman has been perverted into … demonizing a lot of things about … everything about us again. Like, if you're

> beautiful, it's a problem. If you're ugly, it's a problem. If you're heavyset, it's a problem. If you're too skinny, it's a problem. Like, it doesn't fucking matter. So why shouldn't you just do whatever the fuck you want … and, and step into … whatever that that space is for you, that brings you power and makes you magical.
>
> (Medusa)

Late antique incantation conventions and medieval folklore preserved Lilith as a guardian of uncontainment. Her apparition ripples over centuries yet remains stained by contempt. Prior to her development, we must first engage with the biblical creation myth. Genesis 1:27 conceives male and female constructed simultaneously in the divine incarnation (Jewish Publication Society, 1985). However, symmetry collapses in Genesis 2, where woman is fashioned from man to alleviate his solitude, shifting relational ontology from mutuality to derivation. In Genesis 3, Eve's reach for forbidden wisdom incurred God's punishment by way of childbirth pain and relational subjugation (Thompson, 1999) (see Figure 8.2). Further cemented in Christian theology, she is the bearer of original sin, a burden that

Figure 8.2 *The Rebuke of Adam and Eve*

Public domain. Image courtesy of The Metropolitan Museum of Art.

Note:
The Rebuke of Adam and Eve (Natoire, 740), depicts a classical representation of the biblical story of Adam and Eve in the Garden of Eden. The artwork features a serpent-woman hybrid offering fruit from a tree, with symbolic entities and animals surrounding the scene.

reverberates across interpretations of feminine transgression. In midrashic tradition, Genesis Rabbah (3rd–5th century CE) introduces a rupture within the origin tale, proposing a division between the woman of Genesis 1 and the one sculpted from Adam's rib (Genesis Rabbah 17:4). This exegetical schism births Lilith as a prelapsarian figure formed equally, yet unwilling to yield in the *Alphabet of Ben Sira*.

By the 6th century CE, the Babylonian Talmud positions Lilith as a night demon associated with threat and ritual impurity (Shabbat 151b; Patai, 1990). Her appearance coincided with high rates of infant and maternal mortality (Ulmer, 1994), rendering her a scapegoat for reproductive failure and maternal deviation. Projected as both cause and consequence of loss (Scholem, 1941; Alexander, 1983), she absorbed the terror of inexplicable death (Secunda, 2013). Formed by a consolidation of rabbinic authority under Sassanian, (Secunda, 2013) prescriptions for feminine conduct were tightly regulated by halakhic codification and communal enforcement. With amplified interpretations of modesty (Boyarin, 1993), menstrual purity (Fonrobert, 2000), marriage laws, and exclusion from public religious life, a rigid hierarchy prevailed (Hauptman, 1998). Lilith surfaced as a symbolic counterforce: The archetype of female malfeasance, untethered from reproductive and legal obligation. As a metaphysical and corporeal threat, Aramaic incantation bowls from Babylonia and Persia bear protective inscriptions intended to paralyze her spirit (Bohak, 2008; Naveh & Shaked, 1985). Placed underneath beds or entryways, vessels served as apotropaic tools encapsulating anxieties; desperate attempts to enclose the unfathomable (see Figure 8.3).

> I think it is because it's an energy that is very difficult to define. Society can try to have these little cages, like an Excel sheet with little boxes, and you have to be one of those. I feel like there is a constant message that because I don't fit into those boxes, something is wrong with me and people reject my lifestyle. I just want to be able to be an authentic me without the stress of what others might think, but I've had shit go down in the past where people have rejected and abandoned me for that. I'm so scared I'll never have a community because of it.
>
> (Artemis)

Centuries after her shadowed existence in rabbinic commentary, Lilith materializes in deserted corridors. She exists as a winged nocturnal demon associated with erotic dreams and infanticide. Her crucible moment crystallizes in the Alphabet of Ben Sira (8th-10th century CE), a satirical folk text originating from Jewish diasporic life under Islamic rule (Dan, 1998). Tradition offers her a cruel choice: Lie beneath Adam or face banishment. She refuses. To escape her bind, she utters God's ineffable name (Shem ha-Mephorash), committing a sacred transgression. Condemnation follows in deaths of one hundred of her children each day. Overcome with grief, she endangers newborns, nursing vengeance. Striking fear in the Jewish communities, living as dhimmi, where rates of infant mortality

Figure 8.3 *Incantation Bowl with Aramaic Inscription*

Public domain. Image retrieved from The Metropolitan Museum of Art.

Note:
A Sasanian-era incantation bowl from 5th–6th century CE Mesopotamia (The Metropolitan Museum of Art, n.d.-a), crafted from ceramic and paint, was traditionally used to ward off malevolent spirits, including Lilith.

remained high, Lilith absorbed dread. An archetypal severing; a mythic rupture binding her fate to the fatal expense for obstination (Ginzberg, 2022, 1:2:43).

> And then so to tie that into your question of like, what sorts of stereotypes women have, I think about, like, uh. They're—I feel like there are positive ones and then negative ones, like a negative one would be like, 'slut prostitute.' A crazy woman. Overly emotional, psycho. Somebody who's like, mysterious and trying to, like, trick a man into getting what she wants. And then there's the positive ones of like, the mother, the nurturer. Um, oh, the beauty queen. I don't know, like I feel like the good traits are more like, what can feel constricting? Like trying to fit into these things? And then for me personally, like trying to be the sexy good girl, it causes a lot of problems for me.
>
> (Lamia)

Connecting the archetypal to biblical lore, Lilith and Eve are inverses: One penalized for sovereignty, the other for wisdom. Psychically, the dichotomous bind exemplifies women's plight. Damned if they submit; damned if they subvert.

FROM DAUGHTER TO DEVIANT

> Some people might be annoyed at an overly aggressive or not aggressive, that's not the same word ... overly assertive woman, because they might perceive it as aggression because it's coming from her. And that's the only thing I can think of with the question that you asked. Gosh, I remember as a child that my mom and I just had to do our best not to upset my dad. Whatever specific actions he took were beside the point; in her eyes, his anger was our fault. I know now that this was a pattern I learned in all my relationships with others.
>
> (Nyx)

Early socialization framed emotional regulation as appeasement. Rather than naming male volatility as destructive, girls learned to manage themselves. The lesson: Assertion invites consequence. Women discuss how they muted emotional depth in the face of familial harmony, where they are deployed as mediators, losing themselves to an authoritative household regime.

> And then she [mother] would point out, "Hey, look at those guys looking at you." She would say, "I'm walking with my personal harem" because she had three daughters and all that. I know that was not a great message to send me, but anyhow, that's why she would say things like that, or when I was maybe 13 this one guy followed me in the mall as we were walking. And she's like, "Oh, he's following you because he must want to date you or be with you!"
>
> (Hera)

Hera's account underscores how early indoctrination saturates ordinary moments. Her mother's remarks, steeped in male validation, trained her to interpret attention as affirmation. Beneath veiled humor, appeal surmounted to currency. Tracing early objectification, a unifying thread woven in abusive heteronormative romantic relationships. Sexuality mutates into a constricting device, where men wielded power in their claims over women's bodies. However, when seeking individual pleasure, parents met them with corrective surveillance.

> I feel like in my culture, there's no room to be sexual or you're a slut. My family always gets mad at me because they want me to sit a certain way or be a certain thing. It's like right now I'm sitting with my legs open, but that would be considered really bad if I did it in front of my parents. I would probably be slapped, honestly.
>
> (Guan Yin)

Unregulated sexuality threatened morality. Guan Yin's reflection reveals the collision between bodily autonomy and respectability mandates. The pressure to remain *ladylike* operated as an imperative, constricting curiosity. Indicating an interconnected web, participants highlighted how constrictive notions of purity pervaded their lives.

> You think of abortion … the 'Most Evil?' Is the dude in that scenario ever going to show up for that kid or not? There's nobody else who gives a shit about this kid in the world, and it's all on her. All the dude has to do is have sex with her. So it's pretty easy for her to be evil. It reminds me of when I had my abortion. The guy I was sleeping with was so upset about it, but he wasn't even willing to commit to me. It was bizarre, honestly.
>
> (Hestia)

Moral outrage targets women disproportionately, with interviews revealing that society considers their behavior perverse. Abortion condemnation, like modesty mandates, functions as societal mechanisms that reframe choice as selfishness. Interviews illustrate how effortlessly one can embody wickedness within this systemic guillotine. Recollections outline subtle demonization, as society condemns femininity based on how close it is to sacrifice. To assert opposition is to risk excommunication. Girls learn to mold themselves to please, to survive. A precarious love arises from external sources rather than being nurtured from within. The result is psychic fragmentation: A dissonant subjectivity that splits the performed from the repressed.

Stage 2

Shapeshifting

Fractured Identities

SHAPESHIFTING: INTERNALIZED PERVERSIONS

> This idea of power and subservience was my identity, and that created perfectionism inside of me as a woman, and I had to be a specific way to survive or thrive going into my next stage of life.
>
> (Hestia)

Shapeshifting constitutes an internal reorganization enacted in response to implicit socio-cultural demands for legibility. In place of authentic self-expression, individuals reflect dominant projections that associate femininity with passivity, agreeableness, and emotional regulation. Ideological imprints, internalized at a preconscious level, operate as structuring forces that shape behavior, fundamentally implanted in survival imperatives (Woodman, 1982).

Emergent as context-specific adaptations, behavioral recalibrations solidify into enduring performative scripts. The designation may alternate between exaggerated displays of normative femininity and overt self-armoring, yet both expressions reinforce intrapsychic division. Gradually, repetitive gestures displace instinctive responsiveness. The resulting self-effacement contributes to the formation of one's shadow, as individuals downplay their strengths, desires, or unacceptable traits to fit societal expectations.

Culminating in shadow development, the progressive dissolution of coherent self-recognition ensues. In contexts where deviation elicits threat, performance evolves into a mechanism of self-preservation. However, the cost is profound: Increasing alienation from interior authority. Such fragmentation forms the latent substrate for the Perverse Feminine Archetype (PFA), whose activation signifies entrapment characterized as projective perversity.

DOI: 10.4324/9781003455837-12

SHADOW FORMATION AND THE TOLL OF SHAPESHIFTING

> And that's a point … for a man to say the feminine or the female is perverse, which is a weird way of saying that intuition is wrong. I think a lot of people think that certain aspects of people are bad just because they don't understand how they work. And they're not taking the time and effort to connect and understand it.
>
> (Kali)

When moral imperatives encode femininity, the psyche cultivates defensive bifurcation, constricting possibility towards presence. This intrapsychic split functions as an adaptive defense mechanism forged in early encounters with conditional acceptance. Gradually, evaluative scrutiny suppresses instincts, compelling them into subterranean domains, where they forestall integration and individuation (Johnson, 1994).

> I don't want to talk too much about my relationship with my mother. But she doesn't know that I do this [dance]. This is an image she would never find out; it would probably kill her. So I, you know, yeah. But I feel like I have two people. The person that she raised, and the person I have now that's like, bold and outgoing. And, you know, all of what I do is conservative, and my mother is in the south, just a Black woman, heavily religious.
>
> (Oshun)

The maternal gaze functions as an inaugural mirror filtering subjectivity through a lens of acceptability. In this early reflection, psychosomatic dissociation begins. The shadow morphs into a phantom limb, a severed constellation of instinctual drives and unarticulated longings. Operating beneath the liminal edge of consciousness, this sublimated architecture leaves a spectral imprint (Jung, 1928–43/1966; von Franz, 1980). Buried beneath the infertile ground of Social Indoctrination, occluded fragments lose vitality, casting spectral traces that outline the cost of compliance.

ADAPTATION AND REPRESSION

> There are days when it feels like it's eating away at my self-esteem. Because I'm not enough as I am, I have to be something else to be accepted, which is also coming back to her last. For a while, it felt like I wasn't especially accepted everywhere because I was a plus-size performer.
>
> (Ala)

Beneath adaptive comportment lies a more elusive form of psychic erosion. In a recursive, internalized imperative toward self-monitoring, the process masquerades as moral rectitude or cultural fidelity. This surveillance mechanism, often bound to normative ideals of feminine restraint and modesty (Neumann, 1994), sustains a compulsive pursuit of external affirmation. The drive for perfection, rather than cultivating stability, amplifies disconnection from instinctual knowing.

> It's like not being grumpy or not being mad or not super tired or not imbalanced or overly sexual or underly sexual, just like sort of the perfect, harmonious female who can glide in and out of all situations. Like, what are the words, a tremendous capacity for adaptability, that I think is inhuman. It's like an inhuman model of being a woman.
>
> (Lilith)

External expectations often impose narrow conditions for acceptance and belonging. In this climate, a compulsion ascends from the incomprehensible tension between conformity and authenticity. The internal cost accumulates as an erosion of volition.

> I think, as a whole, the woman learns her place. We end up performing, constantly, like we're in a play we didn't audition for. It's this strange, endless act where we learn to accept what's actually not okay as if it's normal.
>
> (Artemis)

Encased in emotional repression and codified gendered norms, personhood undergoes a recalibration oriented toward survival. The internalization of external demands installs a regulatory apparatus that disciplines desire and constrains imaginative range, fostering a persistent undertow of dissatisfaction. What initially functions as an adaptive strategy calcifies into a fragmented performance of selfhood, wherein compartmentalized roles offer short-term protection at the cost of long-term coherence. Each role functions as a survival tactic. Fragmented by persistent dissonance, the soul cleaves to manipulation to guarantee security. As fragmentation deepens, internalized sexism gains traction both as a social force and structure shaping one's sense of legitimacy. What remains obscured is how Shapeshifting itself becomes mistaken for truth.

INTERNALIZED SEXISM AND THE PERSONA

> I can't really say I have a full idea of who I am. That's really embarrassing to admit, but it's true, and I think that a lot of people are often perplexed by me. I don't know. I try my best to be normal, but I think this just leads to a lot of resentment because maybe I'm not normal. I don't even know how to face that idea because all of my life I've just wanted to fit in.
>
> (Ixchel)

A form of disorientation often arises from a preoccupation with social adaptation, characterized by a slow erosion of inner clarity resulting from cumulative self-editing. What may initially appear as subtle accommodation gradually ossifies into a reflexive performance, increasingly severed from instinct. Jung designated this mechanism as the persona: A socially constructed mask that facilitates recognition and a sense of belonging (Jung, 1928–43/1966). While essential to navigating collective life, the veneer risks hardening into a fixed placation. Judith Butler's performativity posits that gendered characteristics are a set of stylized acts, replicated under social regulation (Butler, 1990). Jung and Butler converge to illuminate the Shapeshifting mechanism that fractures the relationship between internal life and public image.

> I don't feel confident about who I am, and I can't remember a time when I ever did. I've noticed a lot of self-hate and anger tied to these ideas. When I talk about them, it just makes me want to shut down because my inner voice is so negative. I want my best to be able to become more of a whole person, but what does that even mean? How am I not whole? Does that mean I'm broken? Ugh. I wish I could just be content and stable in myself.
>
> (Inanna)

Self-criticism frequently reflects the internal residue of adaptation. Fear of exclusion entangles perception, acting as a precondition for acceptance. The toll of such vigilance results in self-monitoring, producing heightened emotional constriction (Fredrickson & Roberts, 1997; Szymanski et al., 2010). Shapeshifting acts as the psychic toll of internalized sexism, where individuals pay the price of visibility by disconnecting from their instinctual lives.

Chapter **9**

Shadowed Formation

> If jealousy, malice, and ill intention weren't taboo. Hmm, for me, um, I think I wouldn't feel so stuffed down when I feel them. When I feel jealous, I feel like I've just stuffed it in, and when I … I feel like doing something not perfect. I must always hide these more negative emotions and retreat to the top layer of a hidden castle. I hate it, but I won't be accepted if I don't shove these feelings down.
>
> (Lilith)

Ceaseless concessions reshape women's psychological orientation, driven by insidious repression that seeps into the personal unconscious. Early inhibitions embed internalized sexism by etching subjectivity with tension and submission, fracturing instinctual responses to interpersonal limits. Concessions accumulate, generating tensions that settle beneath awareness. Dissonant strata of the psyche generate an interior rift, where a gorged repository manifests in the psychic underworld, housing contradictory and unsanctioned impulses (Jung, 1916; von Franz, 1980). Repressed material condenses, molded by repeated internal prohibitions and their emotional weight. As socially unacceptable traits recede from cognizant reach, they accumulate tension. Such characteristics, burdened with shame, signal an imposed severance from instinctual response. Arising from formidably destructive psychic conditions, the Perverse Feminine Archetype (PFA) appears as a consequence of prolonged disavowal. Her existence unveils the psychic toll of distorted norms: Traits such as assertiveness, anger, erotic desire, or intuitive resistance, ingrained in the unconscious, categorized as dangerous or excessive.

BINARY BINDS

> I find myself in the US, mainly because of this definition of the feminine as weak, and there's all kinds of interesting institutions built around that essential notion,

DOI: 10.4324/9781003455837-13

> right? I feel like people who are self-defined as women going through pregnancy and birth often have a very difficult time determining whether they're vulnerable or not vulnerable, weak or not weak, strong or not strong. Another binary, right? If you're weak, you're not strong. If you're strong, you're not weak.
>
> (Hecate)

Hecate's reflection draws us into the realm of outworn binaries that tunnel fault lines in the psyche, leading toward mental contortion. Strewn in contrasting directions, urged to assimilate to resilience, women cultivate constructs based on perceived strength and weakness. Competing demands spawn a crossroads, where fragments of the Self denote illusions of security, each carving a separate allegiance. In the internal unrest, instinctual repression occurs, cultivating mass and expelling divergent qualities. A breeding ground for compensatory abandonment, perversity coils in the recesses of the mind, where inhibitions counteract authenticity (Jung, 1970). External critiques from caregivers, cultural narratives, and peers reinforce the early construction of polarized gender associations that fracture identity, tethering worth to performative traits (Weiner et al., 2012). Distinguishing the PFA from the broader Jungian notion of the shadow, which encompasses all repressed psychic content (Jung, 1916), clarifies specificity as a construct rooted in gendered social order. Rather than acting as a broad vessel for all disowned traits, the PFA crystallizes a narrower set of feminine qualities often targeted for repression, such as assertiveness, sensuality, and unyielding self-trust. Such traits disperse into fragmented psychic compartments in response to relentless scrutiny and moral condemnation (Perera, 1981; Woodman, 1982; Estés, 1992).

> I work in the tech industry, and there's a lot of sexism and harassment, mainly because I have a big personality. Even before the whole burlesque thing, I, you know, it isn't like your typical sassy black woman kind of thing. I, I don't bullshit. Because a lot of it is connected, like with a big personality as a woman, I can't be boss, but a man can. Oh, he has leadership skills? Shit, I have leadership skills! I used to fight this, but now I just do my job and stay quiet.
>
> (Oya)

When in powerful positions, women raise suspicion. Men's leadership behaviors receive praise, while the same behaviors in women are often criticized or perceived as abrasive or threatening. In response, many recalibrate their behavior, muting instincts and reshaping themselves to align with acceptable versions of professionalism. When externally imposed ideals are absorbed, the psyche begins to split, severing connection to intuitive knowing and inner continuity (Neumann, 1994). With each act of compliance, individuals pare down their constructed personas to fit what others find legible and palatable, adhering to a narrow range of approved traits (Grosz, 1994). Gradually, this erosion of agency depletes the inner world, constricting the ability to act with autonomy (Becker, 1997). Psychic boundaries tighten through daily acts of personal betrayal, many too subtle to name. Conditioned imperatives, shaped by familial expectations and institutional codes, corrode intuitive discernment.

Butler (1997) argues that prolonged performance erases the distinction between the actor and role, until the veneer overtakes a sense of inwardness. As vigilance accrues, ambition grows suspect, emotional articulation feels perilous, and instinct sharpens into liability. Participants describe disconnection from a once-reliable inner compass, a rhythm that previously informed choices and convictions. Fragmentation follows. With sustained self-surveillance, the animating force recedes, collapsing into a persona that performs, pleases, and protects, yet struggles to feel alive. Spiritual vacancy carries the cost, siphoning vitality. A fragmented inner world reflects the slow disintegration of personal conviction, a strategy for endurance honed through repetition. Shadow formation takes root in these habitual distortions of subjectivity, where the pursuit of acceptance demands a forfeiture of one's inner orientation.

> I've lost all connection with myself because, well, I mean … everyone has always looked at me like I am completely out of my mind for trying to follow my intuitive pulls. I don't know. I've always had this connection to some higher power, but people have abused that so much that I have had to hide it. I think I've hidden it for so long that I don't even know how to connect with it. It makes me fucking sad. I feel so lost all of the time.
>
> (Ixchel)

Prolonged disconnection from intuition generated a cognitive vacancy, one that pursued security in superficial markers of significance. Without a stable tether to inner vitality, women often turn to masculine-coded metrics of success, such as logic, productivity, and material achievement. Mastery in these domains offered a fleeting sense of control while introducing a profound fracture. As interviewees described attributes cited by dominant structures, many shared a distrust or diminished value associated with stereotypically feminine expression.

> I'm really good at getting things done and very practical, and all those things that are attributed to men, so I feel like that has always been in my favor. Because I could fit into the man's world somehow and could be a really valuable part of their world and draw the value there, and I never really fit in with women until recently, like I never had girlfriends.
>
> (Nyx)

The early tilt away from a seemingly feminine community led to feelings of isolation, reinforcing the need to adapt further. Participants described role-switching, calibrating their presence to secure belonging or authority, and concealing ambitions whenever their presence disrupted the prevailing order. In doing so, traits such as softness, emotional complexity, and interdependence became sites of inner scrutiny and unease.

THE PARADOX OF FEMININE IDENTITY

> There's a stay-in-your-place kind of thing. And I think it's really subtle. Like, I'm 66, or almost 66. So I was born into that, like, small and quiet. When I was little, I was the firstborn, and my dad told me he wanted a boy, so he taught me 'boy' things like chasing salamanders in the stream behind the house. He taught me how to hammer a nail and fix engines, but it was really hard for my mom. I think that she was angry about never getting her little girly girl.
>
> (Hestia)

Shapeshifting is a persistent narrowing; a precarious balance uncovers relentless strain, resulting in internal erosion. Emergent as a rejection of customary femininity, individuals developed personas set apart from familiar stereotypes. A yearning to appear low maintenance led to a deliberate act of distancing from what they deemed overly expressive, complicated, or dramatic tendencies in others. In rejecting traits associated with femininity, they sever associations to instinctive clarity, stunting affective attunement and growth.

> I always felt I had to be 'one of the guys' to be accepted. I downplayed my emotions, avoided talking about 'girly' things, and even dressed in a more masculine way. It's like I was trying to erase any trace of femininity within myself.
>
> (Medusa)

The male gaze coalesced throughout conversations, illustrating a pronounced inward vigilance that measures worth against unattainable ideals. Under the oppressive grip of aesthetic domination, beauty becomes an obligation. Youth, symmetry, and favored and unique attributes can lead to insecurity. Such calibration inflicts consequences that ripple beyond the individual psyche. Dominant beauty standards elevate Eurocentric features and marginalize all others. Wolf (1991) underscores how the steady drumbeat that bodies are too much, or never quite enough, exacts a complex system of compulsive surveillance and behavioral regulation (Kite & Kite, 2021).

> I felt really pressured about that. And all those stars look perfect. They have, you know, this kind of body shape. And now I know that's Photoshop! I didn't know it was Photoshop, but it put me under pressure. I thought, "There's so many, like beautiful, perfect faces. But I'm far away from that." This kind of pressure.
>
> (Guan Yin)

Critiques that target physical appearance reinforce the belief that aging bodies or those that resist normative ideals must be corrected or hidden. Woven into reflections, participants voiced escalating anxiety about visibility, desirability, and self-worth.

> I noticed an internalized sexism around aging in women, and, like women, becoming of less value when they're older. And unless I'm young and supple, I'm thrown out like an old piece of Tupperware, and suddenly it's like, well, this is outdated. Like, we can dispose of our elders and their wisdom because it's no longer a value at death. So yeah, I think women start to become less appreciated after a certain age, or fertility is passed.
>
> (Medusa)

Medusa's reflection reveals how women come to internalize the belief that their worth diminishes with age. Such erasure limits the presence of elder wisdom and initiates a more corrosive shift, intensifying fears of fading significance. As tensions accrue, they manifest in lived struggles through compulsive body scrutiny and disordered eating. The shadow collects insecurities, constricting mental energy.

> I feel quite like a fraud very often because I struggle so much with looking at myself in the mirror. And like, my self-esteem is so shot. Getting older is very difficult for me, and I feel like I didn't get a chance to be young and hot for long enough. It's like what the hell … that's over? So how can I, you know, get a little bit more time, like what can I inject into my face to get that feeling of being young again? That's a daily struggle, and I know that it's from things that I've consumed.
>
> (Aphrodite)

Shadow neglect initiates a recursive distortion, as patriarchal valuation reshapes instinct and perception. Displays of anger, erotic impulse, or the will to act with authority mutate into chronic longing. Aphrodite's desire to restore youth through aesthetic intervention reveals an effort to establish worth amid pre-established, external terms. Her words reflect a broader psychic wound, where sustained exposure to ideals that collapse worth into youthfulness and surface appeal erodes a sense of self-assurance over time.

SUPPRESSION OF THE SELF

> When I was growing up, I learned that you want to be pretty and sexy. But then it's that same dichotomy—if you're too sexy, then you're the bad girl, right? Like 'ooh, she's too dominant or sexy' or whatever. I think it's that tightrope I mentioned before … that you just can't win whichever way you go.
>
> (Ala)

Harris and Harris (2015) liken the search for the feminine archetypal to fumbling for an unnamed object in darkness; a metaphor that captures the psychic confusion imposed by generations of conflicting expectations. Overarching demands to be sensual yet modest, nurturing yet emotionally restrained, divide inherent intelligence. Archetypal images such as the temptress, witch, and hysteric (Goldenberg,

1993) form a deep-rooted landscape, restricting psychological development and fostering a state of continual vigilance. Rather than trusting their impulses, women described gauging tone, filtering reactions, and contorting the spirit for social acceptability. Suppressive aims lodge internally, corroding perception and unsettling clarity. As fragmentation augments survival, it undermines cerebral cohesion (Perera, 1981). With each act of withdrawal from desire, emotional honesty, or embodied resistance, core instincts retreat into hidden psychic chambers. Exiled but not extinguished.

> Growing up, I was always told that girls should be quiet and polite. My parents told me that when I was mad it was unfeminine so I buried it deep down, but it sort of always comes out in one way or another … unless I try really hard. When that happens it takes me a long time to recover. It just feels like sometimes its hard just to be me to be honest. I feel so uncomfortable with myself and wish that I didn't have these feelings, life would be a lot easier.
>
> (Gaia)

As aspects of the psyche are exiled into unconscious terrain, shadow formation begins to solidify (Jung, 1916). With each severance, the persona shifts from a porous mask to rigid façade designed to preserve social legibility. Women absorb and enact survival patterns in response to demands, shaped by suppression; a surface curated to deflect scrutiny and preserve proximity to approval. The shapeshifting participants describe unfolds as a constant recalibration of voice, body, and presence.

> At work, I'm a strong, confident leader. At home, I'm a nurturing, caring mother. With my friends, I'm the fun-loving, carefree one. It's exhausting trying to be all these different people. Sometimes I wonder who I really am, and I just want to say fuck it and throw all these pressures to the wind, ya know?
>
> (Hera)

Participants learn to navigate social terrain through continuous adaptation, subtly recalibrating their presentation depending on circumstantial demands (Jung, 1971). Hera's account indicates how roles adjust to manage competing ambitions, frequently at the expense of an integrated Self. The more rigorously one upholds socially sanctioned roles, the more disconnected they may become from instinctual drives and personal longings (Kernberg, 1975; Winnicott, 1960).

BECOMING THE MASK

> I hate to say it, but when I need to get away with something, I guess it's kind of like the quote-unquote, damsel in distress syndrome. Like, when I travel, for safety reasons, I need to be a lot more aware. Being in a strange place as a woman, especially

> depending on where [I'm] traveling to, [I] really need to act like a dumbed-down version of myself so I don't get extra attention.
>
> (Lamia)

The 'damsel in distress' underscores a familiar script: A woman cast as insecure, waiting for a man to intervene, which preserves old hierarchies of power and dependency (Warner, 1994). This trope exploits vulnerability, using helplessness as a calculated survival tactic. Participants discussed shifting between masculine and feminine modes, taking pride in their heightened vigilance periodically. This exchange is inherent in the equation, which minimizes their intellect by suppressing cognition to maintain acceptance.

> If I'm talking to a guy, I feel like my personality becomes more feminine than if I'm at work, per se. It's a benefit when I need to. I hate to say it, but when I need to get away with something, like if I'm late, or if I want to jump a line, or I really need a favor done, or I'm, like, in an emergency situation ... I don't know, the airport or something. And like, I feel like people are nicer to women in situations like that.
>
> (Athena)

As she discussed her travels, Persephone notes her emphasis on obscuring her perceived intellectual threat:

> You know, but, like, when I was traveling, it was awesome. I didn't really have an issue getting help if I was in trouble. Somebody always showed up. You know, and they were there because I don't look like a threat, right? My intellect is a threat, but I am not physically present as a threat. I think a lot of times I will change who I am based on my company. That's normal, right? I don't know, I don't think it's so bad to manipulate situations in a good way, but I've found that sometimes I forget that I'm pretending. I just have shaped some sort of version of myself and now have morphed into that person.
>
> (Persephone)

During the Shapeshifting stage, multiple archetypal roles surface, each reflecting distinct modes of permission seeking: The damsel, helpless yet desirable; the housewife, loyal to her disappearance; the cool girl, radiant on the surface yet hollowed out beneath (Mulvey, 1975). Narrowed aspirations constrict imaginative space, leaving women to yearn for external rescue while overlooking their latent strength. Conditioned to prize dependency and acquiescence, consistent compromise initiates shadow formation, where survival mandates disowning instincts (Jung, 1969b).

Chapter **10**

Internalized Sexism and the Personal Unconscious

> The only thing I could think of is, of a woman being treated as an object, is if she puts herself in that type of situation, like women who do professions that are very, like, scantily clad, like, dancers can be like, regular dancers or exotic dancers, but anything that shows less clothing, I feel like they can be people [that] don't have control of how people view them. People can view them as more of an object than a human, and that's just on the person. I feel like that's their fault.
>
> (Oya)

The personal unconscious forms through diligent construction, absorbing external transmissions that embed themselves as psychic imprints. Without conscious consent, the psyche organizes into implicit hierarchies that influence merit. What begins as ambient messaging hardens into gut-level judgments, deemed credible, rendered suspect, silenced. Detrimental instincts are mistaken for moral clarity when, in fact, they mirror conditioned surveillance. Sexism insidiously acts as a mechanism for displaced continuity, threading domination into thought, affect, and relation. Disentanglement requires symbolic reckoning with the structures that once felt protective but were invariably regulatory. Contemporary digital platforms frame visibility as a form of empowerment. In actuality, they operate as a calculated capitalist performance, curated through and against collective insecurities. Legitimacy is quantifiable, measured in metrics of aesthetic conformity. What appears to be an autonomous presentation is a rehearsed performance designed to conform to patriarchal standards of legibility (Caso et al., 2020; Fredrickson & Roberts, 1997). Platform architectures commodify the female body, recasting performative presence as agency while reinforcing historical hierarchies of control (Manago et al., 2008). The resulting symptoms result in passing of blame, an urge to silence, and an impulse to question another woman's exposure. Seemingly minor responses such as hesitations, deflections, and second-guessing

DOI: 10.4324/9781003455837-14

demonstrate how surveillance masquerades as intuition. The resulting distortion influences how women perceive others and evaluate themselves.

> I don't know. I feel like we absorb it, you know? Like, we grow up seeing it, and, you know, start believing it. I used to think, "Well, maybe she *was* asking for it," or "Maybe I should just be quieter, be smaller, not draw attention." And then you realize ... wait, why am I thinking this? Who told me this? And why did I believe it?
>
> (Inanna)

Sexism manifests as absorbed blame, prompting women to question one another's choices and assign fault for their own or others' harm. Essentially, to shame victims. Conditioned behavioral patterns reinforce themselves over time by censoring emotional responses, camouflaging visible discomfort, and stifling public disagreement (Glick & Fiske, 1996). Antifeminist movements demonstrate the pattern (Totenberg, 2021), circulating stereotypes such as the overly emotional woman, manipulative victim, or attention-seeking feminist. Such tropes reframe resistance as pathology. Resistance to objectification provokes veiled correction or professional reprimand, blurring the line between social control and institutional discipline.

> So, I was in New York volunteering with the crisis response team, and we have a lot of students that come from really underserved neighborhoods and families, and this young kid committed suicide. It was so awful for me, and I just burst into tears. My supervisor was so furious with me because she said I'm supposed to have thicker skin in this line of work. She threatened to write me up for it. I mean, she could have just helped me through it, right? Instead, I got in trouble for expressing a very valid feeling. I think about that moment when I had trouble crying because it wasn't just that one time; it's happened my whole life, and people have been a lot meaner than she has.
>
> (Hestia)

Compensatory blame encourages restraint, touted as professionalism and rooted in learned discipline. Women begin to monitor their reactions, fearing judgment or reprisal (David, 2013). Suffering, irritation, and distress act as an irreverent nuisance. Over time, a narrow affective range can produce psychological strain, and women may learn to limit their emotional range (Rahmani, 2020). To be human becomes a calculated risk, vulnerability, a potential infraction.

PERFORMING SAFETY

> And I think that is a small example of internalized misogyny, but it's fucking everywhere. It's in the way that I work out. It's in the way that I eat. It's in the way that I conduct myself on a walk. It's in the way that I bake. It's in the way that I listen to music. It's in everything. For example, I love my cat. ... She's one of the best things

> that ever happened to me. I take nothing but joy in this cat. There is a small part of my brain now and possibly forever dedicated to not wanting to be perceived as a cat lady because I'm a woman of a certain age who has a cat.
>
> (Demeter)

The fear of appearing as a cat lady reveals a cultural bind in which femininity is tantamount to failure. Whether a woman follows convention or carves an unconventional path, her choices are saturated with judgment. What forms as external scrutiny settles inward. Over time, women rehearse their behavior, justify their joy, and anticipate critique before it arrives. Participants described such burdens as early and persistent. An internal tension narrowed the scope of personal articulation. Desire, once spontaneous, shifted into something to manage. To avoid punishment, women reshaped their desires to conform to societal expectations. Safety required performance and authenticity twisted into preemptive control, a strategy to prevent rejection. Compromise converted into strategy.

> My sister's boyfriend, who is very lovely and great, and I find myself, when we were having impassioned discussions that are not hostile, not aggressive … we're even talking about stuff we agree on, and I say, "Oh, I'm sorry I didn't mean to get so loud about that. I'm just passionate about this topic." Even these sorts of apologies that fall out of you that aren't even necessary or required or even, when I'm not doing anything wrong. Even if it were aggressive, I wouldn't be doing anything wrong, but the need to apologize for being too big or loud or being too emotional about something is something I catch in myself that's been ingrained from the very beginning.
>
> (Persephone)

Reflexive internal calibration demonstrated conditioning that compelled women to shrink themselves. Vocalizing passion or conviction activated internal alarms, as if assertiveness required an apology. Loudness, visibility, or unwavering clarity constituted breaches of propriety. With repetition, the compulsion to soften chipped away at their sense of legitimacy. Confidence trimmed into acceptability, reshaped until it could be articulated without threat. Women who aspired to leadership described how their authority was frequently questioned or dismissed. Strength, ambition, and decisiveness were recast as unacceptable traits. Discomfort with power frequently surfaced through indirect signals. Tone, appearance, or likability eclipsed merit, diverting attention away from substance and toward social compliance.

> I voted for Hillary Clinton back in 2016. And I don't know if you remember, but people would yell at her to iron their shirts—you know, the fact that she was so qualified, overqualified, for the job, and that she didn't win. Seems to me that society is not ready to hear from a strong woman who's extremely smart and, you know, could have done the job. I mean, that's certainly one way.
>
> (Hecate)

History repeated itself in 2024 when resistance to electing Kamala Harris, a qualified woman of color, eclipsed concern over installing a convicted felon as president. Among my peers, I heard a familiar refrain: *Why does she have to act like a man? Can't she be a woman? What's with all the pantsuits?* As conversations unfolded, an internal conflict revealed a devastating oscillation between praise and critique. The bind of a female leader. Rather than focus on her accomplishments, fixation on her wardrobe took precedence. Without recognizing internalized judgments, the entrenched ideology condemns certain traits as crazy, wrong, taboo, or dangerous. Interspersed throughout the conversations, women spoke of their choice to distance themselves from other stereotypes, engaging in what Means (2021) calls the 'not like other girls' phenomenon.

> I think my defense mechanism pretty early on was to not really identify with all of the woman stuff that other people are identifying with me because I went so much into my masculine that I was like, like, these girls are dealing with stuff, and like, I don't have to deal with that. I'm not like them. I'm quirky. I'm loud. I'm like, all of the things I valued about myself were all my masculine traits. I never really felt like I was part of that crew.
>
> (Kali)

Participants articulated a patterned tendency to judge expressions of need or vulnerability in other women, recognizing how such traits had come to signify weakness within internal frameworks. Disavowal operated beneath conscious awareness. Competence, composure, and emotional detachment became aspirational as perceived immunity from critique. Modulation transformed into containment. Absorbed pressure sedimented in the psyche, structuring perception, behavior, and relational orientation. A disconnection from the community resulted in isolation, and with it, a craving for sisterhood. However, detrimental beliefs enveloped the mind, distorting the capacity to connect. What appeared as internal governance concealed internalized fear. In learning to distrust one another, women disconnected from themselves.

INSTITUTIONAL POWER, INTERPERSONAL HARM, AND INTERNALIZED CONTROL

> Okay. I think I internalized, like, I need to be beautiful. That's my only value, right? So, I'm pretty sure I spent a lot of time worrying about either my clothes or, you know, in college, like, I lost a lot of weight, I lost probably more than I needed to because I was worried about how I looked … because that was my value. And then, if guys made, like, random comments to me, I kind of, you know, I didn't act angry, I just kind of dismissed them, because, oh, that's just guys. That's what they're just going to do. This is how it works.
>
> (Guan Yin)

The emotional toll of appearance-driven vigilance diminishes women's sense of agency, narrowing mental bandwidth and breeding pervasive hesitation. Persistent hypervigilance reflects a broader trend of social conditioning where traditional femininity is rewarded, especially when it conforms to narrow standards. Situated in the complex terrain of inherited hierarchies, socially sanctioned expectations conflict with a holistic sense of well-being of womanhood (Lerner, 1987). Persistent uncertainty and shame corrode the unconscious, entangling with repressed affect, inherited wounds, and generational memory (Jung, 1964). Projection functions as a key consequence of internal imprinting, where unresolved anxieties are cast onto others, reinforcing the legitimacy of dominant ideologies (Jung, 1928–1943/1966). Power embedded in dominant systems twists through institutional hierarchies, relational expectations, and internalized psychological structures (David, 2013). Pharmaceutical ads targeting girls with appetite suppressants sell shame, masquerading as health (Aslam & Mehboob, 2023). One participant recalled starting diet pills at age thirteen, "because my mother told me I overate." These overarching violences accumulate. Perpetuated through knowledge systems privilege whiteness (PBS, 2023), domestic abuse slips that avoid accountability (UN Women, 2024b), and in states like Texas, children endure the burden of carrying pregnancies (Aratani, 2023). Each example lives as an interconnected constraint, constructing a pressure-filled daily existence.

> It's one of those things like, how are you supposed to empower women if you don't give women power? If you don't give them power, you're not giving them the space to be in leadership positions. And we're seeing this in reproductive care, too, like with the laws … I mean I don't even know what to do about it anymore. We just don't have power anywhere, it seems.
>
> (Oshun)

The 2022 reversal of Roe v. Wade (Mangan & Breuninger, 2022; Fuentes, 2023) punctured the illusion of secure progress. The ruling stripped reproductive agency and activated a collective sense of fear around bodily autonomy. In parallel, the resurgence of Barbiecore aesthetics underscored a normative vision of womanhood (Cary, 2022). While ostensibly disparate, an implicit confluence between these phenomena prevails. Overall, systemic influence permeates gesture, aesthetics, and expectations. Inequality becomes ambient; an unrelenting presence manifesting in restricted access to healthcare, the relegation of marginalized groups to undervalued labor, and a diffusion of ideological bias through education (Hill & Silva, 2005). Such infrastructures extend beyond policy, colonizing the intimate spaces of everyday life.

> Abortion is seen as so wrong, but who are they protecting? They don't care about the baby after they're born, and people certainly don't give a shit about the mother. You know what I mean? In Texas now, with all these anti-abortion laws, I've found women who refuse to go there because they're afraid they'll get sued for the way

> they look. Like, if they *look* a certain way, people assume they're going to help someone get an abortion. And for me, there's nowhere in the country that feels safe anymore.
>
> (Persephone)

Interpersonal sexism situates itself at a crossroads, where the intimate meets the institutional. Entrenched in daily lives, women shoulder subtle and corrosive burdens, revealing persistent dismissal (Crawford, 2021). Early familial dynamics often lay the groundwork: One parent valorizes stoicism and assertiveness, the other rewards deference and emotional restraint.

> Lots of people get very intimidated by me. Like, once I open my mouth, you know, if I just stay quiet, and I like to keep to myself, and I'm, like, making muffins in the kitchen, like that stereotype, then I'm cool. I'm not a threat. As soon as I switch and open my mouth, people realize that I have a lot more going on in my brain, and the whole vibe changes. Like 'whoa, that's not what I was expecting, calm down, you're being too much'. It's honestly such bull shit.

The recursive entrapment between institutional and interpersonal sexism constitutes the foundation of internal persecution. What originates as external enforcement gradually embeds itself within the personal unconscious, where hegemonic gender mandates operate as mechanisms of internal regulation and inhibition. As Rahmani (2020) contends, internalized sexism fosters chronic internal questioning, cultivates tolerance for boundary violations, and transforms the body into a locus of discontent and scrutiny (Tiggemann & Slater, 2013; Chrisler & Caplan, 2002). Conditioning constrains ambition and discourages resistance, as women begin to second-guess their worth and sidestep opportunities (Swim & Hyers, 1999). In effect, systemic control migrates inward, sustained not only through sociocultural structures but also through the individual's psychological compliance.

THE COST OF VISIBILITY

> I, frankly … I think I've experienced enough setbacks. I'm not so sure if I dream as big anymore. I think now, I just want to get my work into a museum. I just want it to have some value before I die. Because I know this is a really difficult path for a woman artist. So, I think I've … I think I've kind of lowered my expectations a little bit.
>
> (Medusa)

Persistent disappointments narrowed the scope of ambition, leading to weakened confidence and recognition that the dreams were unattainable for those in a female body. Structural and psychological constraints perpetuated these challenges, contributing to the glass ceiling effect, a barrier to professional advancement (Barreto et al., 2009).

> I wonder if things would've played out differently if I hadn't been a woman; if I had gotten along better with this producer, because he had a boys club thing going on. So, I've questioned it, absolutely. I wonder if, in certain circumstances, things would have been different if I had been a man. I have a couple different *Me Too* experiences. When I was the executive assistant for two producers on a very notable show, I was newly 21 and was working with the producer who had actively tried to sleep with me, kissed me a couple of times … and then I got fired. It's the only job, to this day, that I've ever been fired from. And it's still something I question. If I remember correctly, they told me that I wasn't experienced enough as an executive assistant, even though I had been doing the job for a year.
>
> (Kali)

Participants view career goals as unattainable. Riddled with memories of sexual harassment in the workplace, Artemis's story illustrates this dynamic. Although qualified for her position, she was promptly fired for rejecting sexual advances.

> She only exists to be sexually appealing to the man and help him on his journey of realization, or whatever. I'm an actor, but I did not pursue acting until my late 20s. As a kid, I wanted to be an actor, but even then, I looked at the screen and concluded that I would never look like the leads I wanted to play. I would never be pretty, white, or thin enough … So why try?
>
> (Athena)

The cumulative effect of discrimination, bias, and microaggressions further complicates internal struggle, culminating in a sense of learned helplessness:

> I definitely think it inhibits my creativity. I haven't put my [art] work out into the world because I've thought it wasn't enough. As a larger cultural stigma, I think women are constantly feeling like we're never enough. Right? Like, there's no winning. You can't win a game that's already been rigged. And the more I tried—one way or the other—it never worked. I could never win, right? Because if you're not feminine enough, they're not gonna want you anyway.
>
> (Lilith)

A recurring undercurrent of diminished conviction surfaced throughout the discussions, manifesting as a patterned erosion of internal authority. A living experience of impostor syndrome, as conceptualized by Clance and Imes (1978), demonstrated appropriate responses to chronic invalidation. Ongoing pressure to achieve perfection constricted the capacity to channel their energy into personally meaningful work, draining their vitality and replacing it with resignation. What might have emerged as creative expression often became muted under the weight of continuous surveillance and anticipatory judgment.

SELF-SURVEILLANCE AND THE FRAGMENTED FEMININE

> I feel like I'm always looking at my appearance. When I walk by a window, there I am looking at the way I'm walking … stand up straight, tuck it up … or if I pass by my reflection on a fucking toaster, I have to look. It's so bizarre because I'll even take something well-known as distorted, like my front-facing iPhone camera, and see it as truth. I want to look perfect despite the lighting; I want to achieve some weird perfectionism that doesn't even exist. I'm tired of it. I'm tired of waking up every day with a focus on the way I look. I'm tired of avoiding making memories and taking photos because of my insecurities. I mean, damn. I wish I could just live.
>
> (Ala)

Self-surveillance serves as a habitual response. Rehearsed, socially rewarded, and psychically taxing. What appears as internal governance is more often an embodied form of submission, where women view themselves through the lens of anticipated judgment. Objectification theory (Fredrickson & Roberts, 1997) clarifies how the internalized gaze fragments the sense of self and narrows the capacity for spontaneous action. Despite an influx of detrimental images, women seek an understanding of energetic fluidity, where they can connect beyond the dualistic representations of masculinity and femininity.

> Yeah, I mean, from my experience of growing up in a female body, I feel like there's been a lot coming up in the media lately about female energy, or, like, this feminine force, and things like that. And I think that energy flows through all of us. Like, everybody has both masculine and feminine energy, and they're not separate within the body, no matter what form we have. We just have to learn how to utilize and balance them for different purposes. So, with energy, I feel like both are always there, and we can work with them differently.

Competing ideals generate psychic dissonance, where an effort to balance opposing demands obscures access to instinctual clarity. Quality offered participants a temporary safety, yet beneath it, an unease surfaced: How to inhabit oneself without defaulting to performance. Cosmetic, emotional, or behavioral adaptations, often suppressed emotional or psychological breaks. The cost was not merely the effort to conform, but the loss of a coherent center.

> I grew up in the era of skinny, skinny girls who … moved in the direction of … self-harm in order to meet a very angular kind of figure, which is the male, right? Skinny hips, you know, skinny, like skinny—*skinny*—some of us worked really hard, never should have gotten involved in it and never met it, right. And that whole process of grief and self-denial and attempts to control ourselves, the way we were being controlled by the masculine in our culture. So, as you can see, I can apply this to every single little thing in life.
>
> (Nyx)

Internal objectification develops incrementally, conditioned by ongoing exposure to systems that tether value to attractiveness, compliance, or muteness. Such erosion distorts the ego, exacerbating long-established restraint. Dissonance illustrates heightened disconnection from underlying wisdom, demanding a direct reckoning with repressed psychological scaffolding; the inherited voice that chronicles one's perceived unworthiness (Becker, 1997).

> I guess I would say I'm not very expressive about my sexuality. And I know, I guess there are examples of women who are, like, more outgoing. Because I don't know, I feel like that kind of is a society thing. Like, oh, you're not a lady if you're too sexual. Like, it's kind of like, portrayed as, I don't know, like Nicki Minaj or Cardi B or something. They're very expressive women. I could never be like them because I'm more concerned about how I'm perceived.
>
> (Athena)

Contemplations illuminate surveillance as a conditioned response. Vigilance transitions from deliberate effort to ambient reflex, sculpted by early criticism, splintered quintessences, and the necessity for relational safety. Societal conjectures calcify into internal decrees, manipulating how perception suffocates growth. Desire is scrutinized, instinct silenced, and somatic cues weaponized. Internalized sexism arises as a perverse fracture, with the archetype implanting itself into selfhood, veiled beneath a relentless censorship.

Chapter **11**

Contemporary Madness

The Pathologization of Feminine Power

> In some ways, it feels like being a woman who talks too much about her feelings is taboo because then you get labeled that, you know, "oh, she's that crazy woman who's like, you know, still upset about this or that" or whatever. I would say that would be kinda crazy. I mean, even as someone who is very progressive, I will often call certain women crazy. It's like … the crazy ex of some dude, where I believe his story, or the woman who walks around without a bra. I feel ashamed, but often find myself a little appalled. Like, what is she doing? Is she okay? Is she crazy? Does she need help?
>
> (Oya)

Though heresy persecution retired from church courts, the imperative to regulate nonconforming femininity endures. Psychiatric discourse now encodes previously condemned spiritually, restructuring dissent through diagnostic classification. Behaviors attributed to possession or hysteria reappear as symptoms within a clinical framework highlighted with a stigmatized demarcation classified as Borderline Personality Disorder (BPD). Those who meet these criteria are frequently interpreted as untreatable, their distress dismissed as volatility. The label itself functions as symbolic defilement, echoing the enduring cultural residue affixed to hysteria or witchcraft. Once diagnosed, it shapes not only how care is delivered, but whether it is delivered at all.

> My ex-husband always used to tell me I was crazy. He would compare me to his mom, who had bipolar disorder, and would just gaslight me to all hell. I was scared that I was crazy, so we went to a therapist together, and then, guess what? The therapist took my side and pointed out that he was abusing me! I got the fuck out of there, but there is still this small fear that maybe I am crazy, and I have a hypervigilance about it.
>
> (Athena)

DOI: 10.4324/9781003455837-15

What if BPD reflects a survival strategy driven to its limits, a psychic structure shaped by contradiction? Rather than framing the individual as disordered, this perspective prompts an interrogation of psychiatric models (Shaw & Proctor, 2005).

> When you express yourself emotionally or have a passionate opinion about something, you end up being shut up as being overly emotional. My mother used to call me dramatic. I wouldn't call it a trigger, but it's a memory pervasive throughout my childhood. If I got upset about something or felt such a certain way about it, it was like, "Don't be so dramatic, you're being dramatic," and all this emotional outpouring was just like squashed … Whenever I have strong feelings, either, you know, I get mad or upset or whatever, I always wonder to myself, like, "Am I overreacting? Like, was this reaction really justified?" So, I think it's made me doubt my own emotions and how I react to things, that I typically will second-guess myself.
>
> (Demeter)

Applied primarily to women, borderline psychiatric language reframes emotional intensity and instability as defect, often enacted through clinical documentation and practitioner bias, obscuring structural and developmental origins (Modeste, 2019; Ussher, 2006). Although only 1–2% of the population meets criteria for BPD, they represent up to 20% of psychiatric inpatients, and 75% of those diagnosed are women (American Psychiatric Association, 2013). The diagnosis flattens trauma histories, ignoring intersecting factors like neurodivergence, abuse, racial stereotyping, and economic precarity (Shim, 2010). Feminist theorists argue that, like hysteria before it, BPD pathologizes adaptive responses to trauma, translating survival into symptomatology (Shaw & Proctor, 2005; Roth & Fonagy, 2006). As a residue of disciplinary regimes, it recasts the Perverse Feminine Archetype (PFA) in clinical terms, inheriting the historical stigma once reserved for the witch and the hysteric.

Containment in a New Key

> I think humanizing the reasons why someone might seek out or be pushed into a mental health facility would ground it and make it more relatable, instead of turning them into trauma porn characters. Like, if the emphasis was less on the traumatic event itself and more on the strength of processing it, that would be good. The first thing that came to mind was *Girl, Interrupted.* I remember mental illness being framed as women dealing with different mental health issues, but none of them were perceived as particularly good or whole. Maybe I'm grasping at it too hard, but that's what flashed to mind—like, "Oh, they're supposed to be intricate characters, and yet …" Thanks, 90s.
>
> (Persephone)

Adolf Stern first coined '*borderline*' in 1938 to describe patients whose suffering defied neat classification as neurosis or psychosis (Wirth-Cauchon, 2001). In

1980, the American Psychiatric Association introduced Borderline Personality Disorder as an official diagnosis. While not a direct replacement, its emergence coincided with the removal of hysteria, recasting longstanding anxieties about uncontrolled femininity through a new clinical framework (Becker, 1997; Ussher, 2006).

> I never understood until later that expressing emotions isn't a weakness; it's crucial for processing feelings. Initially, I thought, "Why whine about everything?" because I believed boys don't cry. I do cry, and being with women like friends and my mother helped me recognize different emotions. I think women express pain differently; they naturally share. Sitting with women without trying to solve their problems has been my biggest lesson … it's really hard, because I might think I'm helping, but I'm really just shutting them down.
>
> (Medusa)

Psychiatry sustained its authority by redefining emotional expression, sexual agency, and resistance to social norms as symptoms of mental illness, severing distress from its social and structural origins. By the late twentieth century, feminist scholarship (Showalter, 1985), trauma theory (Herman, 1992), and critiques from the anti-psychiatry movement (Szasz, 1961; Laing, 1960) had begun to expose the psychological consequences of systemic harm. Nevertheless, institutions maintained containment-based paradigms, embedding historical stigma in clinical discourse and diagnostic practice.

From Exorcism to Electroshock

> I go through this back and forth about my mental health every day. I remember that after my breakup, I was sad, and all of my male co-workers treated me with kid gloves. They kept saying that I would fuck things up, but I was just fine because I've learned how to put my emotions away and get business done. I must. Otherwise, I may fall apart because I haven't felt fully in so long that I don't even know what might come out.
>
> (Kali)

From inquisitorial decrees to nineteenth-century medical classification, psychiatry absorbed and transformed systems of control, sustaining a legacy of regulation that migrated from ecclesiastical judgment to scientific authority. As psychological discourse evolved, diagnostic categories inherited the disciplinary logics of their religious antecedents, reframing spiritual disobedience as mental pathology (Micale, 1995; Showalter, 1985). Though the witch trials waned, the imperative to subdue nonconforming femininity persisted. Psychiatric diagnoses supplanted theological accusations. Public execution, once justified by a need for social order, has now shifted to pharmacological sedation; instead of exorcisms, we use involuntary commitment to address what we once considered demonic possession. Spiritual affliction was rendered as a psychiatric crisis (Moscucci, 1990). Psychiatric institutions addressed women's suffering with coercive interventions, such as electroshock therapy, hysterectomies, and involuntary sterilization disguised as eugenics. Clinical frameworks pathologized premenstrual symptoms, non-reproductive choices, and queer desire, reasserting moral discipline through medical authority (Shorter, 1992; El-Hai, 2005).

> I find myself saying things like, "oh I'm sorry, I didn't mean to get so loud about that. I'm just passionate about this topic," so even these sorts of apologies that fall out of you that aren't even necessary or required, or even when I'm not doing anything wrong. Even if it was aggressive, I wouldn't be doing anything wrong, but that need to apologize for being too big, or being too loud, or being too emotional about something is still something I catch in myself that's been ingrained from the very beginning.
>
> (Hecate)

Asylum admission records cite diagnoses such as *moral insanity*, domestic troubles, and excessive study, gendered pathologies used to justify female incarceration (Appignanesi, 2008; Chesler, 1972; Micale, 1995; Ehrenreich & English, 1973). Nearly twenty years later, Nellie Bly's exposé, Ten Days in a Mad-House (1887) (see Figure 11.1), revealed conditions at Blackwell's Island asylum in New York. Committed under pretenses, she observed the systemic neglect of women, including overcrowded quarters, forced ice baths, soiled bedding, verbal degradation, and prolonged silencing (see Figure 11.2). Though a grand jury investigation followed, it resulted in no structural reform.

> I was never so tired as I grew sitting on those benches. Several of the patients would sit on one foot or sideways to make a change, but they were always reproved and told to sit up straight. If they talked they were scolded and told to shut up; if they wanted to walk around to take the stiffness out of them, they were told to sit down and be still. What, excepting torture, would produce insanity quicker than this treatment? … I would like the expert physicians who are condemning me for my action … to take a perfectly sane and healthy woman, shut her up and make her sit from 6 A.M. until 8 P.M. on straight-back benches, do not allow her to talk or move during these hours, give her no reading and let her know nothing of the world or its doings, give her bad food and harsh treatment, and see how long it will take to make her insane. Two months would make her a mental and physical wreck.
>
> (Bly, 1887, Ch.12)

Bly's exposé seeded the trajectory of feminist mental health advocacy, presenting a foundational critique of gendered psychiatric abuse later taken up by second-wave feminists and survivor-led movements. Organizations like the National Women's Health Network and figures such as Phyllis Chesler challenged psychiatric misogyny, fighting for women's autonomy in diagnostic and treatment processes (Chesler, 1972; Nelson, 2015).

Figure 11.1 *View of the Lunatic Asylum and Mad House*

Public domain. Image courtesy of The Miriam and Ira D. Wallach Division of Art (1853), Prints and Photographs: Print Collection, The New York Public Library.

Note:
Wood engraving of Lunatic Asylum on Blackwell's Island, highlighting 19th-century institutional architecture and its historical connection to mental health treatment. Created by William Wade (artist) and Joshua H. Peirce (engraver), the work is part of The Eno Collection of New York City Views.

INHERITANCE OF INSTABILITY

> So like, because we've been told, if we speak up about something, or we try to make adjustments or stand up for our rights or say this is "not what I want," then it's our feeling that we didn't try enough, that we're not good enough, that we're not pretty enough, that we're not *this* enough, or that we needed to do more of this or that … if we were, that he would stay. You know, again, it feels like, for me, all of this always comes back to a partner. Like if I were better, he wouldn't hit me.
>
> (Nyx)

Nyx's account underscores how psychological distortion festers when accusations of instability surface in intimate relationships. Despite confirmed abuse, she attempts to modify herself; a vigilance shaped by patriarchal conditioning that teaches women to distrust their own perception. This dynamic reflects the internalization of blame often seen in survivors of prolonged gaslighting.

Figure 11.2 *An Insane Hall*

Public Domain.

Note:
19th-century drawing of an asylum ward (Bly, 1887). A black-and-white line drawing depicts rows of seated women, illustrating medical interventions.

> In the culture, if you're a slut, they won't marry you, and women cannot accept a slut—oh my god, especially older women, they cannot accept, you know, young sluts. Yeah. Oh, men love sluts, but they won't marry you because they feel like you're a public bus or something. I think when I was young, you know, my family just didn't have, you know, many, like, expectations for me to have a good grade or you know, good work because they think, I'm a woman; I'm a girl. When I grow up, I will just get married and you know, find a good person and get married.
>
> (Guan Yin)

With pronounced frustration, participants described their reliance on external approval as a conditioned survival strategy. Though often pathologized as dysfunction, codependency here signals an adaptation to environments that reward suppression and emotional caretaking. Collins (2000) argues these tendencies stem from systems that valorize self-erasure. Participants internalized scripts of the self-sacrificing mother and compliant partner, appearances conflated with feminine virtue. Boundaries were selfish. Desire invited shame. Sexual autonomy marked one for exile, with the slur *slut* serving as a cultural warning. These patterns, shaped by gendered social codes, expose a system that blames women for abandonment.

> I think a family member's relationship with death can vary widely among different family members. But if I were to take a stab at a larger theory, I believe the capacity to truly grieve and genuinely experience that raw grief helps. Being really sad allows me to process the sadness because, in my mind, the sadness shouldn't exist, and it really messes with my expression.
>
> (Lilith)

Lilith's account illuminates the sorrow that accompanies suppressed grief. Her difficulty mourning is not rooted in incapacity, but in a learned compulsion to regulate emotional visibility in environments where sadness risks judgment or rejection. To avoid being labeled unstable, she internalizes her pain, cultivating restraint instead of release. Repeated invalidations became internalized, forming an internal critic that questioned the legitimacy of emotional truth, echoes of an inheritance of invalidation. As they reflected on their path toward authenticity, they traced the roots of disconnection to the atmospheres of their upbringing, conditions in which emotion signals fragility and compliance functions as currency.

> I didn't know how to do that and didn't know how to get any of my needs met. Because of the environment I grew up in, my mother was very emotionally cold and was never emotionally reliable. I think this has ingrained in me a weird relationship with my inner world. Like, I'm so used to instability that I can't imagine what it would be like without it … and like, I would say that a lot of women are perceived as weaker so I feel more like the need to not be like that, so I cannot fall into that stereotype. I feel like if I am in a situation, and I'm feeling emotionally weak, I feel like I have to hold it in or not ask as many questions about it, because I feel like people are automatically gonna say, "Oh, she can't really do it because she's a girl."
>
> (Hera)

The fear of being *too much, too loud, too emotional, too visible* crystallizes the psychic cost of shapeshifting. From an early age, boundary transgressions normalize, justified as essential for acceptance. What initiated as an adaptive skill ossifies into identity, displacing intellect with doubt. Distortions fracture perception. The trajectory from witch hunts to hysteria to modern diagnoses indicates a connecting theme: Female affect is dangerous when it resists authority. While mental health discourse has evolved, the impulse to sanitize remains. The Perverse Feminine Archetype (PFA), then, is not a remnant of obsolete medicalization but a present incarnation of condemned potency.

Chapter **12**

Lilith as the Queen of the Shadow

> The first evil woman I can think of is Maleficent. When I was very young, I wanted to be Aurora. I wanted to be the pretty princess with a beautiful voice, of course; now, I realize that it taught me that this is my goal as a woman. I need to be pretty and adored by people. Otherwise, I'm doing something wrong.
>
> (Medusa)

The perverse materializes in myriad forms, where penalized articulations of excess and lack exist, formulating as disobedient mythic creatures. Lilith rises as an aberration of scorched earth. Her wings, long clipped by dogma, now stretch toward self-determination. Branded by refusal, she haunts the divide between obedience and instinct. Jewish folklore (Otzar Midrashim, n.d.) portrays her departure from Adam as a defiant act, a threat to the fragile order of feminine submission (Patai, 1990). Later, Zohar and Lurianic Kabbalistic she becomes disorder incarnate: A demonic seductress, Samael's consort, wreathed in the husks of the Kelippot (see Figure 12.1). Tracing her lineage as Queen of the Shadows, we awaken her as a conduit for the Perverse Feminine Archetype (PFA). She beckons us toward the uneasy terrain of the repressed psyche, illuminating how persecution begets fragmentation.

> The reason is that she was the great seducer not only of men but also of spirits and demons. R. Isaac said: "The 'sons of God' mentioned in the Scripture (Gen. 6:4), who were Uzza and Azael, were seduced by her." R. Simeon said: "She was the mother of the demons, being of the side of Cain, and it is she who in company with Lilith brings epilepsy on children." Said R. Abba to him: "Did you not say before that her function is to seduce men?" He replied: "That is so; she disports herself with men and sometimes bears spirits from them. And she still exists to seduce men."
>
> (Sperling & Simon, 1933, *Zohar Bereshit* 94b)

DOI: 10.4324/9781003455837-16

Figure 12.1 *Lilith*

Currently housed at the Atkinson Art Gallery in Southport, England.

Note:
Painted by John Collier (1887), this artwork features a nude representation of Lilith, with long red hair and fair skin, entwined by a serpent in a dark, foreboding forest, symbolic of her dangerous and enticing presence.

Envisaged in myth, reinterpretations of Lilith's presence resurged in mystical texts between the 12th and 17th centuries, where writings from Spain and Safed (Scholem, 1965, 1974) portray her as a pivotal character in a complex cosmological network (Sperling & Simon, 1933). She appears as a seductive force, a mother of demons, and an entity subdued due to her jurisdiction over the spirit realm. In contending with her exile, a resounding fragmentation vibrates throughout the earth, followed by a longing for reintegration (Koltuv, 1986; Hurwitz, 1992/2009; Patai, 1990). Participants' narratives reflect this yearning, unearthing how her image animates their daily lives. Extending Kabbalistic tradition, we trace the evolution of her figure as a disruptor in the *Emanation on the Left* (1260–1280 CE), positioned in sacred cycles of separation (Dan, 1980), to her later framing in the Lurianic school of Kabbalah (16th century, Isaac Luria). Here, she develops into a detailed, mystical structure connected to the divine break at the core of creation. As her story progresses from earlier representations, it surfaces a shared human urge to reconcile division and pursue totality.

> You already know that evil Samael and wicked Lilith are like a sexual pair who, using an intermediary, receive an evil and wicked emanation from one and emanate to the other. I shall explain this relying on the esoteric meaning in the verse "In that day the Lord will punish with His great, cruel, mighty sword Leviathan the twisted serpent and Leviathan the tortuous serpent"—this is Lilith—" and He will slay the dragon of the sea" (Isaiah 27:1) … The masters of tradition said that just as this serpent slithers without eyes, so the supernal serpent has the image of a spiritual form without color—these are "the eyes." The traditionalists call it an eyeless creature, therefore its name is Tanin'iver. He is the bond, the accompaniment, and the union between Samael and Lilith. If he were created whole in the fullness of his emanation he would have destroyed the world in an instant.
>
> (Isaac b. Jacob ha-Cohen, 1986, pp. 172–182)

The primal breach cleaved light from darkness, mirroring the original split in the psyche: A division between the Self and its shadow. As the primordial force overflowed its bounds, the vessels, formed to receive and channel the emanation from the Infinite (Ein Sof), shattered (Shevirat HaKelim), scattering luminous fragments into the Sitra Achra, the Other Side, a distorted echo of holiness (Drob, 2000). From shards arose the *Kelippot*, husks that conceal the hidden light, giving rise to both Shekhinah and Lilith: Divergent responses to cosmic fragmentation. Unlike Shekhinah, who incarnates the sacred feminine, Lilith hovers at the edge of sin, as the disowned feminine; her tension resists containment, calling forth the shadow's disruptive potential through the concept of Tikkun Olam (harmony restoration). Although earlier Midrashic and Zoharic texts (see Figure 12.2) portray her Edenic estrangement as defiance, her placement in Lurianic Kabbalah positions her outside the cycle of restoration, a force of division that remains (Frederick, 2015).

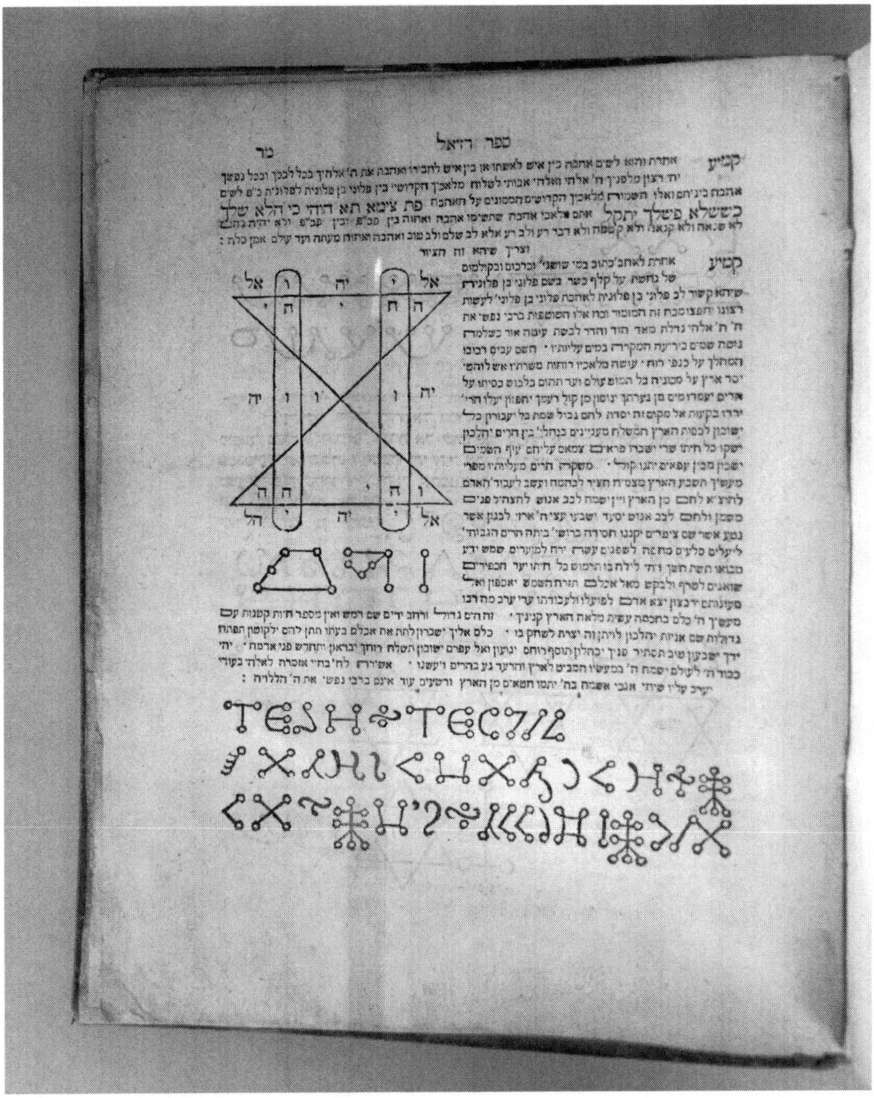

Figure 12.2 *Zohar Hadash and Sefer Raziel*

Figure is in the public domain and freely accessible for educational and commercial use.

Note:

Created in 1701 (Mendes Coutinho, 1701), this manuscript contains the *Zohar Hadash* and *Sefer Raziel*, which are pivotal to Jewish mysticism. The document, characterized by its intricate Hebrew script, mystical symbols, and geometric diagrams, is preserved at the Jewish Historical Museum in Amsterdam.

The Kelippot presents a sharper view of Lilith's mythic tension. Suspended between concealment and revelation, estrangement and return, she emulates the projected profane. She rises as a cosmic instigator, who frames chaos as essential to redemption, memorializing her as a necessary force of disruption. From a Jungian perspective, Lilith represents an early encounter with the psychological underworld, initiating a reintegration cycle (Jung, 1928–1943/1966).

> It seems like men can get away with anything ... they don't have to explain because they're men. They can do whatever they like, just like when men are promiscuous, they're not looked at as bad because they're men, but if a woman is that way, it's like, 'oh my god she has no values, oh my god she is trash.' Oh my god, I wish I was a guy, I could get away with anything. I could get married a hundred times, and no one would question me.
>
> (Hera)

Lilith's banishment illustrates a psychic burial of archetypal material deemed incompatible with collective conventions. Her descent into the *Sitra Achra* mirrors how women dull their fury, dim their appetite, and smooth their wildness to remain acceptable, often disconnecting from their innate authority and silencing forbidden eros. Reminiscent of the Kelippot, women learn to reshape themselves. The persona functions as an internal enforcer, imposing the need to patrol from within. Lilith's exile makes visible the aspects of the feminine that require concealment to survive under social constraints (Jung, 1928–1943/1966, 1907–1909/1969b). What is disavowed gathers in the unconscious, saturated with silence and self-monitoring. Integration commences when internal severance is consciously reconnected, disrupting the illusion of socially acceptability.

Emerging from the Shadow

> And then you think of Mother Mary, and she's, very classically, like, the *good woman* sort of archetype of like, "oh, I'm loving, and I just am gonna nurture you" and stuff ... I think each woman is such a different blend of all sorts of archetypes, and they blend into masculine and feminine.
>
> (Demeter)

Navigating the divide between purity and complexity, participants contended with the pressure to embody an impossible maternal ideal. References to the Virgin Mary actively illustrated the challenging internal divide. While praising obedience, they condemned seemingly unruly desire, resulting in a devotion to sacrifice. Restriction acquired meaning. People use a rigid diet, engage in compulsive caretaking, and pursue relentless appeasement as forms of social currency. The illusion of harmony dulled perception and trained the psyche to value suppression over authenticity. Beneath performativity rested a demand for composure, where strength equated to emotional stunting. Each small act of denial left a trace, shaped by ancestral expectations that once promised safety in exchange for disappearance.

> I feel like I will be this Amazonian, and if other women aren't, then they are weak; it's like some memory of trauma from the past. I don't know; it's like this sort of discomfort, where I wish I could be courageous and speak from a place where I can fully *be*, authentically. I'm so scared of saying no because I don't know how someone else will react. Even when I feel uncomfortable, I just let people think they can do whatever they want because I'd rather not get into some weird argument.
>
> (Aphrodite)

Internalized sexism inflates judgments that interfere with development. When confronted with countercultural peers, a sense of dissonance surfaces where defensiveness acts as a shield to preserve the coherence of a constructed reality. Desire numbs within the psyche with layered, albeit faulty, protective mechanisms. As participants turn inward, survival mechanisms fester. Intuition and attention erode inherited beliefs. Recognition of the damaging impact that religious dogma has on early developmental stages operates as a persistent undercurrent, perpetuating protective evil.

> I don't know if it influences the expectations, but I think that such a story that we all know is this primer of biblical knowledge. I think that it's having that age of limiting; it really does place the ownness of women as being 'the other' in the sense of being somebody that didn't listen. It's just a light influence; it's planting a seed in people's minds that women are 'the other' in some regards. I hesitate to use the word evil because it doesn't feel that way necessarily to me, but I think it is more of an influence than an expectation.
>
> (Lamia)

Religious influence pervades the psyche subtly, not as a mere belief, but as an ingrained sense of morality. Ethical injunctions settle preverbally, scripting contours of unnamed permissibility. Good and evil, often framed as divine law, settle into the mind, governing instinct and emotion alike. When these absolutes fracture, the primal spirit festers. Internal scaffolding that once offered coherence trembles in a liminal space between obedience and awareness. Lilith appears as a broken mirror reflecting both distortion and insight. Her image carries centuries of projection, serving as a foundational insight, where memories surface as lost opportunities. Boundaries, or the lack thereof, underscore a heightened sense of disorientation. A system of moral surveillance indicated a suppressed voice, inducing a state of mourning. Damaging internal denial demonstrated how silence replaced authenticity, which cost them self-trust.

The Price of Appeasement

> It's easy to do it [masturbate] around men because I can see that they really like it. Like, I'm getting some validation here. It's good to do this. When I try it by myself, it's not as easy. It's easier when you have somebody physically there with you. I barely ever do it, and I think it's probably because of shame. It's like, there's a part of me that still is like, oh, it's shameful to be that.
>
> (Kali)

Interviews illustrated how negative body perceptions limited the capacity to assert sexual agency without a male observer (Clayton & Humphreys, 2017). Forfeiting personal pleasure, women recounted difficulty establishing boundaries in intimate contexts, shaped by an almost involuntary impulse to appease others. Torn between longing for connection and anticipating its emotional cost, they described a persistent focus on preserving emotional safety. Hypervigilance consumed mental energy, diverting it from creative expression and fracturing access to inner coherence. As Lilith notes,

> It's not safe to be sexual in this world. I've always felt like I've had to defend and protect my sexuality from men because they were going to hurt me. I don't have any trauma there, but I just, like, have a warning from my world, "Be careful." So, there's an element of just, super, like, feeling like this is an unsafe place.

Attempts to remain diminutive, muted, and nonchalant surfaced as patterned strategies. Several interviewees described behavioral censorship as a form of self-preservation, cultivated through habitual vigilance (Sharma, 2015). Identifying social movements, such as #MeToo, provided language to name explicit infringements in the workplace, and discomfort infiltrated everyday decisions. Scrutiny about how one dressed, moved, and approached intimacy constricted intuitive. Although the shift in discourse signaled change, much of the psychic architecture remained unexamined.

> I don't know, I feel like that is a society thing. Like, "Oh, you're not a lady if you're too sexual." And I feel like that's probably one thing that affects me, that I feel like, certain things I don't really want to do, because I don't want to be seen a certain way, or I want people to think that I am more concerned about how I'm perceived. Because I feel like when you act a certain way, it's perceived as, "Oh, you're asking for it." It's considered an invitation like, "Oh, you're acting like that so it must be okay," but it's not.
>
> (Hecate)

Stalking, coercion, and repeated intrusions normalize as routine. Over time, shapeshifting hardens into psychic armor: A preemptive adaptation to anticipated harm. Unwanted attention recast as proof of value. Encoded expectations conferred status through desirability, regardless of consent, leaving some to equate sexual attraction with value. The internalized belief that one should feel "grateful" for objectifying behavior distorts one's sense of worth. As appearance became paramount, ambition eroded. Assault justification arose, absorbing culpability for violations they neither invited nor deserved.

> It was some internalization of men being entitled to our bodies, especially when it wasn't someone jumping out of the bushes. We had been kissing, we'd been drinking, and I had no idea I was only doing these things; that he thought I was leading him on … and it was almost like, oh, well, he's touching my body in this way because he likes me, he's interested in me. I'm desirable.
>
> (Athena)

Psychoanalytically, acceptance of oppressive systems emanates from an internalized belief in male entitlement. Anxiety, guilt, and eroticism intertwine, vividly illustrating how the shadow appears in the gradual erosion of personal boundaries.

> Women are a piece of meat, which means I get looked at all the time that way. That's why I said 'stereotype.' You know, and I noticed it, that kind of stereotype puts me on the defense a lot, even when I don't need to be on the defense, you know, I can be chillin', but that stereotype just, people treating women like a piece of meat, it's like, I don't want a piece of meat. I can't go grocery shopping over here!
>
> (Persephone)

Repeated boundary violations calcified into a pattern of appeasement, minimizing needs, and folding interiority into a palatable form. Adaptation becomes a performance of safety, where individuals frame desire as strategy and instinct as costume. Lilith's banishment reverberates when refusal invites punishment, and compliance becomes the safer wager. She animates the moment longing is clothed in guilt, when 'no' folds under coercion, when fury presses against the performance of sweetness. As Queen of the Shadow, her presence is revelatory. She governs the remnants of the denied, fragmented, and irreprehensible, compelling confrontation with illusory obedience. Each encounter with the interior is a summoning, and her return demands recognition.

Stage **3**

Awareness

Awakening the Perverse

> There's no one path for everybody. But asking the question is the first step on the path. Just start to bring yourself into every situation even more, asking yourself, What do I need right now? What do I want? And that just bleeds into everything, just bringing yourself, more of being more present with yourself.
>
> (Nyx)

A murky signal registers in the psyche, exposing terrain shaped by chronic repression and moralized silence. In this space, perverse countenance functions as a compensatory adaptation, a learned response to the disavowal of instinct required for one to follow rigid social roles. As internal scripts lose traction, awareness interrupts conditioned patterns and initiates a reckoning with contradictions previously absorbed as truth.

This cognitive shift arrives through atmospheric unease as familiar conventions falter. Disorientation gives way to shadow upheaval, where embodied tension and spiritual fatigue reveal fractures in belief systems and the construction of identity. A *frog in the throat* might indicate a repressed opinion, while a gut-wrenching jolt could imply a need for boundaries.

Externally, arguments with friends and family, a death, or a series of unlucky events might uncover an unavoidable archetypal invitation. Resulting emotional volatility, if followed, allows seekers to dismantle detrimental beliefs, permitting complexity to guide self-awareness. Ignited by a growing dissonance between prescriptive teachings and felt experiences, participants revealed moments of awareness throughout their lives. Interviews served as a conduit for epiphanic reflection, where recognition of habituated responses fell flat. Experiences formerly interpreted as dysfunction were followed by an emotional release.

DOI: 10.4324/9781003455837-17

CATALYSTS FOR AWARENESS

> I had no education surrounding it. I knew what it was, but I didn't know nuances like consent, boundaries, and pleasure. And I became super numb. I thought that I had to have sexual intercourse for it to feel good continuously. And I didn't feel good because I didn't know what to do. And I just ended up thinking that this was something that I had to do almost as a favor to my partner. This was expected of me.
>
> (Ixchel)

Compliance, emotional muting, and strategic withdrawal developed early, shaped by expectations that made self-erasure feel like survival. Awareness rarely arrived as clarity. Instead, it presented in moments when resignation no longer soothed, or fatigue sharpened into refusal. Women began to turn inward and took action towards unadulterated honesty. In therapy, they revisited the lessons that taught them to equate worth with silence. Feminist texts reoriented their questions. Relational conflict exposed where performance had long stood in for presence. Artistic expression asserted authorship over their lives (Mc Mahon, 2019). These unbound practices disrupted silence, allowing for novel interpretations of self-hood and a profound sense of agency (Burn et al., 2000).

> A lot of people's idea of burlesque is skinny, white, and young; that is, that's the typical body that they seem to think about. And they call it the burlesque body. More recently, people have come around to the fact that everybody has a burlesque body. So, if you've got, like, cellulite, and you've got, like, extra pounds ... that's okay, it's very empowering, as you're showing off your body. When you get naked in front of an audience, sure, you're showing your body, but you're also baring your soul.
>
> (Ala)

Participants articulated a fierce yearning to reshape their lives as a personal reclamation of voice, desire, and agency. For some, this began with the recognition of the emotional toll of thinness or performed harmony at the expense of self-expression. Others recounted how a lifelong instinct to serve made joy feel inaccessible. Realizations surfaced through moments of dissonance, where buried shame collided with emerging clarity. What followed was a gradual turn inward.

THE EMOTIONAL LANDSCAPE OF SHADOW CONFRONTATION

> So, I remember being in high school. My friends telling friends about, like, the first time I had sex, which was nonconsensual and not a nice experience, and then being like, ah, everybody's first time is like that. And that just never sat with me, right?

> Like, I didn't want that to be true. And it had to be for me because I had to understand how to move on ... These disappointments that I had; I wanted my first time to be about love. And it wasn't for me, and it was something very different. And so I remember my friends telling me that, and just that, they never sat with me, right?
>
> (Aphrodite)

The PFA whispered beneath the shame, not to seduce or revolt, but to entice. Sexual trauma catalyzed awakening, uncovering the fractured components of their minds, prompting a challenge to deeply ingrained dichotomies. Awareness provided the transitional movement as participants examined the polarities within themselves. The research tracked their reflections, and four pertinent characteristics emerged: A desire to change, innate challenges, recognition of external validation, and internal expansion. Peeling back layers of distortions generated a sense of connection to themselves and community supports. A compassionate resolve replaced harsh expectations for change.

> At first, I was so angry with myself and society that I tried to burn everything down—every relationship, every belief. I thought awareness meant rejecting everything. But I realized awareness is softer than that; it's about noticing, not punishing. It's about love ... something I don't think I ever realized.
>
> (Lamia)

Confrontation sparked moments of clarity but demanded continued effort and conscious action to yield change. The swiftness of transformation proved slow and often painful, requiring an unrelenting patience. Participants described returning psychological fragments shaped by repression, grief, or shame. Each moment of awareness, however subtle, carried the charge of revelation. Rage, once explosive, formed into a more deliberate, embodied drive for change.

> I've realized that if I really want to be there for my friends, I need to empathize and not try too hard to solve the problem or give them a solution, but sit there, feel what they feel, and allow myself to do so. I understand that they need deep [support], and none of those women need to be safe or need a solution. They were doing the natural process of expressing themselves to move through whatever they were experiencing. So, I think that [expressing emotions] was something that I just learned over time.
>
> (Athena)

As participants reflected on their emotional lives, they mourned the erosion of embodied intuition, ancestral knowledge, and relational sensitivity once central to their inner guidance. Emotionality invited them towards personal insights. Recognition of attempts to distance themselves from femininity indicated an internalized sense of judgment when vulnerability arose. Heightened awareness indicated a transition in self-discovery. Confrontation, here, required an uncomfortable investigation of their hearts and minds. A subtle unease signaled the descent with the PFA, where suppressed emotion, disavowed instinct, and internalized shame surfaced. Shadow gave way to an intimate reckoning with parts once buried, gesturing toward a fuller presence.

Chapter **13**

Shadow Confrontation

> I think it feels impossible to ignore what's happening with our Earth, and it really does create a tremendous sense of sorrow and depression. Like, I can never do enough to fix our tremendous collapse. Um, and it feels like an attack on the feminine because it's an attack on our Earth. On a micro level, I think it has affected my creativity. It just feels like we're in a traumatic moment on the planet. And I think women can feel it, and there's extra pressure where what women should be in the media makes my internal critics much larger, louder, and larger. Why can't I fix this ecological crisis? I'm not matching up to the divine feminine. And then it feels like the sort of slippery slope of inadequacy, and I guess that's internalized sexism. And though I've, and then I feel like, well, why would I offer anything if what I'm offering is so inadequate?
>
> (Gaia)

A mental and emotional burden arises from preoccupation with prescribed virtues, the expectation for composure, and the perceived responsibility for repairing the world's challenges. Accumulating as a prescriptive model of femininity, where centuries of mythopoetic histories drip into the mind. Satisfaction proved elusive as efforts to meet such heightened expectations proved unsatisfactory. Diminished agency within affective and relational domains intensified a pervasive sense of shame, exacerbated by the relentless visibility of idealized deities. Figures idealized for their serenity, nurturance, and transcendence came to dominate, positioning intensity as a decorum breach, as though deviation indicated deficiency or moral failing. Striving for perfection, internal conflict accumulated until it gave way to a yearning for a return to self. Standing at this brink, one could succumb to disappearance or begin to unearth and examine the penalizing embedded directives. These beliefs stripped desire and stifled dreams, revealing them as a farce.

DOI: 10.4324/9781003455837-18

Surmounting in a sense of grief for the lives they knew and the authenticity they discarded for performance, interviews indicated a constriction of voice, an erosion of desire, and a compromised ability to maintain internal cohesion. Turning inward revealed fragments of selfhood estranged by the pressure to meet culturally exalted containment. Rather than serving as a source of solace, the sacred operated as a disciplinary force, extending belonging only to those who conformed. Articulating the unspeakable, latent shadow material, surfacing as a tension between inherited dogma and the dissonant multiplicity of lived experience; of a glorious imperfection, of what it means to be a human. However, the disconnection from community and internal sense of self evoked a sense of urgency to deliver collective salvation, to forsake needs for the greater good. If she only tried hard enough, was healed sufficiently, and was vibrating at the highest frequency, then she could save the world. Such depictions permeate spiritual circles, where divinity is held to be the primary source of knowing.

The Perverse Feminine Archetype (PFA) emerged in moments of recognition, where a pit of despair, a well of discomfort, trumped the latent expectations; exhaustion solidified, igniting a charged primordial field, where collapse rendered the split visible and unignorable (Jung, 1970). Shadow confrontation required dismantling absorbed scaffolds that once offered safety and instead perpetuated erasure. Naming inadequacy signaled a refusal to remain governed by silent codes of a ladylike disposition. In voicing the unspeakable, participants initiated a confrontation with the split between internalized judgment and unacknowledged need.

NAVIGATING INTERNAL FRICTION

> I can't even tell you when I started to realize that there was this little voice that always expected me to be perfect. I mean, I don't really even know where it came from … it's been there since, well, forever. I wish I could just shut it up but if I try it gets louder. I also wonder if it's part of me, like, crying out for help or something? I don't know, does that sound stupid?
>
> (Medusa)

Stories embedded in the psyche surfaced across interviews, illustrating how individuals contended with an inner persecutor who demanded flawlessness. Attempts to muffle its insistence failed as the hungry ghost arose from the graveyard of repressed instincts. Once anointed, women recognized their breaking point, where vulnerability unlocked a doorway towards insight. Interrogation exposed unmet needs, and the fearsome voice revealed a demand for recognition. A forgotten child screaming for reprieve. In fleeting memories of freedom, the cost of approval gave way to distorted perceptions. Awakened by a refusal to shrink further, the PFA provoked conflict; clarity from unrest. Transitioning out of the familiar meant encountering a paradox: How to shed a persona that ensured safety through limitation.

> I am still working on shedding those conditions. I think it's something I'm consistently working on as a woman. I mean, I really, really hate that I am so judgmental of other women and myself, but I also don't know what to do with that. I don't think it's useful to experience such *hate* because that tends to turn into shame. I don't know if that's a forever thing, if that's the right thing, or if our society holds the perceptions of men and women in such a way that I will always have that dichotomy. There will always be some kind of divide where I'm always kind of walking a line … like a tightrope, but the degree of awareness may change.
>
> (Hera)

Craving for unfiltered authenticity, elusive performance faltered. Each laugh or outburst felt precarious, overpowered by the menacing perfection. Memories of shame illuminated how early conditioning etched into neural pathways, resulting in an inability to distinguish between genuine perception and entrenched expectations. Judgments directed at unapologetic women reflected a punishing cycle. Lateral aggression bubbled within projective states, where a refusal to claim disavowed traits opposed compliance. Outward scorn festered inward, dividing desire from acceptability. As participants longed for simplicity in a life marketed as ease, an ache for something more captivated their souls. Amid their disillusionment, they acknowledged how they sacrificed themselves for a fabricated dream.

> I just wanted to be a good wife, and that led me to bleed my bank accounts dry. I was a successful woman with a full life, but I really craved his approval, so when he asked for money, I gave it to him. Ugh. I remember being so sick during that time that I was super skinny and lost my period. I believe that this all was a result of giving my power away, and my body fucking knew. I do wish I listened, but at the time, I didn't want to.
>
> (Ala)

In hindsight, interviewees strive for change:

> I realize now that I just didn't have the voice to speak up and say enough is enough. I did everything to the detriment of myself because I thought he would leave if I didn't. At the time, I really thought it was worth it to go bankrupt for this loser. Now that I've done a lot of self-work, I realize where that came from. I'm still sorting it out, and I hope this new awareness will help me build more strength.
>
> (Aphrodite)

Bodily collapse often preceded psychological disparity. Ala's account of weight loss and menstruation mirrored the body's rebellion. Within an uncontainable internal dialogue, the shadow communicated through psychosomatic symptoms. Mental overload gave way to depletion, where overlooking the call would no longer suffice. Validation proved elusive, lacking an internal foundation. Tracing a collapse of spiritual sacrifice, the PFA manifested in moments of unease, where turmoil reached the surface.

> Jealousy, nastiness to other women, being mean—that's evil. Being mean is evil to me. Women being nasty to other women is evil to me. Those kinda like … I don't know if I even want to call them power plays amongst women—something I consider evil. At the same time, I guess it probably comes from survival. You know, on some level people may not even be conscious of it. I have a woman in my circle who has a very big job at IBM. She's mean, and there's a rumor she doesn't like other women. I don't know her personal story, but now that I think about it, I feel like maybe she has had to be that way for survival. I never thought of it like that.
>
> (Aphrodite)

Formulated as a patriarchal device, women perpetuate oppression through judgments of themselves and others. Circulating in subtleties: A vote cast against one's interest, the unraveling of a friendship, the casual slur that deems another woman crazy. Measures offer the illusion of safety, but function as tools of intimidation. Such measures offer no protection from violence or assault, nor do they shield against subjugation. Instead, they isolate women, eroding the shared strength necessary for resistance. Dropping into the shadow, inciting spiritual insurgency where women sought connection. The fog of persistent projection gave way to an increased understanding of interpersonal dynamics (von Franz, 1980).

UNRAVELING FALSE SELVES

> I know that I've been codependent with both parents and with my mother. It's kind of—even though she doesn't recognize it as much and has not sought out therapy, and she's very different in that she is codependent in different ways herself, so I feel like giving this attention … It could be inherited through women in a sense that gets shaped and shifted as we go through everybody's varying traumas and experiences, and it can turn into codependency from caretaking. To be honest, this isn't something I've given too much thought to until right now, so thanks.
>
> (Persephone)

Codependency emerged as a behavioral imperative; a psychic inheritance, built by a moralized logic of sacrifice. When nurturing is upheld as the ultimate virtue while abandonment is dismissed or left unacknowledged, the inner compass is distorted, trapped between care for others and the need to protect oneself. Disobedience is danger, autonomy is betrayal. Uncontained emotion disrupts internalized principles, exposing a fracture between accustomed traits and individualism. A split in the psyche unraveled conformity (Jung, 1989), summoning what had been repressed (Hillman, 1979). Eruption superseded composure. Roles once performed with precision began to collapse under the weight of their falsehood.

> Like, I feel so hindered within boxes and stuff in certain areas that, like, I want to burst out of them and see what's beyond that. And then for me, spirituality is, like, what is beyond everything, and you know, the current structure is so toxic. And, like, it's repressing people and making people feel bad about who they are. And then I'm interested in how to unleash people's full truth of who they are. And their full authenticity, instead of just like, having a frickin' glimmer of it, just like a little fraction of it.
>
> (Kali)

Mijares et al. (2020) argue that fragmentation within the feminine archetype functions as a liminal fracture, less an affliction than a gateway to inner authority. The wound arises where external systems flood the psychic landscape, distorting instinct and eroding coherence. Articulation became invocation, coaxing falsities into view. Electrified encounters with rejected memories open a path towards the exiled. Pursuits of pleasure flood daily interactions, revealing an aching clarity.

> My pleasure and sexuality don't just exist on their own. When I'm with a partner, especially in the past, I assume they only exist to be with someone else. But I want to challenge myself, to keep pushing and seeing if there's anything I still consider taboo. Right now, I don't feel that way because exploring what society deems undesirable or taboo excites me. I love diving into that—because why? Why is it being rejected? Why is it being disempowered? Why is it hidden?
>
> (Lilith)

Dismissed deviance seduces the shadow, calling forth discomfort with heightened clarity. The feminine no longer conformed to prescribed postures; it lurched, insisted, provoked. Instinct surfaced as appetite, as audacity, as the refusal to remain contained. Eminent demons illuminate a return to wholeness through deliberate reweaving.

THE COST OF ADAPTATION

> I feel like there are more good traits. What can feel constricting? Like trying to fit into these things? And then for me, I like trying to be the sexy 'good girl.' Like, yeah, be a, be a sexy, like, a woman who's going to please her man and attract everybody. But then, like, don't be *too* sexy, and be sweet and nice.
>
> (Lamia)

As erroneous identities unravel, what rises to the surface is a heightened entanglement with external expectations. The tension between inner dissonance and outward conformity sharpened. Conflicting impulses collided in daily life as women slip between personas, revealing how they mute their voices. Femininity functioned as performance, unfolding as a choreography of placation, helplessness, and appeal. Driven by clashing expectations, falsity unravels. The fear of rejection risked tearing open a fragile sense of self.

> I have a lot of close male friends, and sometimes I worry I'm not a girl's girl. I get very nervous about what kind of woman I'm being by having male friends, which is internalized sexism, because a man would never in a million years think about who he's friends with. They just wouldn't. It makes me mad because I end up judging people left and right based on this skewed idea of gender, and I wish I could just chill.
>
> (Inanna)

Resistance often coexisted with complicity. A woman might decline a date, then apologize for being cold. She might speak up in a meeting, then berate herself for taking up space. Allegiance to external expectations persisted as reflex: A bitten tongue, a softened critique, a preference swallowed to preserve harmony. Apologizing for assertiveness, softening opinions, and retreating from conflict served as inherited generational survival strategies.

> I think it's because there's a binary around it. Individuals are constantly looking for ways to define themselves in terms of those things, right? They're not just who they are. They're looking for, oh, this is something about me that is feminine, that's defined as feminine. Do I play with that? Do I work that up? In my being? Or do I play it down in my being? How do I do that? Do I do it in my voice? In my mannerisms? In my clothing choices? In whether I wear makeup? I mean, all these trappings, right? Some of them are more embodied. Some of them are more put on.
>
> (Nyx)

Internalized policing extended into numerous facets of participants' lives, from friendships to workplace dynamics, shaped by fears of rejection and scrutiny. Moments of discomfort gradually uncovered constraints, prompting a meaningful shift in behavior. Boundary renegotiation, contending with a persecutory inner dialogue, and the quiet refusal to comply with outdated gender standards marked a transitional state of contention.

> I have female colleagues and some close friends … or girlfriends, but I feel there's some negative connotation to shopping. And you know, as I have gotten older and thought about retiring, I thought, "Oh my God, to be the 'ladies who lunch' would be horrible!" And so that's feminine, right? It's this lack of meaning and purpose. And I do associate that with a certain kind of woman. I am doing my best to shift this type of thinking. Like, what's wrong with women who like traditional feminine activities?
>
> (Hestia)

For some, the confrontation with their ingrained beliefs marked the beginning of dreaming beyond the need for external validation, where a source of power masquerades in simple questions of the inner world. Acting on the instinctive desire to create a life of joy and curiosity, individuals discover a pathway toward creative effusion.

> I started painting again, which felt strange because I had left it for a long time. I honestly am shocked, but I still know how. At first, it felt really scary, and it was difficult for me to get back into the habit, but what drives me is the desire to show my daughters that they can create whatever is deeply part of who they are, and no one can tell them any different.
>
> (Oya)

Prompted by a quiet resolve, participants pivoted toward neglected eros, effectively dismantling segmented psychological wounds. By examining concealed affective layers, they initiated a disruption of detrimental regulatory habits. This shift splintered a performative reflex to adjust, suppress, or disassemble in response to social scrutiny.

> I'm always returning to that feeling of inadequacy, and that … I'm misunderstood on a very basic level. I've been thinking about this a lot and feel so angry, but then I reject that anger in a weird slingshot way. It's like my feelings of grief and loss—I shouldn't be feeling so sad or mad. Or I shouldn't be depressed, or I shouldn't be craving. How could I crave? How could I yearn? How can I be so sad at the loss of, you know, a lover or a species?
>
> (Hera)

Certainty gave way to contradiction. The urge to submit accompanied an intimate revolution. Strength arrived erratically, uncontained, alive. No longer filtered through performativity, selfhood arose as unscripted spiritual unease.

> There was a lot of fear in the past; I think fear in terms of rejection. Because of how much I weigh, or not shaving enough, or not being appealing enough, and something that was a revelation for me in the last year or two, was that my pleasure and sexuality don't only exist when I'm with a partner. In the past, I would have assumed that we only exist in a relationship with someone else. That all changed when I began to explore the freaky shit I want. Haha!
>
> (Demeter)

Shadow confrontation requires standing bare before unacceptability. Rather than bypassing discomfort, participants entered moments of shame, anger, craving, and grief, allowing them to surface without modulation. Their voluntary exposure disrupted coping strategies, indicating that pursuits of safety shaped presentation. In this disorienting atmosphere, the PFA surfaced viscerally: In conflicted desires, creative awakening, disrupted relationships, and resistance to roles once perpetrated for approval.

Chapter **14**

Catalysts and Challenges

> I think they're just scared. You know, like, I think they're scared, and, you know, I don't think it's just from being scared. I think it's deeper than that. When you start getting into the patterns, the generational karmic patterns get passed down, and then, you know, some of the humans that are trying to eradicate this, in whatever form throughout history, have done that. It's a generational karma that continues to be passed down. And it's, it's what these humans have learned.
>
> (Kali)

Beneath initial discomfort lived entrenched patterning. Generations shape fear as individuals transmit repressed pain through their behaviors, gestures, and gazes. The psychic patterns recalled in narratives often reflected more than individual struggle; they bore the mark of a profound ancestral trauma. Contemporary political ruptures stirred long-dormant wounds, surfacing throughout the interviews through compassion and anger. For example, the reversal of Roe v. Wade (Mangan & Breuninger, 2022), alongside the political climate of the Trump administration, appeared repeatedly, igniting existential unease. A widespread rejection of fundamental rights destabilized participants' inner ground, prompting them to reckon with their past. Consequently, wounds fester as reservoirs of wisdom, where women seek self-determined clarity. Articulating memory summons a process in which change insists upon confrontation. Leveraging a sense of authority when the world feels uncertain through work with the PFA can supply an opportunity for stability and faith.

CONFRONTING INTERNALIZED CONFINES

> When I was seven or eight, my father was with his friends, passing by and playing with my things. And he said, "My biggest frustration is not having a son because

DOI: 10.4324/9781003455837-19

> a woman will never be able to achieve what a boy or a son will achieve." And I remember looking at him and saying, "I'm going to prove you wrong," so that instead of making me feel disempowered, it activated a huge amount of, I would say, anger, resentment, and years of therapy.
>
> (Lilith)

Early memories revealed how familial and cultural messages pressure adaptation. As participants' persistent devaluation led to the development of an oppositional drive, rage became indistinguishable from liberation. Yet, cultural narratives that appeared to celebrate feminine strength often reproduced the very constraints they claimed to resist. The tension between external representation and internal truth generated dissonance that many described as formative, where neither rebellion nor conformity offered refuge. What appeared liberatory on the surface frequently obscured patterns of control, reigniting the unresolved conflict between power, performance, and self-definition.

> What was so upsetting about *Wonder Woman* is the whole premise! Everybody's excited that *Wonder Woman* (Jenkins, 2017) is super powerful and whatever. Then, they put her in a position where Chris Pine had to help her everywhere. Because she's helpless. For most of that movie, I felt like I was watching Chris Pine help her. It was like a fish out of water story. They took what could have been, and they immediately said, "We can't do that; she needs to be in a situation where she's a little helpless. Otherwise, how are they gonna fall in love?"
>
> (Artemis)

Participants voiced a conflict between early feminist promises and lived contradictions. For some, feminist ideals once offered relief from inherited narratives of inferiority. Over time, those same standards came to feel scripted and exclusionary. While allegorical progress occurred, it often coexisted with subtle forms of erasure, particularly for women whose experiences did not fit a singular mold of resonance. Apparent in their early exposure to resilience, they spoke to the grief of acknowledging that movements of liberation replicate the constraints they sought to dismantle.

> I have a hard time identifying as a feminist. I think it's great, but it still puts these weird categorizations on women. Like, a feminist looks a certain way, and women who are different are not feminists, and that's not fair. I feel like it's the same thing that men do to us differently, and I am so tired of it.
>
> (Hestia)

The cultural coding of vulnerability as weakness and stoicism as strength imposed a silent metric that actively policed self-expression. Rather than freedom, emotional containment became a survival strategy shaped by early conditioning and disguised as independence.

> I guess because I was more into the masculine, I never understood until I was older that expressing emotions is not a weakness. They're something that is very important and is what allows you to go through the process [of healing]. So of course, at the beginning, you understand and say, "Why are you whining about everything?" But I was raised as a boy, so boys don't cry.
>
> (Ixchel)

Despite attempts to embody equality-driven feminist ideologies, participants were trapped beneath a new set of expectations, revealing a persistent dichotomy. The pressure to reject traditional femininity frequently carries rigid expectations, measuring feminism by a woman's capacity to embrace body positivity, sexual autonomy, or assertive displays of psychic energy.

> An effort to try to help people with trauma has become a slingshot, weirdly. Talking about our bodies has become very taboo. Like talking about if you want to lose weight, we shouldn't talk about that. Because that's unhealthy, or there are two polar dynamics on social media on both sides. And what is happening is that in the middle, no one is allowed, no woman is allowed to talk about her body, ever. There's one group that's fetishizing unhealthy stuff, and there's another group that's saying the same thing but in the opposite direction. In the middle, I can't talk about my body.
>
> (Demeter)

At times, the demand to love oneself unconditionally felt as constricting as the pressure to conform. In attempting to reject imposed ideals, women often encountered a different kind of silence, one that punished desire for change. The body became both battleground and armor. Beneath a confident veneer lay profound exhaustion, cultivated over years of judgment, performance, and containment. Living inside a woman's body offered little space for uncertainty. Many described how this strain carved distance from sensation itself, so that even the question of pleasure felt unreachable.

> I don't quite understand sexuality. I feel like sexuality is not equal to sex, but what does that even mean? It's more like my relationship with it is … honestly, I think it's broken, but I'm exploring it. I'm still shy and feel ashamed when I talk about sex or sexuality. Communicating feels taboo or inappropriate, and I won't even bring up these things to my husband.
>
> (Hera)

Early shame distorts mirrors, glances, and the silence that follows. Over time, what formed as external judgment seeped inward, shaping how women monitored, managed, and mistrusted their bodies. Many spoke to the exhaustion of this surveillance and a growing awareness of its cost.

> I feel like a fraud; there isn't one day that I don't look in the mirror and want to change the way I look. I honestly find it annoying to think about how much energy and time I spend on my physical appearance. Do you know how much I could do if I didn't think about whether I was fat or worry about getting wrinkles in the sun? I would live a much fuller life, but it's embedded so deeply in me that I can't imagine what that would look like.
>
> (Inanna)

As women unfastened the imprint of objectification, many described a return to sensation. Tenderness surfaced as a rupture that breaks through habits of control. Emotional histories marked by shame, abandonment, and silence gave way to unexpected forms of healing. In this view, contemporary ideals of femininity reveal their rigid contours, framing power as a way to distance oneself from vulnerability.

> I think it's a sex bomb, it's, it's, you know, powerless, it's not connected. Or it's kooky. You know, it's like a witch doctor, or, you know, it's an extreme version of something that isn't realistic, apparently, or something. That means it's not empowered. It's not in sovereignty. It's not whole; it's, you know, like, giving some part of itself up to be that, when I see it's quite the opposite.
>
> (Hecate)

For Hecate, her collapse catalyzed the removal of invalidating relationships.

> If I cried, it was looked at as if I was unable to hold myself together or deal with things. Lots of people have said that I'm crazy and weird in terms of how I act and how I feel. I can't believe I listened to those assholes! After a bunch of self-work, however, I finally realized that how I am is part of my gift. If others don't see it that way, they don't need to be around me.
>
> (Hecate)

Across accounts, women described the tension of holding contradictory impressions around strength, desire, and worth. Eventually, each contradiction rippled through their inner landscapes, and many began to exist within them. In that uneasy expanse, what commenced was a hushed loosening of the scripts that once secured belonging. Control softened. Certainty gave way. In that gap, the possibility of unmediated sensation returns.

THE PROCESS OF AWARENESS

> When I was doing my sculpture work, I was working small, but instead, I wanted to go a bit, I wanted to make big things. Then, this shifted when I went to graduate school. I think that was the catalyst that helped me grow mentally, and I started to shed away a lot of these myths, stuff that has this residue that messed with the way I

> expressed my art. It's ridiculous, you know. Like, I can do whatever I want. I'm not hurting anyone; if anything, I'm making the world better.
>
> (Oshun)

From artistic rebellion to educational turning points, participants highlighted the tension between inherited roles and expanding desires. The impulse to reject pre-conceived notions of capabilities often began as an external situation. An argument, political upheaval, career dismissal, or breakup elicited a craving for change. In the wake of difficulties, an unyielding spark ignites individuals to seek previously severed parts of themselves.

> I experience an interesting conflict when I think about the porn I like to watch. It tends to be different from the sex I want to have, which is confusing for me. I wonder what it means about me, and I think about the parts of me that are seeking some expression. There's this very explorative and creative sexual dynamite of a woman trapped inside of a more prudish little lady.
>
> (Nyx)

Conflicts between public behavior and private longing brought dissonance into perspective. Certain beliefs, particularly regarding sex, art, or power, indicated layered contradictions as entry points, thresholds to challenge absorbed normativity.

> I feel like I'm constantly navigating two different worlds. There is an Athena who embodies who they want to be and then an Athena who hides out in the corner. I don't know the difference or how to get them to connect, but it is becoming more apparent as I get older that they are there.

The shape-shifting persona constructed to survive societal demands began to destabilize. In its place, questions unfolded: What parts were inherited, and which were chosen? With growing awareness came the pressure to heal, but that pressure often carried a unique form of violence in the urgency to purify, to transcend, to perform wholeness.

> Sometimes, I wonder if I should give up. Like, what's the use of trying? I think it's difficult to see everything I want to change and feel so useless in fully accomplishing that. When I do this, I realize there's a sense of rigidity that is precisely what I'm trying to get away from, but it's tough because I want to heal already.
>
> (Ala)

As women recognized their internalized, ongoing projections, they gravitated toward archetypal portrayals that had navigated similar challenges, seeking inspiration and validation.

> Even the women trying to smash through the roles still uphold those roles. They're smashing that traditional good girl role, but at the same time, they're in the beauty shop getting their nails done and flaunting their voluptuous figures. So, on the one hand, they're denying, you know, that traditional expectation, but on the other hand, they're still going along with the status quo.
>
> (Hecate)

Participants recounted breaking free from the strictures of societal expectation. In this process of reclamation, the Perverse Feminine Archetype (PFA) surfaced as both provocation and compass, urging a radical departure from performativity. Persephone spoke to this when she described her decision to leave a community that refused to honor her needs:

> Dude, I tell people that it gets better. You have to surround yourself with people who are supportive and care for you and cut out all the bullshit. If you're in a situation where you're not supported, you're depressed and miserable, then you must leave and go somewhere else where you'll be embraced and find happiness.
>
> (Persephone)

She continues,

> It's not easy, and it can be super lonely, but trust that you'll find your people. I used to hope, wish, and hope and wish that at some point, I would be accepted by my family and that if I was just queer and gay for long enough, they would get used to it. But they didn't come around, and I had to leave alone. I joined a traveling circus to get away from them. It was scary as hell, but you bet your ass I found my people.
>
> (Persephone)

The pursuit of authenticity required a shift in community; a departure from inherited roles and obligations. Erupting with a craving for kinship participants leave environments of illusory safety. They gravitated toward relationships that could fully encompass them, mirroring the transformation taking shape within.

Themes of Resilience and Growth

> Once you start to develop awareness, there's no going back. I need to be careful, though, because I've been so used to the harshness that sometimes I treat healing like some militant project. But I've learned I need to allow myself to be vulnerable and that when I start feeling into my emotions and empathizing with others, I can open up a whole new experience of compassion.
>
> (Gaia)

Healing manifested through exhaustion, defiance, and moments of insight that wove together unevenly. Emotional breakthroughs shed light on buried truths, although regressions frequently unsettle momentum, with shame and doubt returning unbidden. Still, the drive toward psychic cohesion persisted. Many spoke of remaining present with discomfort, welcoming softness where hardness once held. Their reflections exposed how the perverse reappeared in memory, subtly urging recognition.

> Growing up in a divorced household was very tumultuous for a long time, the *Rocky Horror Picture Show* (Sharman, 1975) ended up being this weird release valve that I didn't realize until years later, where it was a safe environment, but it still had this flexibility and openness to sex and different sexualities and different cultures in that way, and it was such a melting pot of people and preferences and consent and—like, being. I was even fully aware of these concepts, and so the terms perverse or pervert were constantly bantered about more lightly; I think this helps with my connection to my inner perversity now.
>
> (Hestia)

Cultural encounters stirred recognition. In symbols deemed transgressive, women discovered fragments of themselves. The PFA arrived as a familiar essence. Shame, once imposed, could become a portal. Providing a conceptual lens through which to engage with the shadow, women apprehend the demonized Self (Jacobi, 1942/1968). As interviews untangle varying degrees of apprehension and courage, they illuminate an intricate space of confrontation, where prompting events stir internal angst. Each narrative weaves tension between hardened beliefs and emerging possibilities, revealing moments of recognition.

Chapter **15**

Active Imagination

Engaging the Perverse

> I like to discover what those things are and experiment with them in various ways—not just to explore, but also to work through traumas and the societal constructs that have been imposed upon me. I want to challenge those within myself to see if I still hold any internalized judgments or discomfort. And honestly, through that experimentation, I have encountered some things that have made me realize just how much conditioning I'm still unlearning.
>
> (Medusa)

Active imagination serves as a liminal practice, initiating engagement with the symbolic layers of the unconscious. In Jungian terms, the dialogical method for archetypal connection bypasses abstraction in favor of imaginal presence (Jung, 1997, 1981). Lilith serves as an expressive vessel for the Perverse Feminine Archetype (PFA), providing access to ancestral strata and mythic memory. As desire disentangles from moralization, it animates the body as a source of insight. What unfolds is a psychodynamic strategy in which creative inspiration catalyzes meaning. Once activated, symbolic utterances surface spontaneously: Vivid images, somatic responses, or reconfigured inner narratives.

> It was not until I started exploring my sexuality that I realized I had no idea what consent, boundaries, and pleasure meant. I think before then, I was sort of numb to my body. I've been trying to think, and I think it's an energy thing, where I get to be entirely feminine because somebody embodies the masculine right in front of me. It's like I don't have to incorporate it so much. And so, I get to let my 'Inside Energy' come outside, and the man can act like a cup, and I can see the water flowing wherever I want. And it's, like, this massive, like, it's all my creation energy, like flooding the room. And, like, all my death energy too, like, I don't know, like creeping around the shadows. This is a great way to play with your shadows and let them all come out. And I think allowing our feminine force to be out is very powerful.
>
> (Kali)

DOI: 10.4324/9781003455837-20

Although Jung prescribed conscious and deliberate intention with active imagination, narratives illustrate a more somatic and affect-driven approach to entering the imaginal realm. Rather than structuring their experiences through technique, participants responded to felt shifts of imaginal attunement through internal intensities, whether erotic, melancholic, or ecstatic.

IDENTIFYING THE SHADOW

> When I was younger, I was told that if I showed my body, it would provoke men, and, for the most part, that's what happened. I learned to hide myself in hoodies and baby clothes. I guess you'd call it more of a tomboy style. It made me feel, like, disgusting—like grossed out by my own body, or, like, that it would always be seen that way. I just knew I could feel *something*—like it was attacking me somehow. This set up the idea that I had to cover up who I am for others—make myself small, or they would attack me. But now, I know that's not okay. I try to wear whatever I want and show off my body. I think this practice has helped me heal those hidden parts.
>
> (Hestia)

Participants recounted the psychic burden of an omnipresent threat of harm. A sustained orientation toward safety led to a habitual narrowing of self-expression, reinforcing withdrawal. In voicing the toll of pervasive violence, they surfaced a latent but urgent desire to release emotional residue. The interview space offered a temporary suspension of surveillance, a context where disclosure was neither penalized nor pathologized, enlivening vulnerability.

> I think the first time I was sexually assaulted was at 13. I remember being at this party with all my friends, which was really scary. We all got wasted, and a friend of mine started to aggressively just … you know, finger me in front of the entire group. Everyone egged them on as I said no and kept trying to back away. That was awful, and I still think a lot about how I invited that into my life, and there has been a lot of shame about it all. I think that's when I started to feel mortification around my body. I lost a part of myself during that time.
>
> (Persephone)

When inscribed by trauma, the body registers as a locus of pain and estrangement. To mitigate symptomatic repercussions, individuals often sever ties with innate capacities for sensory pleasure. Participants recognized the psychic costs of their disconnection and angled toward attention as a reparative act. Sitting with painful memories provided a salve for metabolization, granting additional support through discussion.

> I feel like I'm always walking around with a frog in my throat. It's activated when I cry, but it's somewhere underneath my whole facade as a normal person. For a long time, I was afraid to feel the pain there, but it's become so unbearable that I've been listening to it more. I'll put my hand on my throat and visualize it moving out of my body, through a deliberate focus on its presence and the memories associated with it. It sucks, but it seems to be helping it drip out of my body. Maybe someday I'll get relief.
>
> (Oshun)

Active imagination facilitates potent internal imagery, functioning as a conduit through which affective residues and repressed material enter conscious awareness. Throughout the interviews, participants described embodied constrictions, instinctive sensations, and emotional blockages that signaled unresolved psychological material. The manifestations sought attunement; a willingness to remain present with discomfort and to hold states of distress. Reflections on the perverse opened an interpretive space for expressing aspects of experience that remained unspeakable through conventional language.

> I had a lot of guilt and shame related to my late teens, which was promiscuity, where I was exploring my sexuality. And then, of course, I felt just, you know, you know, really ashamed of myself, and that was something that I had to get through and kind of worked out for myself.
>
> (Hera)

Hera's reflection articulates how shame and guilt fracture under the weight of desire. She gestures toward an inevitable split, a moment when the psyche registers the untenability of repression. Suspended between inherited moralism and epitomized yearning, heightened awareness awakens a decision to reexamine the source of self-condemnation. In this fragile terrain, transformation begins with the willingness to acknowledge one's innate contradiction.

> So, I think working with myself, it's all about seeking pleasure, you know? I believe women have learned that they don't deserve pleasure, or they don't deserve to speak up, but that's bullshit. Honestly, if you're not getting pleasure, communicate and know yourself and what you like. You should feel pleasure when you have sex, and this should extend to everything in life. Like, that's your birthright.
>
> (Lamia)

By turning toward the forbidden, participants reinterpret formerly desecrated instincts. No longer regarding satisfaction as indulgence, but a return to the self, the act of conscious engagement with innate desire acknowledges the perverse as a potent ally, guiding towards healing. Her vitality in tandem with emotional risk exposes how vulnerability, when met with attention, functions as a generative force in reshaping shadow connectivity.

ENGAGEMENT WITH THE SHADOW

> For a long time, I've dreamt about having a penis. It's not that I want to be a man or anything; it's just that I want to experience the power that comes from the penis itself. Honestly, I always felt like deep, deep inside, I was a boy and had a lot of lucid dreams about it, honestly, for years. I finally started to listen to these dreams and embody that energetic part of my being, and it's helped me come out of my shell. Just because I'm a woman does not mean that I can't access this type of penetrating and destructive energy.
>
> (Medusa)

Engaging with imaginal configurations enabled participants to access submerged dimensions of their psychic interior, where insurgent agency exists. As they permitted themselves to enter symbolic territory, dreams, intuitive impressions, and internal figures arose, often unsettling and illuminating, obscured appetites (Jung, 1997). The experience paralleled active imagination as an entryway between inner material and archetypal resonance (Jung, 1981). The Perverse Feminine Archetype (PFA) surfaced as a corporeal and cerebrally charged presence, functioning through embodied projection. Narratives revealed how she animated qualities often deemed taboo, guiding women into unexplored territory. Sexuality remains a foundational source of imaginative connection, operating as a tool to support bodily reindwelling after histories of objectification. Rather than existing as a fixed surface for external gaze, their bodies become sites of curiosity and possession.

> It's interesting because I'm still connecting the dots with my sexuality, but when I see people like Cardi B, who are just out there in the world with their shadowy side, I think, yeah, that's pretty cool. She doesn't care. She's like letting it out like a tidal wave. I wish I could be like that, but it's really hard. It's hard to pleasure myself; it's hard to let it all out and dance around. It's easier to do with a partner because I think that's what I'm used to.
>
> (Hera)

Although frequently described as a structured method, active imagination molds in diverse experiential registers. Engaging an archetypal image became a reciprocal process that ushered participants deeper into unconscious terrain. Throughout the interviews, reflections indicated that conscious engagement is situated in various contexts, without formalities. While sexuality served as a vital catalyst, participants also navigated symbolic space through creative modalities, including painting, embodied performance, journaling, and dream inquiry. Called to proceed with generative acts, they enabled connection with submerged aspects of the perverted and distorted mind. Entering a conscious state of confrontation with the shadow, the PFA invites multiplicity, where forgotten dimensions are metabolized and held.

Stage **4**

Redefining the Feminine

An Integration of the PFA

> What am I going to do, be miserable every day? No, like, because what if I ever come back, you know? And so, let's make something happen. *Now*, let's do something with this life. Let's not hope and count on the fact that I might come back because I could be a bug. Who knows? But in this body, in this lifetime, I can do a lot. And why would I waste it?
>
> (Gaia)

The Perverse Feminine Archetype (PFA) surfaces not in fragments or abstraction, but as a unified force made visible through action. Her emergence is in the aftermath of confrontation, a decisive commitment to embody what was once disowned. Participants moved beyond questioning or naming repression; they enacted its inversion. Rather than retreating into prescribed alternatives, they leaned into instinct, contradiction, and desire. Roles that once defined their silence were disrupted through refusal. The audacity to set boundaries and actively oppose compliance, accommodation, and self-effacement helped them reconnect with their compass. A faint inner voice, once dismissed and doubted, began to guide decisions, rituals, and expression. Marking a shift from avoidance to attunement, the shadow provides wisdom beyond willful declarations. Doubt, although present, no longer steers the ship. Moving inward, the PFA exists within its appropriate domain: The soul. In this phase of integration, recovery is erotic, eruptive, and grounded in the sacred mess of becoming.

RETURNING TO THE SACRED BODY

> I was thinking about why I hate it so much when people try to define women in a fixed way. Talking about feminine energy feels different from talking about

DOI: 10.4324/9781003455837-21

> masculine energy because each woman carries a unique balance of masculine and feminine energies, and that balance manifests differently in each of us. I can be nurturing, but I can also be angry and assertive. That doesn't make me any less of a woman or any less feminine.
>
> (Medusa)

Participants described the feminine as an expansive energy that supports fluidity and contradiction. Fixed associations gave way to permeability in ritual, dream-work, and sensual expression, reshaping self-perception. These spiritual and embodied practices fostered a porous sense of self, allowing previously repressed qualities to reintegrate. Lilith's representation took shape as a mythopoetic force, a current of psychic charge that summoned participants toward a felt experience of divinity, rather than a fixed endpoint.

> I think everything is everything. I believe God and sex are intertwined, and we can get in trouble if we try to condense it to some binary language. It's like how we like to explain certain things. I think that women are masculine. And I believe that men are feminine because I feel that we have everything inside of us. I don't think that we could ever disconnect from anything completely. I think we hold every emotion with us, I think that we have every facet of God within us. And one of those facets is always in contradiction.
>
> (Hecate)

Hecate's reflection progressed the dialogue from gender discourse into a metaphysical domain where paradox was the axis of feminine power. No longer reduced to performance or roles, the feminine arrives as a medium to support language. In dialogue, women animated their essence in the philosophical reflections, situating them in a cycle of meaning-making. Adopting an expansive mind, participants allow for immersion with the PFA as they consider memories of trauma and shame.

An in-depth recognition of the ever-changing and multifaceted nature of femininity provided a sense of freedom for critical insight. While facing internal friction between their needs and societal expectations, they remarked that they feel trapped in a cage. The choice to unlock this cage, once imposed by external conditions and now self-perpetuated, illuminates unlocked potency. They yearned to accept and integrate their minds, bodies, emotions, and souls, where limitations could no longer inhibit their creative desires. Although a resolution was not reached in the interviews, creative ventures such as writing, attending graduate school, painting, and participating in healing workshops were indicated as a first step toward healing. Seeking a return to their bodies, self-pleasure became a sacred ritual, leading to a pronounced reconnection.

> So, when I first, which I think is it might be the case for a lot of women when they're starting to, like, to develop, and they get their period, they start to, you know, grow

> breasts, they start to get hips, and they are exposed to a different type of view. I didn't understand what that meant at all. Before, I didn't realize I needed a bra because I never considered it. But somebody mentioned it to me, and like, obviously, that made me like pay attention to my breasts. I mean, I'm a child. I should be able to wear what I want.
>
> (Oya)

The memory of premature bodily awareness reveals a pivotal shift from freedom to surveillance. Though disorienting, such moments often marked the first stirrings of erotic consciousness, a recognition of aliveness beneath constraint. Reconnecting with the inner child, the PFA opens a doorway to a realm of enchantment, activating spirituality as a source of reclamation.

EMBODIED DEFIANCE

> The perverse? Oh God, my instinct is to show you my pussy. Is that okay to say? I mean, just being wholly unafraid and unashamed in being naked and open while you witness what it is to be human. I fuck who I want when I want, and I stop feeling afraid of my instinctual nature. I think that is what perverse is. Completely open and embracing the rawness of what it truly means to be human.
>
> (Kali)

Participants imagined a life without the rigid constraints of social expectations; a life in which they could express the parts of themselves that had long been silenced or surveilled. Vulnerability without consequence. They framed rebellion as both an emotional purging and a rebalancing of their inner world, shedding imposed beliefs to reconnect with intuition. Rejecting inherited roles and deciding to lean into defiance, women voiced an urgent need for liberation. Righteous rage surfaced as clarity. In confronting emotional suppression, many reported greater access to intuition and discernment (Chemaly, 2018). As a return to self-authority, women no longer shaped their lives to meet inherited ideals; instead, they began to embody an internal source of power.

> My mother was so scared I was going to become a lesbian. She did everything in her power to tell me to needlepoint and sew and cook because it would make me look more feminine and more desirable to men. She and her father sent me this birthday card when I was like ten to say, "Here's what ladies do. They lower their voice. They're not loud in a room." Hey, all a whole list of things that I wasn't.
>
> (Lilith)

Several women described moments when they stepped outside of prescriptive roles and followed a voice that had long been suppressed. One joined the fire department; others left stifling relationships, redefined their sexual boundaries, or turned to spiritual practices that honored their interior life. Rebellion, in this context, became a form of remembrance rather than renunciation: A homecoming to the self that had always waited beneath the performance.

> It annoys me that people want me to be a certain way when I'm just not that thing. I remember the first time this triggered me; I was probably eight. I was sitting with my legs spread and playing on the floor. My dad was like, "Don't sit like that. That's not ladylike." And I was like, "Excuse me? The fuck? I'm gonna sit however I want to sit." I think that little girl is somewhere still inside me. I need to listen to her.
>
> (Inanna)

Guan Yin emphasizes her inner call to rebellion:

> There's a lot of pressure from our families to have kids. They feel worried about you if I don't have a baby, so they constantly try to persuade me, but it makes me upset—no, that's not what I want. I'm not little, and you can't tell me what to do. I don't care if you're my elder or not; you cannot force me to have a baby.
>
> (Guan Yin)

In refusals to marry, procreate, or appease, participants echoed Lilith's archetypal defiance. Child-free women recounted pressure from family, friends, and other women, often shamed with accusations of selfishness or narcissism, echoed a growing cultural resistance to motherhood (Kwon, 2020). However, this stance was not merely oppositional. It was generative. In drawing boundaries, participants embodied heightened tonal confidence.

> Well, I think of Ayana Pressley and Ocasio-Cortez. I think they're not backing down, and when women don't back down, that's perverse. Right? As far as the white masculine is concerned, it's perverted, right? That's just what happens when women don't back down. So, whenever we express and project ourselves, regardless of whether it's sexual, personal, or professional, that's perverse; however it shows up.
>
> (Athena)

The choice to rebel catalyzed profound changes. Naming desires, asserting limitations, and abandoning reduction inspired participants to articulate distorted beliefs. Intuitive Inquiry (II) provided a framework for tracing these ruptures and recoveries as a cyclical return to the innate self. The method's integration of intuition, a feminized and long-marginalized mode of knowing, functioned as a rebellion, confronting dominant paradigms of academic investigation (Layton & Leavy-Sperounis, 2020; Miller, 1987). Recalling energetic murmurs awakened a sense of freedom and a connection to a life designed for independence.

> I think it's taken time [to connect with my power], but I know I've always had this energy. Because I'm such a maker, artist, and thinker in that way, working a 'normal' job has always made me miserable. And I'm not the kind of person to sit in that misery. Maybe I did in the past, and that was totally part of a toxic cycle I was stuck in. But I quickly realized I wasn't going to live like that. This is my only life, and I don't want to fucking waste it.
>
> (Artemis)

The PFA unfolded as a strategy for heightened sovereignty. Through speech, gesture, and refusal, participants gave form to the disavowed. In moments of boundary-setting, creative risk, and emotional honesty, a generative source of clarity dethroned conveniences. Generating space for paradox, the following chapters trace how reclamation became ritualized, relational, and sacred.

Chapter **16**

Shadow Integration

> It's been an amazing experience to explore my darker proclivities, and I feel like I'm awakening a feminine force within me. And by feminine, I don't mean soft, gentle, and receiving. That's all part of it, but I feel the feminine force is very powerful and forceful. The force brings the universe down and creates an entire being, grows that being, and pulls it from its source. Like, that's so magical. And when I started working with my sexual force, I grew more out of this hidden and wounded thing that I was stuck in.
>
> (Lilith)

Shadow integration unlocks a threshold in Redefining the Feminine, initiating an intimate reckoning with long-buried psychic material (Jung, 1970). The procedure invites participants to explore their inner world through dreamwork, somatic ritual, imaginal meditation, and a challenging reconnection with aspects they once disowned. Welcoming the Perverse Feminine Archetype (PFA) requires a capacity to navigate emotional volatility and cultivate genuine resonance with her image.

Through narrative and theoretical engagement, I traced moments where the perverse shifted from concept to embodied force. Through deliberate acts of reclamation, participants began to form a reciprocal bond with their ancestors, which echoes in contemporary life. Their accounts enter the subterranean spaces of the psyche, where repressed instincts ignite creative force. What once fractured erupts in ritual recognition. Individuation, as Jung posits, is made possible when the unconscious is actively drawn into awareness (Jung, 1970; von Franz, 1980). Along the arc of descent, women shed inherited shame and awaken an authority born not of mastery, but of intimacy with fear.

DOI: 10.4324/9781003455837-22

RECONNECTING WITH SPIRITUALITY AND INTUITION

> I find value in energetics and things that aren't as physical. If my intuition tells me not to do something, I will listen because I see value in it, like taking in that information that I'm getting from this side of my brain, and I'm finding value in it. I think there's a lot of shame from people who don't understand this feminine energy. And it's like, I feel like this time period is slowly allowing more and more people to see that maybe this supposed 'woo woo' stuff isn't bullshit.
>
> (Kali)

According to Jung (1933–1954/1969a), individuation illuminates omitted corridors of the mind, where disowned fragments await reconstitution. While each level of the unconscious carries personal imprints, it also converges with the collective unconscious, a vast reservoir of shared mythic structures and primordial energies (Jung, 1907–1909/1969b). Within this liminal expanse, participants traced subtle energetic lines that bypassed conventional spiritual doctrine. Intuition led them toward portals of knowing not sanctioned by religious tradition, but through occult practices. A reentry to a connection without dogmatic doctrine supported healing without reexamining religious trauma. What had once been split or pathologized started to reassemble through felt experience. In those encounters, consecrated is visceral in the body, shaped by ancestral memory, and activated in ritual.

> Leaving the religion I was raised in felt like a betrayal at first. But then I found tarot, rituals, and moon ceremonies, and I felt like I was coming home. I don't know how to describe it fully, but it was like some sort of disconnection from my body that ignited and reattached once I started on my spiritual path, where I could discover a source of insight that had long been forgotten.
>
> (Athena)

Participants described a psychic homecoming initiated by spiritual experimentation. What began as estrangement from institutional religion evolved into embodied intimacy with intuitive forms such as tarot, ritual, and lunar ceremonies. Each gesture reactivates dormant wisdom, awakening conduits through which internal guidance confronts doubt. Humor, symbol, and play reframed maligned energies as protective and empowering. Naming oneself as "witch" or invoking energetic boundaries with irony became a method of reclaiming agency.

Rather than a singular moment of awakening, experiences reflected a nonlinear unraveling of psychic disconnection, through which metaphysical contact began to restructure their inner world. In uniting with unseen energies, they formed a reciprocal, evolving relationship with forces that deepened their access to archetypal truth.

> I've had many ghostly things happen in my life, connections with ancestors, and things moving in front of my eyes with other people, not just me being by myself, but that's also happened. And those things, all of those weird stories, have sort of opened my eyes to, like, there's this unseen energy that we, as humans, can, we're not always tapped into, but maybe we could be. And that does play a big role in my work. Like, I am attempting to capture an energy that's unseen around a subject, around a history, around a person, around an object. What could this energy look like if I could manifest it in material?
>
> (Aphrodite)

The PFA catalyzes contact with once-forgotten modes of knowing; a spiritual reawakening. As participants attune to her presence, they describe building intuitive matrices of emotional clarity. Through that connection, obscured healed stirred, enabling a metamorphic strategy where intuition is authority and a gateway to the shadow. Following this pathway ushered in an opportunity to plummet into heightened clarity and courageous action

EXPRESSING BOLD PARTS

> I don't personally find anything perverse. I think that there are people who are uncomfortable with sexuality in general—their own or other people's, who would consider things like that perverse, people who may be more conservative. I believe that I have a very healthy or broad perspective on sexual appetites or sexual proclivities of other people, and to each their own, and I think my perspective is that as long as everybody's happy, healthy, and consensual and of age, then they should be allowed to do whatever they'd like in that regard in the bedroom in the privacy of their own homes.
>
> (Nyx)

Participants examined the taboo dimensions of the self, including desires submerged beneath shame and societal prescriptions. The perverse revealed itself as a mirror of patriarchal distortion, uncovering innate disillusionment with ingrained norms. As layers of conditioning gave way, women animated suppressed aspects of themselves, no longer content to live confined by others' discomfort.

> I became much bolder about exploring these hidden parts of myself, and so I started having lovers. I'm grateful my husband is so supportive because I don't know what to do otherwise. Maybe I would have to leave him. I'm at a stage in life where I can no longer pretend I am something other than who I am. I'm tired of hiding.
>
> (Inanna)

When choice stirred activation, a fearless defiance stood in its place. Navigating layered barriers, women began to recognize the potency of subtle self-claiming acts. One account illuminates how shadow work unsettles ancient arrangements, compelling individuals to choose between prescribed roles and authentic unfolding. The turn inward evolved into both a threat and a threshold.

> I think it is important for us to teach young women to seek pleasure when it comes to engaging in any type of sex act. That means talking about consent and making sure everyone feels safe because it can't be pleasurable if boundaries are crossed, can it? I think that's what my work is all about because I went so long hiding myself out of fear that I never told people what I wanted and how I wanted it. After learning to express these parts of me, I've committed to shouting it from the rooftops.
>
> Lilith

Corporeal instinct, creative will, and spiritual yearning arose into consciousness, reconfiguring self-understanding, illuminating the affective residues of repression (Mijares et al., 2020; von Franz, 1980). Formerly obscured dimensions animated the internal field, culminating in a redefinition supplied with a mischievous revolt.

THEMES OF RESISTANCE AND REBELLION

> As a child … I remember just being like, incredulous. Like, why? Like, um, but then there were other times I would go, like Thanksgiving … I was hanging out with my dad and my brother. And my dad was like, go in the kitchen and help them clean up … And I was like, "I don't want to." And then he was like, "but that's the tradition of what the women do." And I was like, "Well, too bad because I'm not doing it." He was like, "Whoa." Like, "Whoa, my daughter is so bossy" … I think I've shaken up his world a lot.
>
> (Lamia)

Anger surfaced as a suppressed emotional current that, once acknowledged, stirred buried reservoirs of clarity and power (Chemaly, 2018). Despite discomfort, women reflected on moments where boundaries stood as a representation of their intuition. Rather than neglecting communication, it acknowledged its presence as a potent virtue. Forbidden feelings were granted legitimacy, rippling across voice, identity, and relational dynamics.

> I think that for much of my life, I was trapped in this very small box. I got married when I was in my early 30s and had my kids, and my husband was quite abusive. So, this idea of power and subservience was my identity. As I began to understand that this was a marriage that could not be sustained, I joined the fire department. And I think I've been there 22 years, and I think that was the beginning of making the box bigger and eliminating the sides.
>
> (Medusa)

Patterns of early subjugation reveal how patriarchal control curtails personal sovereignty. Bold actions fracture inherited constraints, constructing cracks through which agency seeps. Alchemy embeds in disobedience. Repression loosens its grip. The PFA materializes here, charged with vulnerable force. As the transformation unfolds, resistance ceases to confine and instead embraces the practice of radical becoming.

> At the firehouse, there were a lot of whispers that I was a lesbian. And that's why I was there. Because, you know, short hair, and, you know, whatever masculine clothes I might be wearing. Well, there had been two guys, and this goes back probably 20 years, and they were using the language "homo." And I said, "You wouldn't know that; you can't say that!" And they're like, "Oh, like, why not?" And I said, "You never know who you're going to offend." And they were like, "Oh, like, now we know."
>
> (Hestia)

As participants navigated emotional and societal restrictions, they sought agency through deliberate micro-rebellions. Refusing to apologize for setting boundaries, honoring desires, and confronting internal belief systems. Although challenging, the choice to live authentically outweighed the fear of rejection. Women come to recognize their intensity is valued in communities that share the desire to plumb their edges.

COMMUNITY

> I used not to have a female community because I felt judged by women far more than I did by men in that space. It's like, you're competing for what? Like, who are you competing for? What are you competing for? Why? Why are we doing that instead of having this bond and this creation of magic together with that feminine force and power? Whether it's a man, whether it's a job, whether it's just attention in general. There's a reason that we're put into competition, because it separates us and closes our power. And together, we're so much more magical.
>
> (Oshun)

Shadow forms at the junction of ancestral wounds, lived experience, and public degradation, where layers of pain converge into silence. The resulting disconnection severs relationships, distancing women from one another and undermining communal solidarity with rivalry.

> It makes me really annoyed that people want me to be a certain way when I am not that thing. I was probably eight years old the first time I was triggered about this. And I was chillin' with my legs sprawled out. My friend told me not to sit like that because it's not ladylike. I was like, what the fuck? I'm going to sit however I want to. I was really upset with her, I think I even stopped being her friend. Now, I realize that it had more to do with whatever she was taught. I think these memories guide me to run the women's empowerment circles I lead.
>
> (Demeter)

Subtle conformity disruptions dislodge inherited patterns, inviting women to lean into perversions as clues to profound truths. These acts, often quiet and relational, indicate pervasive judgmental patterns. As they resist expectations, they reanimate repressed desires. Narratives gesture toward a broader reconstitution of feminine power, one no longer predicated on palatability.

> I used to think anger made me weak, that it proved to everyone I was crazy. But when I finally let it out, I realized other people felt the same way. That raw emotion created a righteous sense of connection, like something we had all been longing for but had forgotten. I think through my work, I've seen how we have begun to collectively broaden the term 'feminine' because it's not really about just women or fitting into some fucked up ideal. I think it's evolving, and that's a good thing. Maybe I'm biased because my circle works hard to shatter stereotypes, but isn't that how revolutions are started?
>
> (Nyx)

Internalized sexism severs relational bonds, echoing eras when communion evoked suspicion and retribution (Federici, 2004). The break in sisterhood drained collective power and seeded mistrust. And yet, women reach toward one another. A spirit of revolution endures in visionary dissidents who dare to create connection, who free the condemned without apology. As they confront the weight of isolation, new structures of support take shape. Activated by an embrace of lost connection, the PFA no longer lingers in shadow; she animates in gestures, ignites presence, and manifests in subtle awakenings.

Chapter **17**

Manifestations of the PFA

> Perverse feminine … okay, cool, interesting. Um, well, perverse would mean countercultural. And feminine … I guess just what sort of what our conversation has led us to, after digging around, I think would be this sort of … welcoming of, like, the jealousy and the malignant. It's like bringing those negative qualities into a positive light. For me, it'd be like sourcing back into this feminine space—the benevolence of malevolence.
>
> (Lilith)

The question, "What does the Perverse Feminine mean to you?" revealed how women navigate criticism in pursuit of psychological cohesion. They spoke of her as a force who chooses autonomy over approval and influence over convention. Marked by unfiltered emotion, encounters with detrimental beliefs, anger, envy, and the unsettling pleasure in defiance surfaced as signals of a long-repressed desire. Encounters gradually became interspersed into a shared urgency for change, a breaking point from censorship.

> It seems like women are finally done repressing their so-called shadow selves. We're tired of holding onto the shame society dumped on us and are ready to unleash our wild, chaotic energy. Sure, some haters want us to keep it all hidden away, but it's not the time for that anymore, and it's time to connect with our villain era, which means we need to shed the conditioning of the past and step into a new beginning.
>
> (Kali)

Illustrations of the PFA are allegorical threads running through the research, invoking the charge of she-demons that conjure unease and taboo. Chronologies of witches, rebels, and exiles invite women to consider the possibility of restoration. Amid landscapes deemed barren or broken, they call upon the complexities of mirrored fears.

DOI: 10.4324/9781003455837-23

> I find that women are more compassionate, thoughtful, and intuitive overall. I know that's a generalization, but I find that there's a different connection with other women than there is with men, and I think the complex nature of being a woman is fascinating. It's probably what I appreciate the most in myself and my female-identifying friends. I also like different depths of compassion and emotional pliability. It's weird how people call women crazy for things that are clearly their gifts.
>
> (Hera)

Authors such as Angela Carter (1979), Clarissa Pinkola Estés (1992), and Marie-Louise von Franz (1972) gesture toward a dialogue with the forbidden feminine, reimagining cultural norms through feminist mythopoesis. Whether conveyed through psychological excavation or mythic storytelling, dubious archetypes surface as vivid embodiments of patriarchal residue: Trauma, fury, and the spectral traces of a severed inner world.

> I recently started developing my music, which I think has been linked to finding my voice. It's been a scary journey because I'm honestly afraid of being loud or putting myself out there. I really did internalize some sort of idea that I just needed to be quiet and pretty. I'm trying my best to move out of that space and tune into my strength instead through song. I feel empowered and almost dangerous, but I do it for myself and all women who can't speak.
>
> (Demeter)

In reclaiming the perverse, women trace a demanding path toward cohesion. Drawn by ancestral intuition and instinctive pull, they descend into shadowed terrain where long-buried truths stir. Personality characteristics previously labeled obscene evolve as metaphorical cusps, presenting access to a spiritual underworld—a vision shaped at twilight. As portrayals unfolded, junctures of recovery and reckoning surfaced, illuminating the unconscious architecture that resists erasure.

SEEKING THE PFA

> I think since I've only been with men, my feminine side is really prominent. I've played that sort of 'I'm going to pleasure the man' role, and recently, I'm most curious about letting my more masculine side shine now … whether that's with a man or woman, I don't know; I'm still exploring, but I just want to be more dominant. Like, I think it would be interesting to be a bossy asshole instead of being nice all the time. I want to be in a position of power. I feel like this extends to my work life, too, and I've definitely been more outspoken about my career goals. It's caused some backlash because my boss is really confused about my sudden bossiness, but I don't give a fuck. Fire me if you have such an issue!
>
> (Persephone)

From erotic reveries to bold professional choices, participants tap into subdued instincts. Encounters with internal intensity formed disavowed impulses, altering how they confronted self-sufficiency. In attempting to reshape their lives on their own terms, they explore how nonconformity coexists with individualistic declarations.

> This stage of my life is all about play-pretend, where I can play up certain aspects of my nature, like I did as a kid. I mean, maybe sometimes I want to play up being a boy, and other times I'll be a girl. I know that this all has to do with what I learned in childhood as to what boys and girls are, but that's just what it is. I've accepted this aspect of my identity, and instead of railing against it, I embrace it. I love exploring these roles with my current partner, where we might step into paths of femininity and masculinity, and he is totally down to experimenting with me.
>
> (Ixchel)

Traditionally, societal expectations link femininity to passivity, confining it to narrow roles. Women learn to modify themselves by disconnecting from an innate desire for dominance. As they shift perspective, they challenge previous survival strategies and ignite multiplicity. A choice to reside within previously unexplored territory invites a reframing, where forbidden impulses catalyze agency. Guided by a potent sexual force, they embolden energetic frequencies through a ritualistic form of play.

> So I'm premenopausal, and my hormones are changing, which means my libido is constantly going up and down, and it's kind of been an interesting twist in my sex life. I feel like I crave a power play where I get to act on giving rather than receiving. Like, sometimes, I'll wear a strap-on and peg my partner, and it feels so liberating to penetrate him. It's like, I imagine being encompassed in soft tissue just like a man would be, and it's really invigorating. I've also been asking him to suck my clit as if he's sucking a penis, and that's satisfying in some way. That's when I step into the masculine side of my nature, but still, I feel feminine, like I have both energies coursing through me.
>
> (Inanna)

Courageous experimentation loosens rigidity, giving rise to unanticipated intimacy; unsettling that which had once confined their primal strength. In moments where dominance merged with receptivity, a new association with femininity forms. What emerges here is a conscious reentry into the body as a site of wisdom. The wise woman, no longer concealed or softened, surfaced as a figure of unapologetic presence.

> I feel the perverse feminine is old and just doesn't give a fuck. She's wrinkly and sagging, and, like, her vagina is out. I wish I could be more like that; I wish I could embody her, and maybe, after speaking that out loud, I will become more like her. She is free from the bullshit that fills my mind, and I believe we can all get to some version of her if we try enough ... if we face these inner demons and look at them for what they are.
>
> (Lamia)

Participants longed for a life unbound by purity, where one can conjure the PFA as an unashamed living entity. Her presence disrupts the internalized compulsion to conform, where liberation roots in refusal. Acceptance of aging as a source of freedom exemplifies a desire to uproot aversion, which in turn represents an inner battle. Unapologetic, she reconstructs a connection between the sacred and the profane. Creativity unfolds unexpectedly, calling forth the prohibited inner landscape, where generative acts of revolt stir.

> My paintings explore themes of sexuality and emotions because I personally struggle with a lot of shame around expressing those parts of myself. It's weird because it's not just sadness or anger. I have a hard time even feeling happiness. I guess funneling it through my work is a way for me to just shake that shit out of me, ya know?
>
> (Demeter)

Through imaginative dialogue, raw, untamed emotion matured into a catalyst for renewal. Primordial rage, the erotic charge, the protective force that refused to yield. One such figure, evoked across the conversations, carried the nurturing instinct in destruction, collapsing the binary between violence and care. Her story offered a mirror, affirming that ferocity and tenderness coexist in the perverse; ideals of purity or passivity no longer constrained her.

> If you think about the Goddess Kali, she is so scary. She wants to destroy and rip people's heads off as a way to get rid of what doesn't serve. I think she really speaks to this part of transformation that is all about being nurturing through aggressiveness. Feminine isn't just about being pretty and delicate, but it's about this destructive nature too … I think that's what the perverse is all about.
>
> (Demeter)

Calling upon Hindu mythology, Kali materializes as a symbol of defiant power, inspiring unyielding independence and fierce guardianship (Mookerjee, 1988) (see Figure 17.1). Birthed from Durga's brow in the heat of battle, her rage overtakes the field, annihilating demonic threats with primal force. Blood courses beneath her, and the trembling earth bears witness to her unapologetic force. Salacious and ferocious, she is contradiction; ending and beginning, destruction and creation, rupture and rebirth. As an incarnation of the PFA, Kali channels suppressed forces. Invoking her ferocity evokes a bloodlust that consumes the grotesque. Evident in accounts of strategic survival manipulation, her protection grants entry to unmarked territory.

Adaption; a psychic cunning, wields an energetic trance steeped in suspicion and exile. Following the guidance that emanates from the shadows, a strategic and unruly spell discloses profound brilliance.

> I don't know. I've never had this kind of conversation with anyone. I guess I think about perversity when I think about the witch and, like, just pure evil itself, but I

Figure 17.1 *Goddess Kali*

Public domain. Image courtesy of The Metropolitan Museum of Art.

Note:
Lithograph of *Goddess Kali* (The Metropolitan Museum of Art, n.d.-c), circa 1880–1885, was created in Calcutta, West Bengal, acquired by the Robert and Bobbie Falk Philanthropic Fund Gift, 2021.

> I know it's misunderstood. At the same time, I think the concept of manipulation can be wrapped into the perverse feminine, which is always deemed problematic, but sometimes we need to manipulate to survive. I used to manipulate people a lot when I was younger for the wrong reasons, but now I feel like I have more of an understanding of how I can manipulate for good, like when I need to protect my boundaries.
>
> (Guan Yin)

In reclaiming appetite, audacity, and manipulation as innate skills, participants call upon the PFA, coiled in daily negotiations. She does not hover above as muse or myth. She acts with complication, uncompromising instinct, and the tension of the taboo.

THE SHADOW AS A CATALYST FOR TRANSFORMATION

> I think a lot of times in the past, I've been so worried about how I come across, and it's really built up a lot of inner tension, but as I get older, I'm starting to realize that this is just a part of me that needs some sort of release valve so I can just be my authentic self. I want to be able to transcend whatever the hell has held me back.
>
> (Aphrodite)

Today, the PFA appears as a persistent form of gendered marginalization, nested in detrimental tropes of the incoherent and angry woman. While no longer hanged, burned, or mutilated, the torturous rampages of a historically haunted legacy (Sollee, 2017) remain. For instance, in *Jennifer's Body* (Kusama, 2009), the PFA surfaces as a teenage girl sacrificed by a band pursuing fame. When the ritual backfires, she becomes possessed by a demonic force, prompting her to seduce and devour male classmates. Her transformation reflects the succubus archetype, punished for unchecked hunger and erotic power. Beneath the horror lies a revenge myth born of exploitation. Her brutality is a form of redemption in the face of betrayal and violation. In the same year, 2009, actor Megan Fox, who played the protagonist, was similarly demonized off-screen after exposing director Michael Bay for his predatory and dictatorial behavior. Her frankness resulted in public backlash, reputational dismantling, and industry exile, demonstrating how swiftly defiance is reframed as danger when women challenge patriarchal power.

> When I feel scared, I make myself as big and offensive as possible. I don't care how weird I might look; I just want to be left alone, and I'll do whatever it takes to protect myself. I will talk to myself, tweak out, and scream in public. I will carry a knife and fuck up anyone who even tries me. I think in the past I felt awkward trying to defend myself, but with the state of the world, I have to let these parts of myself out.
>
> (Ala)

The growing precarity of everyday life makes visible how systemic danger is rendered ordinary. For many, rage serves as a tool of survival, a prophecy that speaks out relentlessly. Archetypes once vilified, from witches to sirens, evolve into sources of healing, harboring the voltage required to withstand persistent vigilance and threat (Tilley, 2018).

> Bad female characters give me the power and energy to say, "You know what, you can't define me. I can make my own rules." I think about being a witch a lot and invoke her when I want to connect to my power because that is something nobody can take away. That's what I want, and I'm so tired of feeling like I don't deserve to have it.
>
> (Oshun)

Across their narratives, the PFA surged as an initiator of unruly vitality, stirring up buried instincts and sharpened edges rendered suspicious. What once registered as a transgression now signaled a return. In this final cusp, the archetype shed her spectral frame and stepped forward as a guide. Sovereignty took root in refusal: The decision to rework inherited beliefs without surrendering the heat that once burned them.

Chapter **18**

Embodying the Perverse Feminine

> In my journey, I've connected deeply with astrology. The planets and figures give me a structure for understanding energetic blueprints. So, if I feel a specific energy, like beauty and love, I might say that's Venus's energy. It's nice to have a structure for understanding these things that aren't easy to label so we can use them to grow.
>
> (Persephone)

Personalized archetypal images serve as bridges, connecting the vast, subterranean regions of the psyche with an innate reckoning. They surface beneath ancient myths, woven in scripts of popular culture. Each illustration carries residues of collective significance, tying closely to individual fears, longings, and histories (von Franz, 1999). Archetypal encounters illuminate private truths and coax the renounced into dialogue with the waking mind.

From ancient depictions to a contemporary spirit, Lilith remains on her throne, inspiring a journey of self-discovery. In the depths of unlearning and reclaiming, we step into unfamiliar territory, yearning for transformation. Setbacks collide with insights, pulling us into unhealed wounds. Each return intensifies an unraveling, showing how integration is a dance, alive with passion. Although the integration stage marks a culmination of earlier work, we resist calling it an endpoint. Instead, we live in the whirlwind of becoming, where liminality takes us to ritual. We enter a mythic landscape, the unexposed and unfiltered essence of a cracked doorway, inviting connection. If we choose to enter, we meet the Perverse Feminine Archetype (PFA) as our eager guide.

DOI: 10.4324/9781003455837-24

CONTEMPORARY LILITH: POWER IN POP CULTURE

> I'm blown away by the pagan culture, like earth goddesses ... then I look to pop culture and see Dua Lipa, who's, like, filling coliseums tonight. Like, oh my God, her intense sexuality is worshiped, and it makes me want to tune into that for myself.
>
> (Persephone)

Longings for untamed feminine power reveal a hunger for symbolic uncontainment. Resonating with women who move beyond the status quo, the PFA inspires courage. With a contemporary focus on her manifestation through Lilith, we now revive from the shadows (Ruah-Midbar Shapiro, 2019a). Contending with her portrayal demonstrates that redemption requires an active re-narration of the cultural and psychological scripts that have historically shaped the feminine psyche. Lilith oscillates between being demonized and embracing defiant renewal, reflecting the internalized ambivalence that many women experience. She operates as a psychic entry, a figure through whom perversity is power. Her dwelling in the chasms illuminates a possibility of transformation from within the shadow. Through her, the PFA is a deliberate reworking of inherited shame. Constituted as a provocative illuminator, her dual nature tears open doorways for transcendence, unsettling into theology and popular culture (Hurwitz, 1992/2009).

> They always say, "Don't be too loud," and "Be more like a lady," but what if I don't want to be like a lady? What if I want to be like a man? Then what? I say fuck it and just live my life by my terms; I don't care anymore what other people think because I can't win anyway, so why not just let it out? Let out the crazy and the weird parts I've been holding back.
>
> (Kali)

Symbolic of the split between containment and resistance, Lilith masters contradiction. During the resurgence of Goddess worship in the mid-1970s, she arose as a feminist icon, fostering an opportunity to integrate spirituality and activism (Ruether, 2006; Christ & Plaskow, 1992; Stone, 1978). On screen, she often appeared as a complicated, restless figure, fiercely independent and riddled with lascivious vitality. In *Lilith* (Rossen, 1964), Jean Seberg plays a psychiatric patient marked by sexual transgression, suicidal impulses, and violence. Embodying her mythological containment through hysterical renditions, the film concretizes her as a misunderstood madwoman. More recent television revives her origins with a layered directive, depicting her as a she-demon who yearns for connection. In True Blood (Ball, 2008–2014), Lilith claims her rightful place as the first vampire; in Lucifer (Kapinos, 2016–2021), she wrestles with a craving for individuation to enliven her soul. Breaking the traditional adaptation, she shifts from Satan's servant to Eve's lover, a nod to Kabbalistic interpretations. In The Chilling Adventures of Sabrina (Aguirre-Sacasa, 2018–2020), she navigates a tension between traditional roles and autonomy, grappling with the dichotomous roles projected upon her. In each representation, she lives as a nuanced character who follows a transformational path. Whether it be to confront the status quo, name the perverse, or search for resolution, her myth remains a potent symbol, capturing the innate eros for freedom beyond persecution.

EMBODIED INTEGRATION: RECLAIMING POWER THROUGH LILITH

> For so long, I've lived as if my body was the enemy, where there was always something to control, shrink, or be perfect. After a while, I realized that my body's wisdom had always been there, and I had just ignored it. Once I started to really think about all of the ways that I hated myself, I felt so sad. How could I say such judgmental things? From then on, I decided to reconnect with my inner self, and I started to dance again, as I did as a kid. I took all my mirrors down and focused on what it was like to live in my skin.
>
> (Nyx)

The movement from self-surveillance to somatic presence denotes a turning point, where integration draws us into a work of restoration. Returning is more than a single act of rebellion or self-assertion; it requires a continuous search for freedom. Aligned with Lilith's shift in the communal psyche, from she-demon to feminist, women discover severed pieces of themselves. Reclaiming the corporeal as a source of attunement fosters her presence. As a renewed connection with hidden cravings looms, the PFA arises through an internal wrestling. Physical sovereignty invites a form of pleasure marked by the deafening sting of criticism.

> I've had a lot of sexual traumas in my life. I can't remember when the dude I was with would listen to my NO. It's frustrating, and, for a long time, I disconnected from my body because I think I associated it with all of that bad shit. I didn't know how to get off without a guy, but one day, I saw Nicki Minaj perform, and something clicked. I wanted to be like her … she's so connected to her sexuality and free, it seemed. She inspired me to communicate with that aching part of my insides, you know? That's why I started this ritual where I masturbate every morning and make sure to tell myself how much I love myself. I'm a little intimidated and can't use my hands yet, so a toy feels more comfortable for now … but I'll get there, and keep trying to reclaim myself.
>
> (Oya)

Reorienting passion after painful experiences requires a new grammar shaped by choice. Courage to commune with past wounds initiates the possibility of joy; it is a tie in pleasure. Met with a disorienting inner world, a resounding inquisitiveness underlies the sense of detachment.

> I think women have the taboo of sleeping with a partner too soon. I think that's more to men than women, in that if you are a woman sleeping with a man, that if you slept with him on the first date, the second date, or third date … there is this weird gatekeeping of how many dates. My mother instilled in me, and I have a tough time moving out of that mindset, where, you know, I am afraid to get notches on my belt. Still, I want to explore a lot of stuff, so I am slowly taking steps by just putting myself out there on dating apps. I haven't met anyone yet. Still, I have put in my bio that I'm interested in dating a couple; that's a start to awakening and exploring these interests.
>
> (Hera)

Sexual inquisitiveness, once regarded with shame, unveils itself as long-repressed urges constrained by inherited admonishments. Through practices such as dance, art, and nature-based rituals, participants dismantle the flagrant lies cast upon their feelings, cultivating discernment and reestablishing personal boundaries.

> I was never taught healthy boundaries and believed that it was my job to satisfy everyone else … sexually or otherwise, but I think the space where I realized all of this was in the bedroom. I started to realize that if my boyfriend is aroused, it's not all my responsibility to finish that sexual thought for him. It's not my responsibility to bring you to orgasm just because you're in the mood and I'm not. So that's kind of where that started. That, you know, everyone can kinda be their sexual partner and take responsibility for their sexuality on their own.
>
> (Medusa)

By revitalizing their relationship with the physical realm, women shake loose the silencing shame, a quest for vitality. Reconstituting fabricated stories, Lilith lingers in the tender spaces, alive with excitement. Women discover refuge, permitting worn messages to lose their grip. Extending beyond the personal, the ignition feeds a quiet revolution, a collective resurgence

CONNECTION AND UNITY

> Yeah, I think feminine nature is just really open and curious. It's intuitive, sets boundaries. It feels kinda agile and warm, you know? Nurturing, joyful, playful. You know what I mean? It's channeling, in purpose, and support of the community and other women and the collective, and it's doing its work, showing up, and being kind and gentle first and foremost to themselves. Not only are we in full sovereignty over who we are, what we want, and what we're doing, but we are also the creators of our realities.
>
> (Gaia)

As a vessel for reckoning, the archetypal image holds potential. When engaged consciously, she transmits the PFA, calling forth rejected demons and emotional turmoil. Her intoxicating potency requires a delicate yet firm approach. Positioned as a transgressive conduit, she embodies the enduring representation of the perverse, challenging normative boundaries, and animating societal fringes.

> Some people just struggle with others who aren't mainstream, right? And sure, some behaviors are good or bad, but people? I don't think so. Like, take kink—it's considered perverse, but there's this whole community, here in the Bay Area and worldwide, that embraces it. They have this huge knowledge base on bodies, sensations, differences, acceptance, and how to play with it. And I think that's really valuable, though, yeah, not for everyone, but it's definitely for me, and I'm going to live that truth.
>
> (Inanna)

The invigorating potential of authenticity invites a call to an underworld, one we deemed inappropriate. As we enter this unclaimed penitentiary, we engage with the perverse, vibrating with the thrill of defiance. While in her domain, each uncovering manifests as a rejection of distorted legacy. Lifting the veil of indifference, she encourages us to take a stand. Why is she problematic? Why is she inherently flawed? Why does a light shine on the wicked while condemning her essence?

> Let's just say I'm Trump, right … and I'm looking at a perverse group of women, they are the female lawyers fighting for human rights, or they are in the church running a congregation. Those women would be considered perverse, feminine, you know. And it's again, it goes back to this upholding of quote, unquote, certain traditions and then going against that, and even the naked female body goes against that.
>
> (Ixchel)

Beneath provocative reversals, the question of threat arises as a mark of femininity. Shared confidence and deliberation initiate a wealth of discovery of unidentified feelings, beliefs, and long-neglected needs. Inviting language to frame the tender ferocity of lost time, women search for a framework to support their journey. However, unbeknownst to them, they curated the matrix without intervention. Gradually unlocking the doors to authentic expression, interviews indicate the path situated in a symbiotic strength in the unexplored.

> True power is when you understand yourself so well that you unlock all this energy within yourself without taking it from anybody. You did it because you just are. You found little pockets of light. You've done deep research into the shadows to see who you are. And then all that light and the resources you gain from knowing yourself so well make you powerful.
>
> (Kali)

Illuminated by a willful self-discovery, we recognize the extent of indoctrination and subtle performance. Grieving the girl of the past; unwilling to allow energetic will to slip, women form the perverse ethos, where echoes of past, present, and future converge.

PART III

BROADER IMPLICATIONS AND REFLECTIONS

Expanding the PFA Beyond the Personal

Part III concludes the study with two final chapters, serving as touch points into the external. Recommendations for future research alongside critiques of the present study encourage a critical demand for an intersectional approach. Additionally, the researcher provides a brief reflection of her journey with the four stages of the framework.

DOI: 10.4324/9781003455837-25

Chapter 19

Beyond the Framework

Future Directions for the PFA

TOWARD A LIVING ARCHETYPAL FUTURE

Materializing as a response to the persistence of internalized sexism, the Perverse Feminine Archetype (PFA) yields an opportunity to investigate uncharted territory. Catalyzing myth as a method, an archetypal representation of her force extends throughout stories of exile. Seeking a resurgence of repressed memories, Lilith enters here. As she evolved in this study, her historical context provided a dynamic force that shaped the structure and rhythm of the research itself. Magnifying the connectivity between personal longing and collective condemnation, she serves as a tool that functions as a disruptor and container for the contradictions and chaos inherent in humanity. She reanimates the rejected and leans into rage.

Findings illuminate how she fosters duplicitous comprehension of oppressive institutions through a mythological arc. Illuminated as a bridge to intergenerational trauma, participants expand upon her influence through shared transgression. Cycles of self-surveillance and moral rigidity require emancipation. Repressive practices choreographed shame, obedience, and gendered discipline. Participant narratives intertwined with emotional containment and persistent internal wounding. These patterns resonate with established frameworks of developmental trauma (Fanon, 1961/1965; Gilligan, 1982; Yehuda & Lehrner, 2018), underscoring the need for clinical models that conceptualize psychic suffering as both historically embedded and symbolically charged.

Contextually, what arises in a psychocultural blueprint is a map of sacrificial entanglement. By placing the PFA within both therapeutic and societal matrices, the research demonstrates how internalized sexism is absorbed. Feminist theories, while intersecting, remain irreducibly distinct. Each illustrates how structures of race, gender, and culture shape development, emotional labor, and modes

DOI: 10.4324/9781003455837-26

of self-regulation under patriarchal pressure. Contributing to a theoretical undertaking, working with the PFA invites a reimagining of method, application, and reach. What begins as symbolic disruption must now extend into interdisciplinary domains.

LIMITATIONS AND EXPANSIONS

Intersectional Viability

Although Chapter 3 briefly introduced study limitations, the most pressing remains the lack of intersectional representation. Race, disability, queerness, and gender variance received insufficient attention, resulting in a limited understanding of how internalized oppression operates across diverse positionalities. With demographic narrowness, the research risks reducing the PFA to a reflection of normative psychic structures, rather than a dynamic, culturally contingent phenomenon.

For instance, Black and Indigenous women, queer and trans individuals, and disabled people navigate internalized oppression in ways that reflect both embodied difference and historical trauma. Touch may be perceived as surveillance, harm, or dissociation, while shame can produce hypervisibility or forced silence. Medical systems, family scripts, and cultural narratives encode acceptable desires. Mainstream feminist frameworks frequently universalize experiences of white, cisgender, heterosexual women while ignoring how systemic forces shape divergent realities (Crenshaw, 1989; Collins, 2000). This erasure constrains the symbolic elasticity of archetypes like the PFA, as she remains shrouded in racism. Viewed through Indigenous cosmologies, Black feminist thought, queer temporalities, or disability justice frameworks, we respond to complex lived realities, trauma-informed and culturally grounded approaches must inform all aspects of inquiry, from participant recruitment to interpretive analysis (Chavez-Dueñas et al., 2019).

Reparative scholarship requires a methodological realignment. Beyond extractive paradigms, depth psychological research must embrace co-theorization with participants. Attending to relational power, symbolic inheritance, and the historical legacies offers a pathway forward. Foregrounding epistemologies rooted in communal memory, ritual, and lived resistance can help recover historically neglected voices.

Clinical Imperatives

In conjunction with cognitive-behavioral and narrative therapies, the PFA offers a path to address fragmented identity without pathologization. Infusing trauma-informed practice with metaphor and cultural critique supports narrative repair and meaning-making (Courtois & Ford, 2013; Herman, 1992). Rather than limiting symbolic work to psychoanalysis, this model draws from participatory Jungian thinking to animate depth-oriented insights, while integrating feminist and multicultural nuances grounded in lived experience (Brown, 2008; Moodley & Palmer, 2006). For example, a client navigating religious purity shame might encounter a recurring image of a locked door, signifying repression and choice. In therapeutic discussion, her vivid imagery might invite an investigation into the inner world.

Interdisciplinary Suggestions

Mixed-methods designs can bridge the symbolic and measurable with a nuanced design to balance qualitative richness with psychometric clarity. Existing tools, such as the Internalized Misogyny Scale (Szymanski et al., 2010) and the Ambivalent Sexism Inventory (Glick & Fiske, 1996), offer potential when combined with archetypal multiplicity. Additionally, future studies may draw from neuroscience, anthropology, and developmental psychology to understand how archetypal forces shape lived experience across systems (Jung, 1907–09/1969b; Eisenberger & Lieberman, 2004; Kirmayer, 2006). Results call for longitudinal approaches that can illuminate how psychic injuries are transmitted, interrupted, or transformed within kinship lines and cultural codes (Yehuda & Lehrner, 2018). To engage with investigative integrity, researchers must craft methods that are not only rigorous but also respectful: Approaches grounded in consent, cultural sensitivity, and symbolic attunement (Bloom, 1999). Only then can we trace how the archetypal lives as felt inheritance, possible repair.

CROSS-CULTURAL REPRESENTATIONS

Interrogating internalized sexism through an archetypal lens requires attention to how cultural context informs and conditions mythic representations of feminine power. While Lilith serves as the focal figure, her origins in Jewish and Eurocentric traditions constrain the interpretive reach of the PFA across multivalent cultural contexts (Hurwitz, 1992; Patai, 1990). African diasporic cosmologies, Latin American folklore, and ancient Egyptian theology provide expressions of the PFA across distinct cultural landscapes. La Llorona, Iansã, and Sekhmet render the aberration newly observable, forged in different symbolic and historical flames.

La Llorona

La Llorona (the Weeping Woman) haunts the liminal space between maternal grief and feminine rage, suspended in a cycle of unrelenting mourning. Her legend, rooted in Mexican and Latin American oral traditions, tells of a mother who, in a moment of despair or retaliation, drowns her children and is thereafter condemned to wander the earth in search of them (Perez, 2008). She represents a fragment of the dismembered feminine psyche, one unable to integrate loss. Condemned to endless spiritual recursion. Her cries reverberate across the boundary between living and dead, signaling the danger in disavowed sorrow. As a spectral manifestation of psychic exile, her rage exists in a state of immobilization. Frozen, unassimilated, unredeemed. Her myth articulates the cost of pain that is neither metabolized nor witnessed: A sorrow turned inward, reconstituted as psychic paralysis. She evokes the potency of the maternal shadow: The ambivalence of nurturing, the corrosive effects of invisibility, and the guilt that calcifies in the absence of resolution (see Figure 19.1).

Iansã

A storm deity and warrior spirit, Iansã (also known as Oya in Yorùbá cosmology) initiates chaos in the uncontrollable. Her winds summon disruption, unsettling

Figure 19.1 *La Llorona Árbol Tallado*

Photo by Gabriel Pérez Salazar (2017).

Note:
A haunting tree carving depicting La Llorona (Salazar, 2017), with a face contorted in grief above three skeletal children.

the bound and buried. Unlike static or mournful representations of feminine pain, Iansã refuses to be contained; she confronts repression. Her association with the dead positions her at the threshold between life and dissolution, where disillusionment occurs. She acts as a symbolic agent of psychic reordering, storming the ego's defenses to initiate individuation from within the collective wound. Her relevance across diasporic traditions speaks to her durability as an active, evolving force (Murphy,1995) (see Figure 19.2). The transatlantic movement of her worship, carried under duress, holds the pain of her African diaspora. She is righteous rage; a reparation from a lineage destroyed by coloniality.

Sekhmet

Transmitted by Ra to punish human transgression, Sekhmet unleashes catastrophic violence (Wilkerson, 1991). Bloodlust overwhelms her, and only through deception is her rampage halted. Intoxicated and disoriented, she collapses. No longer

Figure 19.2 *Iansã (Oya)*

Photo by Eurico Zimbres (2006).

Note:
Depictions of Oya from ancient times are rare, as her story is carried through oral traditions. However, this metal sculpture of a faceless, armored figure represents her form as an Afro-Brazilian Orisha. The sculpture is in Parque da Catacumba, Rio de Janeiro, Brazil, and was created by artist Tatti Moreno.

Figure 19.3 *Statue of the Goddess Sakhmet*

Public Domain Dedication.

Note:
A granodiorite sculpture of Sekhmet (contemporarily transliterated) (The Metropolitan Museum of Art, n.d.-b), the lion-headed goddess associated with both destruction and healing in ancient Egyptian mythology. The artifact is part of the collection at The Metropolitan Museum of Art.

a weapon but a force disarmed. Her power turns inward, germinating the roots of restoration. What was once devastation transmutes into discernment. Violence, once indiscriminate, targets the false harmony of illusions built on suppression. The myth memorializes a tension between unbridled fury and ritualized transformation (Figure 19.3).

The PFA materializes in unprocessed grief, culturally pathologized rage, and forms of power that refuse assimilation. She disrupts normative narratives of healing, clarifying what culture disavows. Her presence provokes a confrontation with internalized structures of sexism as an intimate, embodied undoing. Through her, the unspoken unearths form. As a catalyst, she marks an entry point into deeper analysis. Research itself becomes an act of confrontation, where shadow materializes and meaning destabilizes.

Chapter **20**

Reflections on the Perverse

A Researcher's Journey

Note: Although the following accurately depicts my internal world, some details have been condensed or sensationalized for the sake of brevity and evocative storytelling.

SOCIETAL INDOCTRINATION

My earliest memories stitch together, reminiscent of the chaffing sequins of a beauty pageant dress. Even now, I feel my toes crushed into too-small tap shoes, hairspray biting my scalp, and my grin pinned in place while strangers decide if I was enough. I swallowed every story that promised love was the ultimate prize. I dreamt of a man who came along and resolved the dark ache inside of me. I measured my worth against airbrushed portraits of fantasy women. My desire shaped expectations, where a perfect life would arrive in the form of a gallant white knight. The depression and self-destructive behavior? They would fade the moment he arrived. I adapted to a world that conditioned me to measure my value by celebrity magazines, serving as sacred texts. I zeroed in on glossy visions of what a woman ought to be, absorbing the silent command to bend myself. I became fluent in subtle weather shifts, reading danger in every corner. I wore martyrdom like a second skin, offering up my quiet as proof of devotion. I thought endurance meant love, that yielding would keep me safe.

SHAPESHIFTING

At 23, I had finally accomplished my dreams. Or so I thought. A career in Hollywood. A man by my side. Within a year of marriage, however, I would

DOI: 10.4324/9781003455837-27

experience his domineering disposition. The first time he broke me, it wasn't with force; it was the way he carved up my reality. Betrayal alone should have left scars, but his words dug deeper, recasting my pain as proof of my instability. "You're too sensitive. Overreacting. You need help." I splintered under his words, and he watched me come undone. Everything I'd built for approval thinned out under scrutiny, exposing itself as a fragile illusion. No matter how many angles I carved into myself, something skittered beneath it, a low murmur of hunger. Each new shape felt like a gentle assassination of a self I couldn't fully touch. My desire for freedom and my penchant for pain. Who was I? I yearned to know, but I feared the truth. What if I could never find myself again?

AWARENESS

A longing for redemption lingered in my soul. Curiosity poured out of me. I could no longer dampen the questions of who I might become. I could no longer shove my pain into the dark. I had to awaken that monster inside of me: my perversions. I questioned whether it was possible to integrate condemned versions of myself. I wondered if I was lovable. If not by a lover, could I make it alone? A shift in direction arose with clamped hands around my neck. I was done. I was ready to find myself. Discovering the archetypal, the mythic, the rebellious, the fringe became my lifeline. I unfolded the piece of me entangled in the webs of despair and crawled my way back into myself. With desperation, I fought for confrontation, listening to the visceral agony that permeated through my gut.

REDEFINING THE FEMININE

Stumbling upon *Women Who Run with Wolves* (Estés, 1992) served as an initiation. Like an inheritance passed down through blood and bone, her writing permitted an innate sense of wildness and longing, paths back to the rejected. In those pages, I collided with a villainous figure, a wild woman. My desire for unbound creativity transformed into practical manifestations in this reclaimed space, where uncertain risks marked discovery. What existed before conditioning? Where was the girl who once lived in fields of color, who viewed the world with her kaleidoscope eyes? Before the beauty pageants and the obsession with appearance, there had been a time when I could embrace the beauty around me, right? Although I fail to recollect, I feel trapped in an aching call. I want to get back to that place. How? How could I live in truth with my emotional world? Upon reflection, the PFA emerged in those moments as a call. I followed her to San Francisco, where I would enroll at the California Institute of Integral Studies. From there, I discovered my role in the research integration process. My reintegration, my redefinition, is here, with the archetypal and mythological, reminding me of who I am.

References

Aguirre-Sacasa, R. (Developer). (2018–2020). *Chilling adventures of Sabrina* [TV series]. Warner Bros. Netflix. https://www.imdb.com/title/tt7569592/?ref_=nv_sr_srsg_0

Aiwok. (2011). *Burney Relief* [Photograph of terracotta plaque]. British Museum. Licensed under CC BY-SA 3.0. https://commons.wikimedia.org/wiki/File:Burney_Relief_Babylon_-1800-1750.JPG

Akbar, N. (1996). *Breaking the chains of psychological slavery*. Mind Productions & Associates.

Albert, P. R. (2015). Why is depression more prevalent in women? *Journal of Psychiatry & Neuroscience, 40*(4), 219–221. https://doi.org/10.1503/jpn.150205

Alexander, P. S. (1983). The Targum of Canticles: Translated with a critical introduction, apparatus, and notes. The Aramaic Bible, Vol. 17A.

American Psychiatric Association. (2013). Diagnostic and statistical manual of mental disorders (5th ed.). American Psychiatric Publishing.

American Psychiatric Association. (2022). *Diagnostic and statistical manual of mental disorders, text revision (DSM-5-TR)* (5th ed.). American Psychiatric Association.

Anderson, R. (1998). Intuitive inquiry: A transpersonal approach. In W. Braud & R. Anderson (Eds.), *Transpersonal research methods for the social sciences: Honoring human experience* (pp. 69–94). Sage Publications.

Anderson, R. (2000). Intuitive inquiry: Interpreting objective and subjective data. *ReVision: Journal of Consciousness and Transformation, 22*(4), 31–39.

Anderson, R. (2004). Intuitive inquiry: An epistemology of the heart for scientific inquiry. *The Humanistic Psychologist, 32*(4), 307–341. https://doi.org/10.1080/08873267.2004.9961758

Anderson, R. (2011). Intuitive inquiry: Exploring the mirroring discourse of disease. In F. J. Wertz, K. Charmaz, L. M. McMullen, R. Josselson, R. Anderson, & E. McSpadden (Eds.), *Five ways of doing qualitative analysis: Phenomenological psychology, grounded theory, discourse analysis, narrative research, and intuitive inquiry* (pp. 243–278). Guilford Press.

Anderson, R. (2019). Intuitive inquiry: Inviting transformation and breakthrough insights in qualitative research. *Qualitative Psychology*, *6*(3), 312–319. https://doi.org/10.1037/qup0000144

Anderson, R., & Braud, W. (2011). *Transforming self and others through research: Transpersonal research methods and skills for the human sciences and humanities*. State University of New York Press.

Ando, H., Cousins, R., & Young, C. (2014). Achieving saturation in thematic analysis: Development and refinement of a codebook. *Comprehensive Psychology*, *3*. https://doi.org/10.2466/03.cp.3.4

Anzaldúa, G. (1999). *Borderlands/La frontera: The new mestiza* (2nd ed.). Aunt Lute Books.

Appignanesi, L. (2008). *Mad, bad, and sad: A history of women and the mind doctors*. W. W. Norton & Company.

Aratani, L. (2023, August 14). Girl, 13, gives birth after she was raped and denied abortion in Mississippi. *The Guardian*. https://www.theguardian.com/us-news/2023/feb/10/us-south-girls-raped-forced-birth-abortion-roe-restrictions

Aslam, U., & Mehboob, S. (2023). Misuse of Ozempic as a drug choice for weight loss, a potential threat. *International Journal of Scientific Reports*. https://doi.org/10.18203/issn.2454-2156.intjscirep20233563

Bailey, A. (2010). On intersectionality and the whiteness of feminist philosophy. In G. Yancy (Ed.), *The center must not hold: White women philosophers on the whiteness of philosophy* (pp. 51–75). Lexington Books.

Baldissarri, C., Andrighetto, L., Gabbiadini, A., Valtorta, R. R., Sacino, A., & Volpato, C. (2019, August 8). Do self-objectified women believe themselves to be free? Sexual objectification and belief in personal free will. *Frontiers in Psychology*, *10*, Article 1867. https://doi.org/10.3389/fpsyg.2019.01867

Ball, A. (Creator). (2008–2014). *True blood* [TV series]. Your Face Goes Here Entertainment; HBO. https://www.imdb.com/title/tt0844441/?ref_=fn_al_tt_1

Bandura, A. (1977). Self-efficacy: Toward a unifying theory of behavioral change. *Psychological Review*, *84*(2), 191–215.

Bohak, G. (2008). Ancient Jewish magic: A history. Cambridge University Press

Bardo, S. (2003). *Unbearable weight: Feminism, Western culture, and the body* (10th anniversary ed.). University of California Press.

Barreto, M., Ryan, M. K., & Schmitt, M. T. (Eds.). (2009). *The glass ceiling in the 21st century: Understanding barriers to gender equality*. American Psychological Association. https://doi.org/10.1037/11863-000

Barstow, A. L. (1994). *Witchcraze: A new history of the European witch hunts*. HarperCollins.

Beck, A. T., & Haigh, E. A. P. (2014). Advances in cognitive theory and therapy: The generic cognitive model. *Annual Review of Clinical Psychology*, *10*, 1–24.

Becker, D. (1997). *Through the looking glass: Women and borderline personality disorder*. Westview Press.

Best, S. (2003). *A beginner's guide to social theory*. Sage Publications.

Benard, E., & Moon, B. (Eds.). (2000). *Goddesses who rule*. Oxford University Press.

Berger, P. L., & Luckmann, T. (1966). *The social construction of reality: A treatise in the sociology of knowledge*. Anchor Books.

Black, J., Cunningham, G., Robson, E., & Zólyomi, G. (Eds.). (2006). *The literature of ancient Sumer*. Oxford University Press.

Bloom, S. L. (1999). Trauma theory: Abbreviated. In B. L. Levin, A. K. Blanch, & A. Jennings (Eds.), *Women's mental health services: A public health perspective* (pp. 29–50). Sage Publications.

Bly, N. (1887). *Ten days in a mad-house*. Norman L. Munro. https://digital.library.upenn.edu/women/bly/madhouse/madhouse.html

Bowlby, J. (1982). *Attachment and loss: Volume 1: Attachment* (2nd ed.). Basic Books.

Braun, V., & Clarke, V. (2006). Using thematic analysis in psychology. *Qualitative Research in Psychology*, *3*(2), 77–101. https://doi.org/10.1191/1478088706qp063oa

Braun, V., & Clarke, V. (2013). *Successful qualitative research: A practical guide for beginners*. Sage Publications.

Briggs, R. (1996). *Witches and neighbors: The social and cultural context of European witchcraft*. Viking.

Brown, L. S. (2008). Cultural competence in trauma therapy: Beyond the flashback. American Psychological Association.

Burkert, W. (1985). *Greek religion: Archaic and classical* (J. Raffan, Trans.). Blackwell.

Burn, S. M., Aboud, R., & Moyles, C. (2000). The relationship between gender social identity and support for feminism. Sex Roles: A Journal of Research, *42*(11–12), 1081–1089.

Butler, J. (1990). *Gender trouble: Feminism and the subversion of identity*. Routledge.

Butler, J. (1997). *The psychic life of power: Theories in subjection*. Stanford University Press.

Boyarin, D. (1993). Carnal Israel: Reading sex in Talmudic culture. University of California Press.

California Welfare and Institutions Code § 5150 (2024).

Carter, A. (1979). *The bloody chamber and other stories*. Gollancz.

Cary, A. (2022, June 29). Barbiecore is everywhere this summer. *Vogue*. https://www.vogue.com/article/barbie-fashion-is-everywhere-this-summer

Caso, D., Schettino, G., Fabbricatore, R., & Conner, M. (2020). "Change my selfie": Relationships between self-objectification and selfie-behavior in young Italian women. *Journal of Applied Social Psychology*, *50*(9), 538–549. https://doi.org/10.1111/jasp.12693

Centers for Disease Control and Prevention. (2023). Intimate partner violence-related homicides—National Violent Death Reporting System, 48 states, the District of Columbia, and Puerto Rico, 2020–2021. *Morbidity and Mortality Weekly Report*, 73(34), 889–896. https://www.cdc.gov/mmwr/volumes/73/wr/mm7334a4.htm

Chávez-Dueñas, G. N., Adames, H. Y., Perez-Chavez, J. G., & Salas, S. P. (2019). Healing ethno-racial trauma in Latinx immigrant communities: Cultivating hope, resistance, and action. American Psychologist, 74(1), 49–62. https://doi.org/10.1037/amp0000289

Chemaly, S. (2018). *Rage becomes her: The power of women's anger*. Atria Books.

Chesler, P. (1972). Women and madness. Doubleday.

Chodorow, N. J. (1978). *The reproduction of mothering: Psychoanalysis and the sociology of gender*. University of California Press.

Chrisler, J. C., & Caplan, P. (2002). The strange case of Dr. Jekyll and Ms. Hyde: How PMS became a cultural phenomenon and a psychiatric disorder. *Annual Review of Sex Research, 13*(1), 274–306.

Christ, C. P. (1979). Why women need the goddess: Phenomenological, psychological, and political reflections. *Signs: Journal of Women in Culture and Society, 4*(4), 693–710.

Christ, C. P., & Plaskow, J. (Eds.). (1992). *Womanspirit rising: A feminist reader in religion*. HarperOne.

Cixous, H. (1976). The laugh of Medusa. *Signs: Journal of Women in Culture and Society, 1*(4), 875–893. http://www.jstor.org/stable/3173239

Clance, P. R., & Imes, S. A. (1978). The imposter phenomenon in high-achieving women: Dynamics and therapeutic intervention. *Psychotherapy: Theory, Research & Practice, 15*(3), 241–247. https://doi.org/10.1037/h0086006

Clandinin, D. J., & Connelly, F. M. (2000). *Narrative inquiry: Experience and story in qualitative research*. Jossey-Bass.

Clay, J. S. (1984). The Hecate of the theogony. *Greek, Roman, and Byzantine Studies, 25*(1), 27–38.

Clayton, W., & Humphreys, G. (2017). "Keep it to yourself": Shame and female masturbation in American independent cinema. *Sexualities, 22*(1–2), 244–261. https://doi.org/10.1177/1363460717731930

Collier, J. (1887). *Lilith* [Oil on canvas]. Wikimedia Commons. Public Domain. https://commons.wikimedia.org/wiki/File:Lilith_(John_Collier_painting).jpg

Collins, B. G. (1993). Reconstruing codependency using self-in-relation theory: A feminist perspective. *Social Work, 38*(4), 470–476. https://www.jstor.org/stable/pdf/23716975.pdf

Collins, J. J. (1997). *Jewish wisdom in the Hellenistic age*. Westminster John Knox Press.

Collins, P. H. (2000). *Black feminist thought: Knowledge, consciousness, and the politics of empowerment* (2nd ed.). Routledge.

Common English Bible (CEB). (2011). *The Holy Bible, Common English Bible*. Bible Gateway. https://www.biblegateway.com

Connell, R. W. (1987). *Gender and power: Society, the person, and sexual politics*. Stanford University Press.

Courtois, C. A., & Ford, J. D. (Eds.). (2013). Treatment of complex trauma: A sequenced, relationship-based approach. Guilford Press.

Cox, K. (1891). *Lilith* [Collotype]. Public domain (US). The Miriam and Ira D. Wallach Division of Art, Prints and Photographs: Picture Collection, The New York Public Library. https://digitalcollections.nypl.org/items/d91313d0-c5bd-012f-3419-58d385a7bc34

Crawford, K. (2021). *Atlas of AI: Power, politics, and the planetary costs of artificial intelligence*. Yale University Press.

Crawford, M., & Unger, R. (2003). *Women and gender: A feminist psychology* (4th ed.). McGraw-Hill Humanities/Social Sciences/Languages.

Creed, B. (1993). *The monstrous-feminine: Film, feminism, psychoanalysis*. Routledge.

Crenshaw, K. (1989). Demarginalizing the intersection of race and sex: A Black feminist critique of antidiscrimination doctrine, feminist theory and antiracist politics. *University of Chicago Legal Forum, 1989*(1), 139–167.

Crenshaw, K. (1991). Mapping the margins: Intersectionality, identity politics, and violence against women of color. *Stanford Law Review*, *43*(6), 1241–1299.

Creswell, J. W., & Poth, C. N. (2017). *Qualitative inquiry and research design: Choosing among five approaches* (4th ed.). Sage Publications.

Crews, F. (1995). *The memory wars: Freud's legacy in dispute*. New York Review of Books.

Dalmia, V. (2000). Loving paradoxes: A feminist reclamation of the goddess Kali. Hypatia, 15(3), 125–150. https://doi.org/10.1111/j.1527-2001.2000.tb00330.x

Dan, J. (1980). Samael, Lilith, and the concept of evil in early Kabbalah. *AJS Review*, *5*, 17–40.

Dan, J. (1998). The Hebrew story in the Alphabet of Ben Sira. Jerusalem: Israel Academy of Sciences and Humanities.

Dan, J. (2006). *Kabbalah: A very short introduction*. Oxford University Press.

David, E. J. R. (Ed.). (2013). *Internalized oppression: The psychology of marginalized groups*. Springer.

Davis, A. (1981). *Women, race, & class*. Random House.

de Beauvoir, S. (2010). *The second sex* (C. Borde & S. Malovany-Chevallier, Trans.). Vintage Books.

de Beauvoir, S. (2018). *The independent woman: Extracts from the second sex* (C. Borde & S. Malovany-Chevallier, Trans.). Vintage Books.

Dijkstra, B. (1988). *Idols of perversity: Fantasies of feminine evil in fin-de-siècle culture*. Oxford University Press.

Dijkstra, B. (1996). *Evil sisters: The threat of female sexuality and the cult of manhood*. Knopf.

Dilthey, W. (1989). Introduction to the human sciences (R. J. Betanzos, Trans.). Wayne State University Press.

Disney, W. (Producer), & Hand, D. (Director). (1937). Snow White and the seven dwarfs [Film]. Walt Disney Productions.

Doane, M. A. (1991). *Femmes fatales: Feminism, film theory, psychoanalysis*. Routledge.

Drob, S. L. (2000). *Kabbalistic metaphors: Jewish mystical themes in ancient and modern thought*. Ars Aequi Libri.

Dürer, A. (1497). *The four witches (Four Naked Women)* [Engraving]. Cleveland Museum of Art. Public Domain. Wikimedia Commons. Retrieved March 5, 2025, from https://commons.wikimedia.org/wiki/File:Albrecht_Dürer_-The_Four_Witches(Four_Naked_Women)_-1964.22-_Cleveland_Museum_of_Art.tif

Dutton, D. G. (2007). *The abusive personality: Violence and control in intimate relationships* (2nd ed.). Guilford Press.

Ehrenreich, B., & English, D. (1973). *Witches, midwives, and nurses: A history of women healers*. Feminist Press.

Eisenberger, N. I., & Lieberman, M. D. (2004). Why rejection hurts: A common neural alarm system for physical and social pain. *Trends in Cognitive Sciences*, *8*(7), 294–300. https://www.cell.com/trends/cognitive-sciences/abstract/S1364-6613(04)00143-3

Eisenstein, J. D., Mendelsohn, S., & Dembitz, L. N. (2011). *Critical review of the legal articles of the Jewish encyclopedia* (Vol. 1). Nabu Press.

Eisler, R. (1987). *The chalice and the blade: Our history, our future*. Harper & Row.

El-Hai, J. (2005). *The lobotomist: A maverick medical genius and his tragic quest to rid the world of mental illness*. Wiley.

Estés, C. P. (1992). *Women who run with the wolves: Myths and stories of the wild woman archetype*. Ballantine Books.

Evans, J., Heron, J., Lewis, G., Araya, R., & Wolke, D. (2005). Negative self-schemas and the onset of depression in women: Longitudinal study. *The British Journal of Psychiatry*, *186*(4), 302–307. https://doi.org/10.1192/bjp.186.4.302

Fanon, F. (1965). *The wretched of the earth* (Constance Farrington, Trans.). Grove Press. (Original work published 1961)

Fanon, F. (1967). Black skin, white masks (Charles Lam Markmann, Trans.). Grove Press.

Federici, S. (2004). *Caliban and the witch: Women, the body, and primitive accumulation*. Autonomedia.

Fink, B. (1999). *A clinical introduction to Lacanian psychoanalysis: Theory and technique*. Harvard University Press.

Fonrobert, C. E. (2000). Menstrual purity: Rabbinic and Christian reconstructions of biblical gender. Stanford University Press.

Foucault, M. (1977). *Discipline and punish: The birth of the prison* (A. Sheridan, Trans.). Pantheon Books.

Foucault, M. (2003). *Society must be defended: Lectures at the Collège de France, 1975–1976* (D. Macey, Trans.). Picador.

Foucault, M. (2004). The history of sexuality: Volume 1: The will to knowledge (R. Hurley, Trans.). Penguin Books. (Original work published 1976).

Frederick, S. (2015). Disarticulating Lilith: Notions of God's evil in Jewish folklore. In I. Moulton (Ed.), *Eroticism in the Middle Ages and the Renaissance: Magic, marriage, and midwifery* (pp. 59–78). Brepols.

Fredrickson, B. L., & Roberts, T. A. (1997). Objectification theory: Toward understanding women's lived experiences and mental health risks. *Psychology of Women Quarterly*, *21*(2), 173–206.

Freud, S. (2000). *Three essays on the theory of sexuality* (J. Strachey, Trans.). Basic Books. (Original work published 1905)

Freud, S. (2018). *A general introduction to psychoanalysis: A history of psychoanalytic theory, treatment and therapy* (S. G. Hall, Trans.). Lulu.com. (Original work produced 1915–1917)

Fromm, E. (1970). *The crisis of psychoanalysis: Essays on Freud, Marx, and social psychology*. Holt, Rinehart and Winston.

Fuentes, L. (2023, January 31). *Inequity in US abortion rights and access: The end of Roe is deepening existing divides*. Guttmacher Institute. https://www.guttmacher.org/2023/01/inequity-us-abortion-rights-and-access-end-roe-deepening-existing-divides

Gay, P. (2006). *Freud: A life for our time*. W. W. Norton & Company.

George, D. (1992). *Mysteries of the dark moon: The healing power of the dark goddess*. HarperCollins.

George, T. (2020, December 9). Hermeneutics. In E. N. Zalta (Ed.), *The Stanford encyclopedia of philosophy* (Winter 2020 ed.). Stanford University Press. https://plato.stanford.edu/cgi-bin/encyclopedia/archinfo.cgi?entry=hermeneutics&archive=win2020

Gergen, K. J. (1985). The social constructionist movement in modern psychology. *American Psychologist*, *40*(3), 266–275.

Gerwig, G. (Director). (2019). *Little women* [Film]. Columbia Pictures.

Gilbert, S. M., & Gubar, S. (1979). *The madwoman in the attic: The woman writer and the nineteenth-century literary imagination*. Yale University Press.

Gilligan, C. (1982). *In a different voice: Psychological theory and women's development*. Harvard University Press.

Ginzberg, L. (2022). *The legends of the Jews* (4 vols.). DigiCat.

Glaser, B. G., & Strauss, A. L. (1999). *The discovery of grounded theory: Strategies for qualitative research*. Routledge. (Original work published 1967)

Glick, P., & Fiske, S. T. (1996). The ambivalent sexism inventory: Differentiating hostile and benevolent sexism. *Journal of Personality and Social Psychology*, *70*(3), 491–512. https://doi.org/10.1037/0022-3514.70.3.491

Goldenberg, N. R. (1993). *Resurrecting the body: Feminism, religion, and psychoanalysis*. Crossroad Publishing Company.

Green, M. H. (2001). *The Trotula: A medieval compendium of women's medicine*. University of Pennsylvania Press.

Green, M. H. (2008). *Making women's medicine masculine: The rise of male authority in pre-modern gynaecology*. Oxford University Press.

Grosz, E. (1994). *Volatile bodies: Toward a corporeal feminism*. Indiana University Press.

Guba, E. G., & Lincoln, Y. S. (1989). *Fourth generation evaluation*. Sage Publications.

Guest, G., Namey, E., & Chen, M. (2020). A simple method to assess and report thematic saturation in qualitative research. *PLoS One*, *15*(5), Article e0232076. https://doi.org/10.1371/journal.pone.0232076

Gustafson, F. (Ed.). (2003). *The moonlit path: Reflections on the dark feminine*. Nicolas-Hays.

Hand, D. (Director). (1937). *Snow White and the seven dwarfs* [Film]. Walt Disney. https://www.imdb.com/title/tt0029583/?ref_=nv_sr_srsg_0

Haraway, D. J. (1991). *Simians, cyborgs and women: The reinvention of nature*. Free Association Books.

Harris, M., & Harris, B. (2015). *Into the heart of the feminine: Facing the Death Mother archetype to reclaim love, strength, and vitality*. Daphne.

Hauptman, J. (1998). Rereading the rabbis: A woman's voice. Westview Press.

Heelan, P. A. (1998). The scope of hermeneutics in natural science. *Studies in History and Philosophy of Science Part A*, *29*(2), 273–298. https://doi.org/10.1016/s0039-3681(98)00002-8

Heidegger, M. (1962). *Being and time* (J. Macquarrie & E. Robinson, Trans.). Harper & Row. (Original work published 1927)

Hennink, M. M., Kaiser, B. N., & Marconi, V. C. (2016). Code saturation versus meaning saturation: How many interviews are enough? *Qualitative Health Research*, *27*(4), 591–608. https://doi.org/10.1177/1049732316665344

Herman, J. L. (1992). *Trauma and recovery: The aftermath of violence—from domestic abuse to political terror*. Basic Books.

Hesiod. (1914). *Theogony* (H. G. Evelyn-White, Trans.). Harvard University Press. (Original work published circa 700 BCE)

Hill, C., & Silva, E. (2005). *Drawing the line: Sexual harassment on campus*. American Association of University Women Educational Foundation. https://www.aauw.org/app/uploads/2020/02/AAUW-Drawing-the-line.pdf

Hillman, J. (1975). *Re-visioning psychology*. Harper & Row.

Hillman, J. (1979). *The dream and the underworld*. Harper & Row.

Hillman, J. (1989). *A blue fire: Selected writings by James Hillman* (T. Moore, Ed.). Harper & Row.

Hillman, J. (1999). *The force of character: And the lasting life*. Random House.

Hoffmann, D. E., & Tarzian, A. J. (2001). The girl who cried pain: A bias against women in the treatment of pain. *The Journal of Law, Medicine & Ethics: A Journal of the American Society of Law, Medicine & Ethics*, *29*(1), 13–27. https://pubmed.ncbi.nlm.nih.gov/11521267/

hooks, b. (2014). *Feminism is for everybody: Passionate politics* (2nd ed.). Routledge.

Hurwitz, S. (2009). *Lilith, the first Eve: Historical and psychological aspects of the dark feminine* (3rd Rev. ed.). Daimon Verlag. (Original work published 1992)

Irigaray, L. (1985). *This sex which is not one* (C. Porter & C. Burke, Trans.). Cornell University Press.

Isaac ben Jacob ha-Cohen. (1986). Treatise on the left emanation. In J. Dan (Ed.), *The early Kabbalah* (R. C. Kiener, Trans., pp. 165–182). Paulist Press.

Jacobi, J. (1968). *The psychology of C. G. Jung: An introduction with illustrations*. Yale University Press. (Original work published 1942)

Jaggar, A. M. (Ed.). (1989). *Gender/body/knowledge: Feminist reconstructions of being and knowing*. Rutgers University Press.

Jenkins, P. (Director). (2017). *Wonder woman*. [Film]. Warner Bros. https://www.imdb.com/title/tt0451279/?ref_=fn_al_tt_1

Jewish Publication Society. (Ed.). (1985). *JPS TANAKH: The Holy Scriptures: The new JPS translation according to the traditional Hebrew text* (White Leatherette). Jewish Publication Society.

Johnson, N. B. (1991). Primordial image and the archetypal design of art. *Journal of Analytical Psychology*, *36*(3), 371–392. https://doi.org/10.1111/j.1465-5922.1991.00371.x

Johnson, R. A. (1994). *Owning your own shadow: Understanding the dark side of the psyche*. HarperSanFrancisco.

Johnston, S. I. (1990). *Hekate Soteira: A study of Hekate's roles in the Chaldean oracles and related literature*. Scholars Press.

Jung, C. G. (1916). *Psychology of the unconscious: A study of the transformations and symbolisms of the libido* (B. Hinkle, Trans.). Moffat, Yard and Company.

Jung, C. G. (1964). *The collected works of C. G. Jung: Vol. 10, Civilisation in transition* (2nd ed., H. Read, M. Fordham, & G. Adler, Eds. and R. F. C. Hull, Trans.). Routledge and Kegan Paul.

Jung, C. G. (1966). *Two essays on analytical psychology* (R.F.C. Hull, Trans.). Princeton University Press. (Original work published 1928–43)

Jung, C. G. (1969a). *The collected works of C. G. Jung, Vol. 9 (Part 1): The archetypes and the collective unconscious* (2nd ed., R. F. C. Hull, Trans.). Princeton University Press. (Original work published 1933–1954)

Jung, C. G. (1969b). *Collected works of C. G. Jung, Vol. 9 (Part 2): Aion: ResearchRes into the phenomenology of the self* (R.F.C. Hull, Trans.). Princeton University Press. (Original work produced 1907–1909).

Jung, C. G. (1970). *The collected works of C. G. Jung: Vol. 8, The structure and dynamics of the psyche* (2nd ed., G. Adler & A. R. F. C Hull, Eds. and Trans.). Princeton University Press.

Jung, C. G. (1971). *The collected works of C. G. Jung, Vol. 6: Psychological types* (H. G. Baynes, Trans. and R. F. C. Hull, Rev. ed.). Princeton University Press. (Original work published 1921)

Jung, C. G. (1977a). *The collected works of C. G. Jung, Vol. 14: Mysterium coniunctionis* (2nd ed., G. Adler & R. F. C. Hull, Eds. and R. F. C. Hull, Trans.). Princeton University Press.

Jung, C. G. (1981). *The collected works of C. G. Jung, Vol. 17: The development of personality* (2nd ed., G. Adler & R. F. C. Hull, Eds. and Trans.). Princeton University Press.

Jung, C. G. (1989). *Memories, dreams, reflections* (A. Jaffe, C. Winston, & R. Winston, Eds., Reissue ed.). Vintage.

Jung, C. G. (1997). *Jung on active imagination*. (J. Chodorow, Ed.). Princeton University Press.

Kalsched, D. (2013). *Trauma and the soul: A psycho-spiritual approach to human development and its interruption*. Routledge.

Kapinos, T. (Developer). (2016–2021). *Lucifer* [TV series]. Warner Bros Television; Fox; Netflix. https://www.imdb.com/title/tt4052886/?ref_=fn_al_tt_1

Kaplan, A. (1982). *Meditation and Kabbalah*. Samuel Weiser.

Kaplan, L. (1991). *Female perversions: The temptations of Emma Bovary* (American First). Anchor.

Karlsen, C. F. (1987). *The Devil in the shape of a woman: Witchcraft in colonial New England*. W. W. Norton & Company.

Kautz, W. (2003). *Opening the inner eye: Explorations on the practical application of intuition in daily life and work*. iUniverse.

Kernberg, O. F. (1975). *Borderline conditions and pathological narcissism*. Jason Aronson.

Kessler, R. C., Chiu, W. T., Demler, O., & Walters, E. E. (2005). Prevalence, severity, and comorbidity of 12-month DSM-IV disorders in the national comorbidity survey replication. *Archives of General Psychiatry*, *62*(6), 617–627. https://doi.org/10.1001/archpsyc.62.6.617

King, U., Ed. (1998). *Feminist theology from the third world: A reader*. SPCK.

Kinsley, D. R. (1987). *Hindu goddesses: Visions of the divine feminine in the Hindu religious tradition*. University of California Press.

Kirmayer, L. J. (2006). Beyond the 'new cross-cultural psychiatry': Cultural biology, discursive psychology and the ironies of globalization. *Transcultural Psychiatry*, *43*(1), 126–144. https://pubmed.ncbi.nlm.nih.gov/16671396/

Kite, L., & Kite, L. (2021). *More than a body: Your body is an instrument, not an ornament*. Harvest.

Klimt, G. (1904–1907). *Water serpents II* [Oil on canvas]. Public Domain. https://commons.wikimedia.org/wiki/File:Gustav_Klimt_-_Water_Serpents_II.jpg

Koerber, A. (2018). *From hysteria to hormones: A rhetorical history* (*RSA Series in Transdisciplinary Rhetoric*). Penn State University Press.

Koltuv, B. B. (1986). *The book of Lilith*. Nicolas-Hays.

Korsmeyer, C. (2004). *Gender and aesthetics: An introduction*. Routledge.

Kramer, H., & Sprenger, J. (1928). *The Malleus Maleficarum of Heinrich Kramer and James Sprenger* (M. Summers, Ed. and Trans.). John Rodker. (Original work published 1486)

Kristeva, J. (1982). Powers of horror: An essay on abjection (L. S. Roudiez, Trans.). Columbia University Press. (Original work published 1980)

Kusama, K. (Director). (2009). *Jennifer's body*. [Film]. Fox Atomic. https://www.imdb.com/title/tt1131734/?ref_=fn_al_tt_1

Kwon, R. O. (2020, July 7). More women like me are choosing to be childfree. Is this the age of opting out? *The Guardian*. https://www.theguardian.com/lifeandstyle/2020/jul/06/more-women-like-me-are-choosing-to-be-childfree-is-this-the-age-of-opting-out

Laing, R. D. (1960). The divided self: An existential study in sanity and madness. Tavistock Publications.

Lalukota, S. (2023). Adolescent perception of female representation in television and its impact on adolescent views on female gender roles. *Journal of Student Research*, *12*(3). https://doi.org/10.47611/jsrhs.v12i3.4773

Lauter, E., & Rupprecht, C. (1985). *Feminist archetypal theory: Interdisciplinary re-visions of Jungian thought*. University of Tennessee Press.

Layton, L., Hollander, N. C., & Gutwill, S. (Eds.). (2006). *Psychoanalysis, class and politics: Encounters in the clinical setting*. Routledge.

Layton, L., & Leavy-Sperounis, M. (Eds.). (2020). *Toward a social psychoanalysis: Culture, character, and normative unconscious processes* (Relational Perspectives Book Series). Routledge.

Leonard, L. S. (1993). *Meeting the madwoman: Empowering the feminine spirit*. Bantam Books.

Lerner, G. (1987). *The creation of patriarchy*. Oxford University Press.

Levack, B. P. (2015). *The witch-hunt in early modern Europe* (4th ed.). Routledge. https://doi.org/10.4324/9781315685526

Lincoln, Y. S., & Guba, E. G. (1985). *Naturalistic inquiry*. Sage Publications.

Lindenfeld, D. (2009). Jungian archetypes and the discourse of history. *Rethinking History*, *13*(2), 217–234. https://doi.org/10.1080/13642520902833833

Lombroso, C., & Ferrero, G. (1895). *The female offender*. D. Appleton and Company.

Londoño Tobón, A., McNicholas, E., Clare, C. A., Ireland, L. D., Payne, J. L., Moore Simas, T. A., Scott, R. K., Becker, M., & Byatt, N. (2023). The end of Roe v. Wade: Implications for women's mental health and care. *Frontiers in Psychiatry*, *14*, 1087045. https://doi.org/10.3389/fpsyt.2023.1087045

Los Angeles Civil Rights Department. (2023). Violence against Black and Latina women in Los Angeles: A call to action. https://civilandhumanrights.lacity.gov/news/la-civil-rights-releases-new-report-violence-against-black-latina-women

Lurat, A. (1888). *Jean-Martin Charcot demonstrating hysteria in a hypnotized patient at the Salpêtrière* [Etching after P.-A.-A. Brouillet, 1887]. Wellcome Collection. Licensed under CC BY 4.0. Public Domain. https://wellcomecollection.org/works/qrkb3myu

Maes, G. (1680). *Head of Medusa* [Painting]. Art Institute of Chicago. Wikimedia Commons. Public Domain. https://commons.wikimedia.org/wiki/File:Head_of_Medusa_by_Godfried_Maes,_1680.jpg

Maines, R. P. (2001). *The technology of orgasm: "Hysteria," the vibrator, and women's sexual satisfaction*. Johns Hopkins University Press.

Mangan, D., & Breuninger, K. (2022, June 24). *Supreme court overturns Roe v. Wade, ending 50 years of federal abortion rights*. CNBC. https://www.cnbc.com/2022/06/24/roe-v-wade-overturned-by-supreme-court-ending-federal-abortion-rights.html

Manago, A. M., Graham, M. B., Greenfield, P. M., & Salimkhan, G. (2008). Self-presentation and gender on MySpace. *Journal of Applied Developmental Psychology*, *29*(6), 446–458. https://doi.org/10.1016/j.appdev.2008.07.001

Mangold, J. (Director). (1999). *Girl, interrupted*. [Film]. Columbia Pictures. https://www.imdb.com/title/tt0172493/?ref_=nv_sr_srsg_1

Martin, E. (1987). *The woman in the body: A cultural analysis of reproduction*. Beacon Press.

Mason, A. (2017). *Lilith: Dark feminine archetype*. Van Haren.

Matteson, T. H., & Detroit Publishing Co. (1900–1920). *Trial of George Jacobs of Salem for Witchcraft* [Photograph of oil painting]. Public Domain. Library of Congress, Prints & Photographs Division. https://www.loc.gov/item/2016817487/

McCarthy, C., Healey, J. F., Mein, A., & Camp, C., V. (Eds.). (2004). *Biblical & Near Eastern essays*. Continuum.

McDermott, R. F., & Kripal, J. J. (Eds.). (2003). Encountering Kali: In the margins, at the center, in the West. University of California Press.

McKinley, N. M., & Hyde, J. S. (1996). The objectified body consciousness scale: Development and validation. *Psychology of Women Quarterly*, *20*(2), 181–215. https://doi.org/10.1111/j.1471-6402.1996.tb00467.x

Mc Mahon, C. (2019). *The psychology of social media*. Routledge.

Means, K. (2021). *'Not like other girls': Implicit and explicit dimensions of internalized sexism and behavioral outcomes* [Master's thesis, Western Washington University]. WWU Graduate School Collection. https://cedar.wwu.edu/wwuet/1020/

Mendes Coutinho, M. (Ed.). (1701). *Zohar Hadash and Sefer Raziel* [Kabbalistic texts]. Joods Historisch Museum, Amsterdam. Photographed by Vassil (2012). Wikimedia Commons. https://commons.wikimedia.org/wiki/File:Kabbalistic_texts_1701_JHM_Amsterdam_08112012.jpg

Merriam-Webster. (2019). Perversity. In *Merriam-Webster's collegiate dictionary* (11th ed., p. 925). Merriam-Webster, Inc.

The Metropolitan Museum of Art. (n.d.-a). *Incantation bowl with Aramaic inscription* [Ceramic, paint]. Public Domain. https://www.metmuseum.org/art/collection/search/321885

The Metropolitan Museum of Art. (n.d.-b). *Statue of the Goddess Sakhmet* [Granodiorite sculpture]. The Met Collection. https://www.metmuseum.org/art/collection/search/544485

The Metropolitan Museum of Art. (n.d.-c). *Goddess Kali* [Lithograph]. Public Domain. Purchase, Robert and Bobbie Falk Philanthropic Fund Gift, 2021. https://www.metmuseum.org/art/collection/search/849495

Micale, M. S. (1995). *Approaching Hysteria: Disease and its interpretations.* Princeton University Press. ISBN: 978-0691037220

Mijares, S., Rafea, A., Sharling, D., Amponsem, J., & Mallory, M. (2020). *The power of the feminine: Facing shadow evoking light.* The Human Foundation.

Miller, J. B. (1987). *Toward a new psychology of women* (2nd ed.). Beacon Press.

Miller, K. (2024, February 26). Research developing solutions for misdiagnosis of heart disease in women. *MedStar Health Blog.* https://www.medstarhealth.org/blog/cardiovascular-diagnosis-research

The Miriam and Ira D. Wallach Division of Art, Prints and Photographs: Print Collection, The New York Public Library. (1853). *View of the lunatic asylum and mad house, on Blackwell's Island, New York* [Wood engraving]. Created by William Wade (Artist), Joshua H. Peirce (Engraver), and collected by Amos F. Eno. Public Domain (U.S.). https://digitalcollections.nypl.org/items/5e66b3e8-d3cf-d471-e040-e00a180654d7

Mitchell, J. (2000). *Mad men and Medusas: Reclaiming hysteria.* Basic Books.

Modeste, C. N. (2019). *Clinician perspectives on gender bias in diagnosis of borderline personality disorder* [Doctoral dissertation, Walden University]. Walden Dissertations and Doctoral Studies Collection. https://scholarworks.waldenu.edu/cgi/viewcontent.cgi?article=10470&context=dissertations

Monter, E. W. (1976). *Witchcraft in France and Switzerland: The borderlands during the reformation.* Cornell University Press.

Moodley, R., & Palmer, S. (Eds.). (2006). Race, culture and psychotherapy: Critical perspectives in multicultural practice. Routledge.

Mookerjee, A. (1988). *Kali: The feminine force.* Destiny Books.

Moscucci, O. (1990). *The science of woman: Gynaecology and gender in England, 1800–1929.* Cambridge University Press.

Mulvey, L. (1975). Visual pleasure and narrative cinema. *Screen, 16*(3), 6–18.

Murdock, M. (1990). *The heroine's journey: Woman's quest for wholeness.* Shambhala Publications.

Murphy, J. M. (1995). *Working the spirit: Ceremonies of the African diaspora.* Beacon Press.

Murphy, R., & Falchuk, B. (Creators). (2013). *American horror story: Coven.* [TV Series]. FX.

Nado, J. (2014). Why intuition? *Philosophy and Phenomenological ResearchRR, 89*(1), 15–41. https://doi.org/10.1111/j.1933-1592.2012.00644.x. National Gallery of Modern Art, 2010.

Natoire, C. J. (1740). *The Rebuke of Adam and Eve* [Painting]. The Metropolitan Museum of Art. Retrieved March 5, 2025, from https://www.metmuseum.org/art/collection/search/437180

Naveh, J., & Shaked, S. (1985). Amulets and magic bowls: Aramaic incantations of late antiquity. Magnes Press.

Nelson, J. (2015). More than medicine: A history of the feminist women's health movement. New York University Press.

Noll, R. (1997). *The Aryan Christ: The secret life of Carl Jung.* Random House.

Neumann, E. (1994). *The fear of the feminine.* Princeton University Press.

Nunn, J. F. (1996). Ancient Egyptian medicine. University of Oklahoma Press.

Ollerenshaw, J. A., & Creswell, J. W. (2002). Narrative research: A comparison of two restorying data analysis approaches. *Qualitative Inquiry*, *8*(3), 329–347. https://doi.org/10.1177/10778004008003008

Osborne, G. R. (2006). *The hermeneutical spiral: A comprehensive introduction to biblical interpretation* (Rev. and expanded ed.). IVP Academic.

Otzar Midrashim. (n.d.). *The alphabet of Ben Sira*. Sefaria. https://www.sefaria.org/Otzar_Midrashim%2C_The_Aleph_Bet_of_ben_Sira%2C_The_Alphabet_of_ben_Sira%2C_(alternative_version).1?ven=Sefaria_Community_Translation&lang=bi&with=Sheets&lang2=en

Ovid. (2004). *Metamorphoses* (D. Raeburn, Trans.). Penguin Classics. (Original work published 8 CE)

Patai, R. (1990). *The Hebrew goddess* (3rd ed.). Wayne State University Press.

Patton, M. Q. (2015). *Qualitative research & evaluation methods: Integrating theory and practice* (4th ed.). Sage Publications.

Perez, D. R. (2008). There was a woman: La Llorona from folklore to popular culture. University of Texas Press.

Perera, S. B. (1981). *Descent to the goddess: A way of initiation for women*. Inner City Books.

Perez Salazar, G. (2017). *La Llorona árbol tallado* [Photograph]. Wikimedia Commons. https://commons.wikimedia.org/wiki/File:La_Llorona_arbol_tallado.jpg

Planned Parenthood Federation of America. (2020). *Annual report 2019–2020*. Planned Parenthood. https://www.plannedparenthood.org/uploads/filer_public/67/30/67305ea1-8da2-4cee-9191-19228c1d6f70/210219-annual-report-2019-2020-web-final.pdf

Polkinghorne, D. E. (1995). Narrative configuration in qualitative analysis. *International Journal of Qualitative Studies in Education*, *8*(1), 5–23. https://doi.org/10.1080/0951839950080103

Plaskow, J. (1990). Standing again at Sinai: Judaism from a feminist perspective. HarperSanFrancisco.

Raday, F. (2003). Culture, religion, and gender. *International Journal of Constitutional Law*, *1*(4), 663–715. https://doi.org/10.1093/icon/1.4.663

Raday, F. (2012, April). Sacralising the patriarchal family in the monotheistic religions: 'To no form of religion is woman indebted for one impulse of freedom' [Special Issue]. *International Journal of Law in Context*, *8*(2), 211–230.

Rahmani, S. (2020). *Women's experiences of internalized sexism* [Doctoral dissertation, National Louis University]. Clinical Psychology Commons. https://digitalcommons.nl.edu/cgi/viewcontent.cgi?article=1485&context=diss

Roesler, C. (2012). Are archetypes transmitted more by culture than biology? Questions arising from conceptualizations of the archetype. *Journal of Analytical Psychology*, *57*(2), 223–246.

Rapley, R. (2001). *A case of witchcraft: The trial of Urbain Grandier* (New ed.). McGill Queens University Press.

Reynolds, E. H. (2018). Hysteria in ancient civilisations: A neurological review. *Journal of the Neurological Sciences*, *388*, 208–213. https://doi.org/10.1016/j.jns.2018.02.024

Ross, F. C. (2004). *Understanding perversion in clinical practice: Structure and strategy in the psyche*. Routledge.

Rossen, R. (Director). (1964). *Lilith*. [Film]. Centaur Productions.

Rossetti, D. G. (1866/1872–1873). *Lady Lilith* [Oil painting]. Delaware Art Museum. Public Domain. https://commons.wikimedia.org/wiki/File:Lady-Lilith.jpg

Roth. A., & Fonagy, P. (2006). *What works for whom? A critical review of psychotherapy research* (2nd ed.). The Guilford Press.

Rowland, S. (2002). *Jung: A feminist revision.* Polity Press.

Ruah-Midbar Shapiro, M. (2019a). Lilith's comeback from a Jungian-feminist outlook: Contemporary feminist spirituality gets into bed with Lilith. *Feminist Theology*, *27*(2), 149–163. https://doi.org/10.1177/0966735018814674

Ruah-Midbar Shapiro, M. (2019b). The temptation of legitimacy: Lilith's adoption and adaption in contemporary feminist spirituality and their meanings. *Modern Judaism: A Journal of Jewish Ideas and Experience*, *39*(2), 125–143. https://doi.org/10.1093/mj/kjz003

Ruether, R. (2006). *Goddesses and the divine feminine: A Western religious history.* University of California Press.

Russell, D. E. H. (1990). *Rape in marriage* (2nd ed.). Indiana University Press.

Sait, B. (2021). *The indoctrination of the Wehrmacht: Nazi ideology and the war crimes of the German military.* Berghahn Books.

Samuels, A. (1985). *Jung and the post-Jungians.* Routledge and Kegan Paul.

Schleiermacher, F. (1998). Hermeneutics and criticism and other writings (A. Bowie, Trans.). Cambridge University Press. (Original work published 1838)

Scholem, G. (1941). Major trends in Jewish mysticism. Schocken Books.

Scholem, G. (1965). *On the Kabbalah and its symbolism.* Schocken Books.

Scholem, G. (1974). *Kabbalah.* Keter Publishing House.

Schwartz, H. (2006). *Tree of souls: The mythology of Judaism.* Oxford University Press.

Secunda, S. (2013). The Iranian Talmud: Reading the Bavli in its Sasanian context. University of Pennsylvania Press.

Seelig, B. (2002). The rape of Medusa in the temple of Athena: Aspects of triangulation in the girl. *The International Journal of Psychoanalysis*, *83*(4), 895–911. https://doi.org/10.1516/00207570260172975

Shammas, C. (1994). Re-assessing the married women's property acts. *Journal of Women's History*, *6*(1), 9–30. https://muse.jhu.edu/pub/1/article/363318

Sharma, I. (2015). Violence against women: Where are the solutions? *Indian Journal of Psychiatry*, *57*(2), 131. https://doi.org/10.4103/0019-5545.158133

Sharman, J. (Director). (1975). *The Rocky Horror picture show* [Film]. 20th Century Fox.

Shaw, C., & Proctor, G. (2005). Women at the margins: A critique of the diagnosis of borderline personality disorder. Feminism & Psychology, *15*(4), 483–490. https://doi.org/10.1177/0959-353505057620

Shim, J. K. (2010). Cultural health capital: A theoretical approach to understanding health care interactions and the dynamics of unequal treatment. Journal of Health and Social Behavior, 51(1), 1–15. https://doi.org/10.1177/0022146509361185

Shneur Zalman of Liadi. (n.d.). *Torah Ohr. Sefaria.org*. Retrieved October 14, 2021, from https://www.sefaria.org/Shenei_Luchot_HaBerit%2C_Torah_Shebikhtav%2C_Ki_Teitzei%2C_Torah_Ohr?ven=Shney_Luchot_Habrit_by_Rabbi_Eliyahu_Munk&lang=bi

Shorter, E. (1992). *From paralysis to fatigue: A history of psychosomatic illness in the modern era.* Free Press.

Showalter, E. (1985). *The female malady: Women, madness, and English culture, 1830–1980*. Pantheon Books.
Singer, T. (2000). *The vision thing: Myth, politics and psyche in the world*. Routledge.
Skodol, A. E., & Bender, D. S. (2003). Why are women diagnosed borderline more than men? *Psychiatric Quarterly*, *74*(4), 349–360.
Skolnik, F. (Ed.). (2007). *Encyclopedia Judaica* (Vol. 2, 2nd ed.). Keter Publishing House.
Sollee, K. J. (2017). *Witches, sluts, feminists: Conjuring the sex positive*. ThreeL Media.
Sperling, H., & Simon, M. (Trans.). (1933). *The Zohar* (Vol. 1, Bereshit 94b). Soncino Press. https://www.sefaria.org/Zohar%2C_Bereshit.94.353
Spielberg, S. (Director). (1985). *The color purple*. [Film]. Warner Bros.
Stein, M. (1998). *Jung's map of the soul: An introduction*. Open Court Publishing.
Stern, R., & Sundberg, A. (Directors). (2018). *Reversing Roe*. [Film]. Netflix. https://www.imdb.com/title/tt8948614/?ref_=fn_al_tt_1
Stone, M. (1978). *When God was a woman*. Mariner Books.
Streitfeld, S. (1996). *Female perversions*. [Film]. October Films. https://www.imdb.com/title/tt0116293/?ref_=fn_al_tt_1
Strong, D., & Daniels, L. (Creators). (2015–2020). *Empire* [TV series]. 20th Century Fox Television.
Swim, J. K., & Hyers, L. L. (1999). Excuse me—what did you just say?! Women's public and private responses to sexist remarks. *Journal of Experimental Social Psychology*, *35*(1), 68–88.
Szasz, T. S. (1961). The myth of mental illness: Foundations of a theory of personal conduct. Harper & Row.
Szymanski, D. M., Moffitt, L. B., & Carr, E. R. (2010). Sexual objectification of women: Advances to theory and research. *The Counseling Psychologist*, *39*(1), 6–38.
Takakuwa, K. M., Rubashkin, N., Herzig, K. E., & Elders, J. (2004). *What I learned in medical school: Personal stories of young doctors*. University of California Press.
Tasca, C., Rapetti, M., Carta, M. G., & Fadda, B. (2012). Women and hysteria in the history of mental health. *Clinical Practice and Epidemiology in Mental Health: CP & EMH*, *8*, 110–119. https://doi.org/10.2174/1745017901208010110
Thiessen, E. J. (1993). *Teaching for commitment: Liberal education, indoctrination, and Christian nurture*. McGill-Queen's University Press.
Thompson, L. (1999). *The wandering womb: A cultural history of outrageous beliefs about women*. Prometheus.
Tiggemann, M., & Slater, A. (2013). NetGirls: The internet, Facebook, and body image concern in adolescent girls. *International Journal of Eating Disorders*, *46*(6), 630–633.
Tilley, C. L. (2018). A regressive formula of perversity: Wertham and the women of comics. *Journal of Lesbian Studies*, *22*(4), 354–372. https://doi.org/10.1080/10894160.2018.1450001
Tomes, N., & Showalter, E. (1987). The female malady: Women, madness, and English culture. *The American Historical Review*, *92*(1), 131–132. https://doi.org/10.1086/ahr/92.1.131-a
Totenberg, N. (2021, September 2). *Supreme Court upholds new Texas abortion law, for now*. NPR. https://choice.npr.org/index.html?origin=https://www.npr.org/2021/09/02/1033048958/supreme-court-upholds-new-texas-abortion-law-for-now

Ulmer, R. (1994). The evil eye in the Bible and in rabbinic literature. KTAV Publishing House.

United Nations Office on Drugs and Crime. (2024). *World drug report 2024*. United Nations. https://www.unodc.org/unodc/en/data-and-analysis/world-drug-report-2024.html

Unknown Artist. (ca. 117–138 CE). *Relief of Triplicate Hekate* [Marble relief]. National Gallery Prague, Kinský Palace (NM-H10 4742). Photographed by Zde (2014). Wikimedia Commons. https://commons.wikimedia.org/wiki/File:Relief_triplicate_Hekate_marble,_Hadrian_clasicism,_Prague_Kinsky,_NM-H10_4742,_140995.jpg

Unknown Scribe. (ca. 2nd century BCE). *The Great Isaiah Scroll* [Manuscript]. Israel Museum, Jerusalem. Digitized by Google Art Project. Wikimedia Commons. Retrieved March 5, 2025, from https://commons.wikimedia.org/wiki/File:The_Great_Isaiah_Scroll_MS_A_(1QIsa)_-_Google_Art_Project-x3-y0.jpg

UN Women. (2024a). *Progress of the world's women 2024: Gender equality in a changing world*. United Nations Entity for Gender Equality and the Empowerment of Women. Retrieved March 6, 2025, from https://www.unwomen.org/en/digital-library/progress-of-the-worlds-women

UN Women. (2024b). *One woman or girl is killed every 10 minutes by their intimate partner or family member*. UN Women. Retrieved March 6, 2025, from https://www.unwomen.org/en/news-stories/press-release/2024/11/one-woman-or-girl-is-killed-every-10-minutes-by-their-intimate-partner-or-family-member

Ussher, J. M. (2006). *Managing the monstrous feminine: Regulating the reproductive body*. Routledge.

Vaccarino, V., Parsons, L., Every, N. R., Barron, H. V., & Krumholz, H. M. (1999). Sex-based differences in early mortality after myocardial infarction. *The New England Journal of Medicine*, *341*(4), 217–225. doi:10.1056/NEJM199907223410401

Violence Policy Center. (2021). *When men murder women: An analysis of 2019 homicide data*. Violence Policy Center. https://vpc.org/studies/wmmw2021.pdf

von Franz, M.L. (1970). *The interpretation of fairy tales*. Spring Publications.

von Franz, M. L. (1972). *The feminine in fairytales*. Spring Publications.

von Franz, M. L. (1980). *Projection and re-collection in Jungian psychology: Reflections of the soul*. Open Court.

von Franz, M. L. (1999). *Archetypal dimensions of the psyche*. Shambhala Publications.

Walby, S. (1990). *Theorizing patriarchy*. Blackwell.

Walker, B. G. (1983). *The woman's encyclopedia of myths and secrets*. Harper & Row.

Ware, V. (2015). *Beyond the pale: White women, racism, and history* (Feminist Classics). Verso.

Warner, M. (1994). *From the beast to the blonde: On fairy tales and their tellers*. Farrar, Straus and Giroux.

Waters, J. (Director). (1972). *Pink flamingos*. [Film]. New Line Cinema.

Wehr, D. (1987). *Jung and feminism: Liberating archetypes*. Beacon Press.

Weiner, I. B., Lerner, R. M., Easterbrooks, M. A., & Mistry, J. (2012). *Handbook of psychology, developmental psychology* (Vol. 6). Wiley.

Welldon, E. V. (1995). Female perversion and hysteria. *British Journal of Psychotherapy*, *11*(3), 406–414. https://doi.org/10.1111/j.1752-0118.1995.tb00747.x

Welldon, E. V. (2011). *Playing with dynamite: A personal approach to the psychoanalytic understanding of perversions, violence, and criminality*. Routledge.

Wertz, F. J., Charmaz, K., McMullen, L. M., Josselson, R., Anderson, R., & McSpadden, E. (2011). *Five ways of doing qualitative analysis: Phenomenological psychology, grounded theory, discourse analysis, narrative research, and intuitive inquiry*. The Guilford Press.

West, S. (Director). (2001). *Lara Croft: Tomb raider*. [Film]. Paramount Pictures (United States). https://www.imdb.com/title/tt0146316/

The White House. (2025, July 24). Ending crime and disorder on America's streets [Executive order]. https://www.whitehouse.gov/presidential-actions/2025/07/ending-crime-and-disorder-on-americas-streets/

Whitmont, E. C. (1978). *The symbolic quest: Basic concepts of analytical psychology* (Expanded ed.). Princeton University Press.

Wikimedia Commons. (1669). *Title page of Malleus Maleficarum* [Historical title page]. Public Domain. https://commons.wikimedia.org/wiki/File:Sprenger_-_Malleus_maleficarum,_1669_-_BEIC_9477645.tiff?page=1

Wilkerson, R. H. (1991). Sekhmet, in Egyptian mythology. In M. Eliade (Ed.), The encyclopedia of religion (Vol. 13, pp. 287–289). Macmillan.

The William Davidson Talmud. (n.d.). Shabbat 151b. Sefaria. https://www.sefaria.org/Shabbat.151b

Williamson, E. (1985). Plato's "eidos" and the archetypes of Jung and Frye. *Interpretations*, *16*(1), 94–104. http://www.jstor.org/stable/43797850

Winnicott, D. W. (1960). The theory of the parent–infant relationship. *International Journal of Psychoanalysis*, *41*, 585–595.

Wirth-Cauchon, J. (2001). *Women and borderline personality disorder: Symptoms and stories*. Rutgers University Press.

Wolf, N. (1991). *The beauty myth: How images of beauty are used against women*. William Morrow & Co.

Woodman, M. (1982). *Addiction to perfection: The still unravished bride*. Inner City Books.

Woodman, M. (1993). *Leaving my father's house: A journey to conscious femininity*. Shambhala Publications.

Workman, J. (2016). *Demonomania and witchcraft: An occult reference*. CreateSpace.

Yehuda, R., & Lehrner, A. (2018). Intergenerational transmission of trauma effects: Putative role of epigenetic mechanisms. *World Psychiatry*, *17*(3), 243–257. https://doi.org/10.1002/wps.20568

Young-Eisendrath, P. (1999). *Women and desire: Beyond wanting to be wanted*. Harmony Books.

Zimbres, E. (2006). *Iansã* [Photograph of metal sculpture]. Wikimedia Commons. https://commons.wikimedia.org/wiki/File:Iansã.jpg

Zweig, C., & Abrams, J. (Eds.). (1991). *Meeting the shadow: The hidden power of the dark side of human nature*. TarcherPerigee.

Index

Page numbers in **bold** denote tables, those in *italic* denote figures.

Printed in the United States
by Baker & Taylor Publisher Services